be brave to things

wesleyan poetry

THE COLLECTED WORKS OF JACK SPICER
Series Editor, Peter Gizzi

VOLUME 1
My Vocabulary Did This to Me: The Collected Poetry of Jack Spicer
Edited by Peter Gizzi and Kevin Killian

VOLUME 2
Be Brave to Things: The Uncollected Poetry and Plays of Jack Spicer
Edited and with an Introduction by Daniel Katz

VOLUME 3
The House That Jack Built: The Collected Lectures of Jack Spicer
Edited and with an Afterword by Peter Gizzi

be brave to things

The Uncollected Poetry and Plays of
JACK SPICER

Edited and with an Introduction by Daniel Katz

Wesleyan University Press   Middletown, Connecticut

Wesleyan University Press
Middletown CT 06459
www.wesleyan.edu/wespress

Poems and plays © 2021 The Estate of Jack Spicer.
Introduction and Notes © 2021 Daniel Katz
All rights reserved
Manufactured in the United States of America
Designed by Eric Brooks
Composed in Dante MT by Passumpsic Publishing

Library of Congress Cataloging-in-Publication Data
NAMES: Spicer, Jack, author. | Katz, Daniel, editor,
    writer of introduction.
TITLE: Be brave to things: the uncollected poetry and
    plays of Jack Spicer / Jack Spicer; edited and with
    an introduction by Daniel Katz.
DESCRIPTION: Middletown, Connecticut : Wesleyan
    University Press, [2021]
SERIES: Wesleyan poetry | Includes bibliographical
    references and index.
SUMMARY: "The previously uncollected poems and plays
    of a renowned poet of the San Francisco Renaissance"
    —Provided by publisher.
IDENTIFIERS: LCCN 2021033102 (print) | LCCN 2021033103
    (ebook) | ISBN 9780819578150 (cloth) |
    ISBN 9780819578167 (ebook)
SUBJECTS: LCGFT: Poetry. | Drama.
CLASSIFICATION: LCC PS3569.P47 B4 2021 (print) |
    LCC PS3569.P47 (ebook) | DDC 811/.54—dc23
LC record available at https://lccn.loc.gov/2021033102
LC ebook record available at https://lccn.loc
    .gov/2021033103

5 4 3 2 1

CONTENTS

EARLY POEMS: LOS ANGELES, BERKELEY, MINNEAPOLIS, SAN FRANCISCO

MANHATTAN AND BOSTON: 1955–1956

SAN FRANCISCO AND BERKELEY: 1956–1965

THE PLAYS

ACKNOWLEDGMENTS

Coming to this project with no real experience in textual editing or the preparation of critical editions, I needed help. Thankfully, I got it. First, from my publisher: I'm grateful to Wesleyan University Press for their support, encouragement, and exceptional competence throughout the process, and especially to my editor, Suzanna Tamminen, and to Jim Schley, an exemplary copyeditor whose diligence and taste have greatly contributed to this book. I also want to thank the Department of English and Comparative Literary Studies, at the University of Warwick, for providing study-leave without which this project could not have been completed, as well as Warwick's Faculty of the Arts for additional forms of material aid.

Help and companionship were also provided by Joe Shafer, Stephen J. Ross, and David Grundy; thanks to the latter two who made the tedious process of checking transcriptions against the originals not only a relative pleasure but also at times an intellectual event, albeit a remote one, given the new realities of summer 2020. Remote in time as well as space was the aid I received from Aaron Kunin. In 2004 when Robin Blaser first donated his Spicer archives to the Bancroft Library at the University of California–Berkeley, Aaron created preliminary transcriptions of a vast amount of the poetry, creating an electronic archive which was never far from my screen as I went about establishing my own texts. On many occasions his transcriptions solved cruces in Spicer's erratic handwriting that I couldn't, and my debt to Aaron's work is enormous. Likewise, Aaron's edition of Spicer's play *Troilus*, first published in *No: A Journal of the Arts* (issue 3, 2004), was of great help in preparing the text for this volume, as were his prompt, informative, and lively answers to various queries I had on the text, including information passed on to him by Robin Blaser himself.

Thanks too to Miriam Nichols, for sharing with me her extensive knowledge of Blaser and the Berkeley Renaissance with the generosity

I've found to be characteristic of scholars of the subject, as well as her unparalleled insight. Her work and conversation have been indispensable to my understanding of the contexts behind a great deal of the writing collected here. From Berlin, Stan Persky shared memories and stories from the years when many of the works collected in this volume were being written. Beyond the concretely useful information he provided, he conveyed a sense of that time and that place, as well as of the person that Jack Spicer was, as no one else could.

Peter Gizzi knows how much I owe him, but all readers of this book should too. As series editor for the *Collected Works of Jack Spicer* he continues to oversee the entire project with superlative sensitivity and intelligence. His contributions in thinking through the trickiest decisions I faced here are incalculable, as is the quality of his friendship, which saw me through and out of the underworld Spicer insists his readers traverse, even if neither Peter nor I seem able to stop ourselves from obsessively glancing back. His companionship throughout was sustaining and enlivening, and a reminder that there can be no poetry without friendship.

Finally, as anyone who has been reading Spicer in recent years has likely already guessed, my greatest debt is to someone who will not read the record of it here. But no one contributed more to this project, and in so many ways, than Kevin Killian. Kevin knew more about Spicer and his work than anyone, and he put that knowledge at my disposal with the affectionate generosity for which he is legendary. Whether it was actual documents painstakingly found or obscure yet crucial facts only he knew, whatever I asked for was given with alacrity, good humor, insight, and wit. The constant exchange with Kevin that this project necessitated was no doubt its greatest pleasure—working with Kevin was, simply yet crucially, incredibly fun. And my work here is inseparable in my mind from Kevin's inimitable spirit.

INTRODUCTION

Like great kites we are fallen

—Jack Spicer[1]

Unpublishing Jack Spicer

It's hard not to start at the end with Jack Spicer: him drifting in and out of consciousness in San Francisco General Hospital in August, 1965, finally dying of chronic alcoholism, but rousing himself just enough to force out his legendary last words to Robin Blaser: "My vocabulary did this to me. Your love will let you go on."[2] Though Spicer was only forty such a demise was not entirely unexpected when it happened, given how severe his drinking habit had become over the previous years. It also grimly rhymed with the darkness and pain at the core of Spicer's work, which so often derives its dazzling luminosity from these unlikely wellsprings. These often discussed final words are almost too apt to be true, encapsulating his rage and frustration with himself, his grumpy truculence, and the impossible demands that created massive difficulties even with those friends, like Blaser, who were most committed to him. They end with a dialectical supersession of the nihilism that he believed in, which he called love. Spicer, with Blaser and their mutual close friend Robert Duncan, had been at the heart of the Berkeley Renaissance in the late 1940s, and then the San Francisco Renaissance in the 1950s. He was a central figure in the Bay Area poetry scene for nearly twenty years, and during the year he spent in Boston in the mid-'50s he also forged important ties with Boston poets such as Steve Jonas and John Wieners. However, at the time of his death and for many years after, though a local legend and included in Donald Allen's epoch-defining *New American Poetry* anthology, Spicer remained in the shadow of many of the other notable figures of the San Francisco poetry scene: not only Duncan but also poets like Allen Ginsberg and Gary Snyder. In addition to his difficult personality and chaotic life, a major reason for this was that Spicer's preference for very small presses—often informal collectives run by friends

—meant that his work was quite simply hard to find until Blaser, his chosen literary executor, put together *The Collected Books of Jack Spicer* in 1975. Five years later Donald Allen, another good friend, edited a volume of shorter lyrics, *One Night Stand*. By this time Spicer's reputation was growing and expanding, furthered not least by the importance bestowed on his work by the burgeoning L=A=N=G=U=A=G=E movement and especially Ron Silliman, who saw in Spicer a crucial precursor to the core concerns of the 1970s and '80s. Academic interest in Spicer also rose significantly in the 1980s and '90s, and work by Michael Davidson and Maria Damon among others was crucial in establishing Spicer as one of the indispensable poets of the "New American" group. Finally, 1998 saw the publication of two splendid and massively important books for readers of Spicer, outside the academy and within: Lew Ellingham and Kevin Killian's biography *Poet, Be Like God* and Peter Gizzi's edition of the legendary "Vancouver lectures" (with one lecture from Berkeley and other prose included, too), *The House That Jack Built*.

By the turn of the century it was clear that new editions of Spicer's work were needed, and in 2004 when Blaser donated his Spicer archives to the Bancroft Library at the University of California–Berkeley, it also became apparent that his papers contained much unpublished and in some cases unknown work, whose dissemination required serious consideration. A first pass was made by Peter Gizzi and Kevin Killian when they edited *My Vocabulary Did This To Me: The Collected Poetry of Jack Spicer* (hereafter abbreviated *CP*), which made extensive use of this material, as well as including almost all of Blaser's *Collected Books* and much of *One Night Stand*. That volume was the first of Wesleyan University Press's series *The Collected Writings of Jack Spicer*. This book is the second, and its aims were foretold by Gizzi and Killian when they projected a companion volume including student work, poems "Spicer clearly didn't intend for publication" (*CP*, xxxi), others they couldn't fit in, and also his plays. I have tried to follow this program, and below I will describe in greater detail the criteria and processes by which I made my selection and established the texts. In many respects I follow well-established protocols of textual scholarship, especially when it comes to posthumous editions, as would be expected. But Spicer's work and thought in their specificity provoke a particularly pointed set of questions and problems for anyone engaged in a task like mine, and I want to consider these before moving forward.[3]

★

What does it mean to publish a poem? What effects do the conditions of its circulation have on the poem itself? Indeed, is it even possible to conceive of the poem "itself" separated from the conditions of its circulation? To whom does a poem properly belong? Where does a poem come from, and where should it—where can it—go? These are questions likely to occupy any editor of any collection of poems, especially a posthumous one, but few poets have asked them more insistently than Jack Spicer. They are at the heart of his two most famous contributions to poetics—the idea of poetry as "dictation," and the "serial poem" or "book"—and they constantly informed his artistic practice as well. So much is this the case that even if I can't quite claim this introduction is ghost-written or dictated by Spicer himself, the entire project has been conducted in the shadow of problems Spicer posed with a clarity and intensity that remain unique. In thinking of my task, from early on, as a process of "unpublishing," I take my lead from Spicer: his engagement with Lorca led him not only to translate the Spanish poet but also to produce and include in *After Lorca* what he called "untranslations." Throughout my work on this edition, I have been tormented by the question of what kind of publishing, or "unpublishing," does honor to the imperatives that Spicer established.

As with any posthumous edition, Spicer's death inevitably brackets the author's desires and allows them to be superseded by criteria established by an editor whose responsibility is necessarily divided, answering at once to the ghostly author and also to her or his living and even still unborn readers. This is standard, and mediating editors—like translators, their doppelgängers—cannot always parse so easily the distinction between fidelity and betrayal. Yet when it comes to Spicer the course is especially fraught. To create a book of poems, as either author or editor, is invariably to confront a set of questions with massive ramifications if pursued to the points where Spicer tended to push them.

With regard to publishing in the conventional acceptation, in many respects Spicer—like so many of his peers—followed in the footsteps of Walt Whitman, who in disseminating the 1855 *Leaves of Grass* "self-published" in the most radical and literal sense. Not only did he eschew existing commercial publishing houses, but using skills he had acquired in the newspaper trade, he designed the book and set some of the type himself, overseeing the entire production process. For the poet who continually stressed that the body is the equal of the soul, it was indispensable to participate in the physical labor that produced the physical object. For Spicer as for Whitman, controlling the production and conditions of distribution of a collection was almost as fundamental as writing the "works" themselves, while the small, local presses and communal productions of pamphlets, mimeographs, and broadsides that Spicer favored also tied him to practices familiar from the modernist "little magazines" dear to so many of the major American poets of the generation before his. For Spicer, this conception not only of writing but of bookmaking, publishing, and disseminating as a communal, collective, and collaborative practice would remain fundamental.

But an even more decisive precedent is that of Emily Dickinson, whose manuscripts Spicer studied intensively at the Boston Public Library in 1956, and who almost never published at all, at least not in Whitman's sense. Only a handful of her poems appeared in her lifetime, usually in small, local outlets, and largely due to the efforts of others than herself. However, if Dickinson could reassure a worried T. W. Higginson that "I smile when you suggest that I delay 'to publish'—that being foreign to my thought, as Firmament to Fin—," (*Selected Letters*, 174), she hardly saw herself as a hidden creature of the inky deeps, toiling in obscurity on works never meant to be exposed to the bright lights of heaven. On the contrary, Dickinson certainly did not desire to go unread, as her scare quotes around "to publish" indicate, as well as the fact that she herself had sought Higginson out and sent him some poems unsolicited after reading his "Letter to a Young Contributor" in the *Atlantic Monthly*. Yet the conditions under which she would be read mattered enormously to her. Dickinson says more about this in a now famous poem, unpublished in her lifetime, and probably written about a year or so after her exchange with Higginson. It begins "Publication—is the Auction / Of the Mind of Man—" and concludes with the admonition ". . . reduce no Human Spirit / To Disgrace of Price—" (*Poems*, 351). This poem obviously protests against the commodification of literary labor, with the play on "grace" and "disgrace" implying that putting a price on literary creation is more than just shameful, being rather a way of annulling or destroying whatever "grace" is to be found in the writing in the first instance. And for Dickinson it therefore followed that poetry needed to exist within a form of sociality and exchange which was not that of the marketplace. For her, this was above all the medium of epistolary correspondence and the framework of the gift economy: her poems were often enclosed with letters and presented as affectionate offerings. This was how she *unpublished* the vast majority of her poems that were read by others in her lifetime. In the middle of the next century, Spicer continued to push Dickinson's limits and possibilities into confrontation with the different social and economic conditions in which he found himself.

For example, with respect to her proscription against "auctioning" the mind of the writer, here is Don Allen, Spicer's close friend but also editor of the hugely influential *New American Poetry* anthology, writing to Spicer on June 14, 1958, after his first book had been published by friends who started a press specifically for that purpose:

> It's wonderful that you've made three hundred on the *After Lorca*. . . . But, Jack, remember to get the book copyrighted else anyone can steal your stuff. (JSP 2004)

As Allen knew, this was not an oversight on Spicer's part: he was vehemently opposed to copyrighting his own work, and broke bitterly with the tiny Auerhahn Press, which copyrighted his *Heads of the Town up to the Aether* without his permission in 1962. But Spicer's fury at transforming a poem into intellectual property didn't mean he felt his poems might belong to whoever wanted them, for if he refused legal copyright he also tended to tightly control distribution, objecting to having his books sold in stores of which he didn't approve (including Lawrence Ferlinghetti's City Lights Books), and, as a poet of the local, suggesting strict regional boundaries for circulation, for example of the free magazine *Open Space*, which was edited by a member of his circle, originally with the intention that "They wouldn't be given past the East Bay" (*The House That Jack Built*, 166)—the furthest acceptable border of the San Francisco Bay Area. And this, for a reason linked to a very Dickinsonian sense of the poem as tied to a moment and a particular relationship, rather than as a monument preserved in amber: "The idea of making things last is something which just has to be conquered. The idea of *Open Space* was that these things would not last" (*H*, 166). Spicer's belief in the poem as ephemeral and not objectifiable is in complete contradiction with my task here—to preserve and perpetuate the most suitable items of his literary remains, and establish definitive texts to be brought under copyright.

And beyond these already unnerving implicit ghostly admonitions, Spicer's thought and writing explicitly challenge many of the fundamental categories upon which textual editing relies. How does one go about handling the problem of authorial intention when Spicer, through his radical theory of "dictated" poetry, in which the poet is a radio receiver tuning into alien signals from Mars, denied authorship in the usual senses, going so far as to say, just weeks before his death, "I really honestly don't feel that I own my poems, and I don't feel proud of them" (*H*, 15)? How do all the protocols regarding posthumous publication alter for a writer whose poetics are profoundly thanatocratic and posit death as the precondition of the poetic act? This is the premise of his breakthrough book *After Lorca*, written as the title implies from after the fact of Lorca's death, and containing the assertion that the moment of artistic danger is when "The poet . . . ceases to be a dead man" (*CP*, 150). And moreover, how to publish a poet for whom, like Dickinson, *not* being published becomes an integral element of the poetic project? This is explicitly the case with Spicer's last work, the posthumously published

Book of Magazine Verse, divided into sections bearing the titles of various journals and magazines of the day. Describing the book, Spicer explained that the principle behind it was "the idea of writing poems for magazines which would not print them" (*H*, 102), and this was not only conceptual: Spicer kept the rejection slips that went with some of the "Poems for *The Nation*," for example. However, more than just a *folie*, *The Book of Magazine Verse* speaks volumes about some of Spicer's fundamental views of publishing and of poetry more generally. For him, the point of poetic address was not to achieve communication, communion, and understanding. Rather than poetry telling people what they want to hear, or what they like to hear, Spicer insists that poetry must say the very thing that the particular people to whom it is addressed cannot hear—what they refuse to hear, and sends them running in the other direction or mailing rejection slips. Orpheus was a central figure for Spicer throughout his life, for Orpheus, in Spicer's view, was not the one with poems that were "beautiful in and of themselves" but rather the poet who "moved impossible audiences—trees, wild animals, the king of hell himself" (*H*, 230). If Spicer was Orpheus, as *The Book of Magazine Verse* shows, he was Orpheus in reverse. For the premise of this book is that the act of unpublishing it constitutes is a badge of integrity and value, an avoidance of Dickinson's "disgrace" or what Spicer, in a play on worship, called the "whorship of poetry." For Spicer, the converse of "whorship" is to offer yourself for free to those whom you drive into not wanting you; something not entirely different from Lacan's definition of love. This is also for Spicer a political and ethical act, an "admonition," to use his term, of reform addressed at cultural institutions that aren't only that; "a magazine is a society," Spicer affirms, before saying that he doesn't publish in *Poetry* "because I don't believe in the society that it creates" (*H*, 157).

This concern with a poetry that would define the terms of its circulation, and assert a value indissociable from the very negation of its value as a commodity, or as a social convenience, or as narcissistic comfort, returns us to Dickinson. Spicer read Dickinson with great care during the transformative year he spent in Boston starting in late 1955, which culminated in the seeds of his book *After Lorca*, completed upon his return to San Francisco. Working in the Rare Book Room of the Boston Public Library, Spicer accepted a suggestion from his supervisor there that he write a review of the new Johnson edition of Dickinson's poems—a task made all the more interesting as the Library itself contained many of the manuscripts and letters that Johnson had examined, and that Spicer consulted in evaluating Johnson's editing work. In the short piece he eventually wrote for the *Boston Public Library Quarterly*, Spicer dwelled on the special problems Dickinson posed for her editor, in a manner that prefigured some of the most important trends of Dickinson criticism from the 1980s onward, as well as suggesting some of the predicament that is now mine. Spicer paid special attention to Dickinson's letters, noting that "She would often spread out her poetry on the page as if it were prose and even, at times, indent her prose as poetry," with the result that "One of the most difficult problems of the editor has been the separation of prose from poetry" (*H*, 232). But by the time Spicer has examined several acute cases of this difficulty, he reaches a much more radical conclusion: "The reason for the difficulty of drawing a line between the poetry and prose in Emily Dickinson's letters may be that she did not wish such a line to be drawn" (234). This insight, as I have argued elsewhere,[4] was to become foundational for the rest of Spicer's work, as seen in *After Lorca*, which mixes lyric translations and fake translations of Lorca with prose "letters" from "Jack" to the dead poet, or in the "Letters to James Alexander," which insist on being at once personal singular events of address *and* iterable aesthetic objects in a manner that befuddled and disturbed his own entourage. In a July 1955 letter to his friend Allen Joyce, Spicer asked Joyce to share the letters with others, stipulating: "They are personal letters for you and they are also public letters. I measure their success by how well I can succeed in being deeply personal and public at the same time. Like my poems" ("Letters to Allen Joyce," 153). And as Michael Davidson has pointed out, for Spicer poems themselves often functioned *as* letters within his community: "the function of poetry," Davidson notes, "was often to perform and engage social alliances, not represent them separate from the poem" (*Guys*, 17–18). Again like Dickinson's, Spicer's poems were not "about" the social; they *were* the social. And given this conception, poems are in some way literally "unpublishable" as such, while letters are always a form of poetry rather than simply a vehicle for poetry's conveyance. To put it another way, at the core of Spicer's writing is not only a breakdown of the problematic opposition public/private, which is always an embarrassment for any editor ruffling through someone else's personal papers and notebooks, but even more: a breakdown between the opposition "life" and "work." And this is an even bigger embarrassment for an editor, as this involves not merely questions of decency and tact but the very ontological basis on which the choices of what is to be published in a book of "poems" and what is to be left out is founded.

Indeed, this brings us to what is perhaps the crux, for the idea of a random collection of isolated bits of "fine" writing pulled free from any dialogic context, and valorized according to fetishized notions of autonomous aesthetic quality, is precisely what Spicer objected to in his most famous and powerful formulation of the serial poem, or composition by book. Here, in his 1957 work *Admonitions*—also structurally based on the interplay between poem and letter—he writes that his previous work consisting of isolated individual lyrics "looks foul to me. The poems belong nowhere. . . . It was not my anger or my frustration that got in the way of my poetry but the fact that I viewed each anger and each frustration as unique—something to be converted into poetry as one would exchange foreign money. I learned this from the English Department (and from the English Department of the spirit—that great quagmire that lurks at the bottom of all of us) and it ruined ten years of my poetry. . . . Poems should echo and re-echo against each other. They should create resonances. They cannot live alone any more than we can" (*CP*, 163). And yet to a considerable extent, this book consists precisely of poems that Spicer decided indeed "belonged nowhere," which meant for Spicer, as of 1957, that they probably shouldn't be published at all. In one of his famous Vancouver lectures of June 1965, Spicer stresses the importance of throwing away poems when the crucial "dictation" falters, remarking, ". . . there are plenty of poems. One of the nicest things is when you learn that you can throw poems away—that you don't have to save good lines and things like that" (*H*, 88). For Spicer, the fact of a poem being "good" doesn't make it worth saving, as that very criterion of isolated value is what he rejects.

Therefore, let the paradox of titling a collection "uncollected" carry its full burden, and may the energies released in these texts not be bound within their binding here. May these poems in some way be broadcast and dispatched as well as published. There is no escaping the fact that a book such as this violates core principles of Spicer's sense of the possibilities of poetry; it also violates core principles of Spicer's sense of poetry's limitations. Its very form makes fewer claims than those on which Spicer insisted, while at the same time affirming a timeless, ideal potency of the poetic, which Spicer scorned. My hope is that this book will endure, however, not as a betrayal of Spicer, but rather as a failed monument to the failure of the poetic which Spicer paradoxically championed. And that it will serve as a homage to and additional instance of the relentless battle Spicer's work, when at its best, waged against itself. When evoking the desire of the poet, Spicer rejected the conscious desiring of what the poet "wants" to say. On the other hand, there's another "want" which Spicer posits as fundamental to the poetic act, as in the phrase "it wants five dollars being ten dollars, that kind of want" (*H*, 6). It is in this sense that Spicer's strictures notwithstanding, we might want this book.

The Poems

The vast majority of the poetry Spicer published in his lifetime has already been collected in the first volume of this series, *My Vocabulary Did This To Me: The Collected Poetry of Jack Spicer*. There, the editors published all of the "books" that Spicer saw into print in his lifetime, along with the posthumous serial poems included by Robin Blaser in his *Collected Books* and a few additional ones they found among the papers that Blaser bequeathed to the Bancroft Library in 2004. They also included many but not all of the lyrics that Donald Allen had published in *One Night Stand*, a collection of Spicer's shorter works, as well as new finds discovered in the archives mentioned above. For this volume, I have decided to republish every poem from *One Night Stand* that did not appear in *My Vocabulary Did This To Me*, re-edited in light of new manuscript evidence where appropriate.

Further selections from the notebooks and papers were generally made according to the following criteria. First is my sense of the intrinsic quality of the poem—a theoretically faulty and methodologically unstable concept at the best of times, and one rendered even less valid by Spicer's own poetics, as discussed above. As Spicer well knew, however, this form of judgment remains unavoidable. Second, I included some poems which if not entirely successful on their own nevertheless shed interesting light on other works by Spicer, or show different approaches to problems and questions Spicer worked through elsewhere, even if said approaches were ultimately not retained. Third, poems were included that seemed clearly important from the perspective of literary or cultural history. Often, these speak to his consideration of contemporary issues in poetics but sometimes more generally to the San Francisco counterculture, the queer subculture of the 1950s and '60s, current events and politics, or his relationship with other poets, such as Duncan and, in one notable case, Bob Kaufman ("For Bob"). Fourth, weight was given to how important works seemed to Spicer himself: texts included in this volume range from poems whose extant copytext is only one hastily scribbled notebook draft, which Spicer might very well have forgotten ever writing, to those that were preserved in multiple typed fair copies, carefully discussed with friends in correspondence, and presented at large public readings. Obviously, all else being equal, poems like these have a stronger claim, though not a definitive one.

Moreover, regarding this last criterion, considerable evidence exists in the form of several lists of his work Spicer made for himself. The first is a handwritten inventory of twenty-one poems, probably from 1947. All poems on this list that were not published in *CP*, save one which could not be identified, have been included here. More important are two speculative attempts at compiling a "Selected Poems," which date from the mid-50s. The first of these is a holograph manuscript written in pencil on pages ripped out of a small spiral-bound notebook. It begins with a title page reading "A Pook-Up for Rabbi Blasen," followed by the date-line "Sept. 10, 1956, Boston, Masochistic." There follow pencil holograph fair copies of forty poems, ranging from early Berkeley work to pieces which then would have been extremely fresh. "Blasen" is of course Robin Blaser, who later produced a typescript from this sheaf of papers, apparently after Spicer's death. Though the "Pook-Up" manuscript went no further, Spicer relaunched the project of a Selected Poems shortly thereafter. This second collection consists of a pencil holograph table of contents listing eighty-four poems, as well as a complete typescript with occasional corrections in Spicer's hand. The poems are listed in roughly chronological order, again beginning with early Berkeley work, and this time extending into spring 1958, as the title of one of the last poems in-dicates: "A Poem for Dada Day at the Place, April 1, 1958" (published in *CP*). In other words, well after the pivotal letter to Robin Blaser found in *Admonitions*, which rejects the idea of the isolated lyric in favor of the "book" or "serial poem" (and which is included in the "Selected Poems" project!), Spicer was still seriously considering publishing a collection that expressly violated these very strictures. Perhaps it was reservations such as those in the Blaser letter that led him to abandon the idea, and indeed, many of the more recent poems Spicer included in his table of contents were organized into and did appear as the "books" *Admonitions* and *A Book of Music*, if only after Spicer's death.[5] The ultimate fate of these collections notwithstanding, for this edition I have tended to priv-ilege the manuscripts for the "Pook-Up" and the "Selected" in establish-ing copytexts, as well as in selecting poems for inclusion; more detailed explanations are found in the notes to individual poems.

The poems in this book are presented mainly in chronological order, to the extent this can be established. While some of these poems were published in Spicer's lifetime or, as noted above, were the object of sig-nificant attention on his part and well circulated among his friends— for example, "An Arcadia for Dick Brown," "The Trojan Wars Renewed: A Capitulation, or The Dunkiad," "An Exercise," and the poems pub-lished in *J*—many others are from loose leaves classed in alphabetical order in the Spicer papers at Bancroft, and these can be hard to date.

Even more are found in the notebooks of diverse shapes, sizes, and formats that Spicer kept throughout his writing life. As Spicer increasingly turned to longer, extended forms from the mid-50s onwards, the stray pieces I have collected here likewise increasingly appear in perfectly definable contexts: quite literally between the pages and in the margins of bigger projects to which the notebook that houses the strays is dedicated. In this way many of these poems, when read in archival context, can feel like notes on or outtakes from other projects with which they are clearly in dialogue. This is a form of co-respondence (to use Spicer's term from *After Lorca*) which I have wanted to convey, and therefore within the chronological format poems have also often been grouped according to the notebooks in which they are found. There are three main series of notebooks belonging to longer works from which poems have been extracted for this edition: those devoted to the Boston "Oliver Charming" project or to *After Lorca* (both published in *CP*), and those from Spicer's unfinished detective novel, titled by his editors *The Tower of Babel*. Though less numerous, the works found in notebooks relating to *Lament for the Makers*, *A Red Wheelbarrow*, and *Homage to Creeley* (again, all published in *CP*, the latter the first section of *The Heads of the Town Up to the Aether*) also profit from being considered in context. While the dates of the earlier notebooks are often harder to ascertain, to the extent that Spicer finished one notebook before starting another (which doesn't seem to always have been the case) they do allow us to group his work into temporal units, and as a rule I've used the notebooks when possible as a basis for sequencing the earlier work too.

This book begins, however, with a series that presents no such difficulties. Rather, it reproduces in full Spicer's very first extended poetic project, quite possibly the original precursor to the "book" or "serial poem" which was to emerge fully theorized about a decade later. This is Spicer's *Collected Poems 1945–1946 (for Josephine Miles)*, a handmade one-off booklet, sewn together by Spicer and presented to his University of California at Berkeley poetry teacher as a Christmas present in 1946, shortly before his twenty-second birthday. Some of these very early poems Spicer still liked enough ten years later to list for inclusion in the selected poems projects mentioned above; others, understandably, seem to have been left completely behind. Thus the *Collected Poems* made for Miles is included here not on the basis of the quality of every one of its poems, but rather as a general representation of Spicer's earliest mature work, and also as a fully conceived and self-realized artistic project.[6] If it anticipates the "book" and serial poem, it also foreshadows Spicer's predilection for self-publishing, as well as the all important act of dedicating specific works to specific individuals, which was to play such an important role throughout his life. Recognizing the book as an object as much as a collection, Spicer's friend and publisher Graham Mackintosh produced a facsimile edition of it in 1981 with his White Rabbit Press, though this edition inadvertently confused the page order in some places. But it is in the same spirit as Mackintosh that this present volume reprints the book in courier type, as a gesture to the literally unique made object which it is.

The portion of this book devoted to poetry ends with another special case: Spicer's 1958 serial work "A New Poem," which while containing some of the most impressive writing in the entire collection also exists in a state that makes it simply impossible to establish anything like a definitive text. For this reason, as the notes recount in detail, it has seemed best to present the texts in a necessarily incomplete state as an addendum of "texts and fragments," rather than as a putatively finished work.

Not surprisingly, as Spicer's commitment to serial form solidified the number of stray lyrics declined. As of 1957 there are comparatively few individual lyrics, and of those many are clearly outtakes and trial runs from books such as *After Lorca*, *Admonitions*, *A Book of Music*, and *Billy the Kid*. While this is not the case with the *Hokkus* and poems published in *J*, as the notes indicate, here too his notebooks and publication decisions gesture towards the establishment of longer forms. Still, the existence of stray lyrics to the very end, and the manners in which Spicer often tried to bind them into larger structures, deepens the picture conveyed by *My Vocabulary*: the tension between the shorter work and the "book" was never resolved by Spicer. Which of course doesn't invalidate serial form, as for Spicer the "book" in its generative power *is* that very tension, and not its resolution. That said, in addition to the unstable *A New Poem*, this collection contains four other fully fledged serial works: *An Exercise* (probably 1961), *The Clock Jungle* (1957), *For Major General Abner Doubleday Inventor of Baseball and First American President of the Theosophical Society* (probably 1961), and *Spider Music* (1962), the latter three previously unpublished. These all provide interesting supplements and counterpoints to the books of corresponding years published in *My Vocabulary Did This To Me*.

The earlier shorter poems are of course extremely varied in the pleasures and interest they offer, but read in isolation and without the context of *My Vocabulary*, they can give a skewed picture of Spicer's "development." For example, while many of the works from the 1940s or early '50s collected here could seem to bear witness to Spicer's difficulties in "modernizing" himself, as Pound might have put it, one does well to remember that during this period he also wrote poems like "We find the body difficult to speak," "One Night Stand," and "An Answer to Jaime de Angulo." Read in tandem with *My Vocabulary*, among the particularly salient elements that emerge in this volume is the extent of Spicer's Berkeley-era experiments with longer lyric forms already familiar to us from poems like "Psychoanalysis: An Elegy," or Boston poems like "Song for Bird and Myself" and "A Poem to the Reader of the Poem." Poems here such as "I wonder where Orpheus has been . . . ," "We were talking," "We are too tired to live like lions . . . ," and "Whenever I love" expand our sense of Spicer's interest in a longer, reflective lyric form, neither that of the isolated short lyric nor the dialogic but often jagged-edged "books."

As for the short lyrics that Spicer could never stop writing, of those collected here one of the last is "Be Brave to Things," an occasional poem arising from *Open Space*'s Valentine's Day contest, announced in its first issue. In issue number two Spicer's poem took the laurels, published under the title "This Is Submitted to Your Valentine Contest" and enclosed in a clumsily hand-drawn heart, with the editor noting "in lieu of other entries, M. Spicer to be winner by default" (*Open Space* 2). By default, it is perhaps the love that lets you go on that wins in the end for Spicer, in this piece which, to borrow from Simon Smith, might be called a "general purpose love poem," and in which the specificity of the second-person address Spicer so loved to pressure is abandoned for an unlimited, admonishing imperative. The poem seems affirmationist in its trumpeting of resilience, yet it brackets its seeming unconditional call by the repeated phrase "as long as." The poem looks to the future, yet is elegiac. The infinity that Blake imagined as held in the palm of the hand is here, but in the form of one tiny universe whose particularity challenges the concept of universality itself. This poem condenses many of the oppositions that Spicer played against each other throughout his writing, couched in a familiar imperative form that feverishly undercuts the authority from which it commands. And no less familiar is Spicer's pressuring of language beyond univocal meaning, as here the phrase "as long as" oscillates between logical restriction and measure, between the temporal and the spatial, leaving us only with dimension. This poem of the finite gives this collection its name.

The Plays

Although he always identified as a poet first and foremost, Spicer also frequently tried his hand at prose fiction and drama, from his days as a creative writing student in college through to 1958 and the unfinished detective novel. The three plays collected here represent two major projects from the mid-1950s into which he invested significant effort—*Pentheus and the Dancers* and *Troilus*—and the most successful of his early experiments, *Young Goodman Brown*. Interestingly, all three are adaptations, which surely says something about Spicer's general level of interest in narrative or character, or perhaps about his aptitude at handling them in dramatic form, as in the archives can be found several wholly original unfinished plays.

Young Goodman Brown was composed as a creative writing assignment at either the University of Redlands or the University of California–Berkeley, and thus dates from the mid-1940s. Spicer's professor gave him an A−, while acknowledging "This seems to me about the most successful dramatization of the story which could be achieved" (JSP 2004/209). Kevin Killian and David Brazil published it in their *Kenning Anthology of*

Poets Theater 1945–1985, which I have used as copytext (subject to minor corrections based on material in JSP 2004) while adding a Cast of Characters—an element I have introduced to all three of the plays collected here. I've found no further references to the play anywhere by Spicer or his entourage, but Spicer's interest in and handling of the material speaks to his major concerns in significant ways, and also perhaps to his interest in the theater as form. As with both *Pentheus* and *Troilus*, at the heart of *Young Goodman Brown* is a highly charged and ambivalent witnessing of what rightfully should have been veiled—something Spicer's treatment of the material in his adaptation of Nathaniel Hawthorne's 1835 story serves to stress. And Hawthorne remained an important touchstone for Spicer throughout his life.

The copytext for *Pentheus and the Dancers—An Adaptation* (JSP 2004) is a 33-page typescript with "by Jack Spicer" written in pencil by Spicer in the upper right corner of the first page; it also contains a few holograph pencil corrections, and a dateline at the end: "Golden Gate Y.M.C.A., San Francisco, August 25, 1954."[7] Spicer's qualification notwithstanding, this text follows Euripides's *The Bacchae* far more closely than a reader of, say, *After Lorca*, might have expected—the end of the play, where the source text suffers from lacunae editors and translators have always attempted to fill, is also where Spicer's interventions are most visible. It would be interesting to know what he had in mind when he wrote of *Pentheus* to Graham Mackintosh on January 3, 1955: "It's certainly an entirely different play than the *Bacchae* of Euripides which it started out to be an adaptation of" (JSP 2004), as that seems something of an exaggeration. Nor is it clear what drew Spicer to *The Bacchae* in the first place, though the modernist recasting of Greek classics practiced by poets such as W. B. Yeats, H. D., and Ezra Pound must certainly have played a role.[8] As late as early 1956—well after finishing *Troilus*—he was still concerned with the earlier play, writing to his friend Allen Joyce that "I'm now revising my Bacchae . . ." ("Letters to Allen Joyce," 150) but if a revised version was ever completed it has yet to be found. At any rate, around six months previously, in the last stages of completing *Troilus*, he had written to Duncan "I now fully understand your criticisms of my Pentheus.

It seemed good to me because (unconsciously) I knew where I was going after it. Now I've been there I'm sorry I wasted the money having this finger-exercise typed" (*Acts* 6, 14).

Still, whatever Spicer's initial motivations in undertaking the *Pentheus* project, and however quickly it was superseded by other concerns, the play occupies a fascinating place in Spicer's work. At the heart of the play, of course, is the non-recognition of the sacred in the form of Dionysus, and therefore the non-recognition of the sacredness of drunken excess and sexuality. While Euripides's original stresses Pentheus's arrogance and over-estimation of his powers, Spicer's version tends to cast his protagonist's fault more as obtuseness or willful blindness—a repression exposed by Pentheus's sudden eagerness to perhaps see his mother engage in lewd acts. Also, while for Euripides Dionysus himself is a principal character, though disguised and unrecognizable to the other characters in the play, Spicer simply gives him the name he is sometimes called in Euripides too—"Stranger"—at times harping on the root word "strange." At one of the play's climactic moments, the Stranger has been locked away inside Thebes (and therefore offstage) and the Chorus laments, "We are alone outside the gates of a strange city. I do not feel the god anywhere. What if Pentheus is right?" Almost immediately, however, Dionysus announces his presence from offstage, after which the earth begins to quake, lightning flashes, Pentheus's palace falls, the Chorus and Antichorus prostrate themselves, and a stage direction reads: "(Lights brighten and Stranger enters through the gate.)" Spicer seemed to remember these terms. A few years later in a major work he would write "Love isn't proud enough to hate / The stranger at its gate / That says and does" (*CP*, 261) and "Strange, I had words for dinner / Stranger, I had words for dinner / Stranger, strange, do you believe me" (*CP*, 264). More than Euripides, Spicer insists on the strangeness of the god, and the perhaps unassimilable strangeness of the passions the god represents. The uncanny and sacred eruption of an intimate strangeness is also fundamental to the entire dynamics of dictated poetry, and *The Heads of the Town up to the Aether* (*CP*, 247) does the work of drawing *Pentheus* fully into Spicer's poetics.

Spicer must have begun work on *Troilus* soon after completing *Pentheus*. When he left the San Francisco Bay area for New York in the summer of 1955 very shortly after finishing the play, he considered it among the most impressive of the literary accomplishments he was taking with him, and more than two years later, defining his new dedication to serial form in the famous letter to Blaser in *Admonitions*, he grouped *Troilus* with the "Imaginary Elegies" as the only part of his early work worth saving. The earliest reference to it appears to be a letter to Graham Mackintosh of January 21, 1955, where Spicer mentions a "new play" (JSP 2004). On February 2, he informs Mackintosh that he has finished the prologue and is working on the first act. Letters in June to several correspondents mention revisions, and a June 28 letter to Mackintosh, also announcing Spicer's imminent departure for New York, declares "My Troilus is all firmly revised and now only awaits a typist" (JSP 2004). If that typist was ever found, the resulting typescript hasn't been: the copy-text for this volume, a typescript in JSP 2004, was prepared by Robin Blaser and Stephany Judy in the 1960s, though concluding with the dateline "San Francisco, June 25, 1955," which Spicer had used to end his holograph draft.[9]

If *Troilus* was certainly Spicer's major writing project during the first half of 1955, his interest in the story and its previous treatments was long-standing. In college Spicer had written a somewhat desultory essay titled "A Preliminary Excursion into Comparison of Shakespeare's and Dryden's Troilus and Cressida in a Quixotic Attempt to Discover Neo-Classical Poetic Technique, or, Some Little Truth Found Too Early" (for which he received an eminently reasonable B). But in addition to Dryden (whom Spicer largely dismisses in his essay) and Shakespeare, Chaucer looms large. *Poet, Be Like God* relates an anecdote from Larry Fagin suggesting that Spicer knew very large portions of *Troilus and Criseyde*, an 8,000-line poem, by heart (P, 211) as well as another where Gail Chugg remembers Spicer telling him that Chaucer's version was "the greatest poem in English" (P, 203). Meanwhile, if Spicer was not wrong to conclude later that his play was "overcrowded" and a "mouthful big enough for five plays" (P, 86) it's still easy to see why he esteemed it so highly, and was so disappointed when the Cambridge Poets' Theater turned it down in 1956 (*P*, 75). The play is funny, campy, clever, but also serious and reflective, and poses questions that would occupy Spicer for the rest of his life.

From Chaucer, Spicer took the early considerations of the nature and etiology of love, largely absent from Shakespeare, which circle around the "accident" of Spicer's Act I, Scene 1, which itself makes use of a spillage that might also hearken back to *Billy Budd*. However, it is Shakespeare who provides the panorama of the warring armies, each with its own tensions and interpersonal intrigues, which occupy Spicer as much as the love story. The football uniforms and boardrooms within which Spicer places his warriors stress the contrived, ritualistic, and managerial nature of the war no more than Shakespeare does in his astonishing *Troilus and Cressida*. Spicer also felt he was making some serious points about his own times: for Spicer, Troilus reflects the younger generation of students he was now encountering as a teacher, and who, like Troilus, couldn't remember a life before wartime. "I like music," Troilus says in Act 1, Scene 2. "You don't have to believe anything to hear it." As Spicer wrote to Graham Mackintosh just when he was first drafting this scene, Troilus was just a "small kid" when the siege of Troy started—a "war child" like Mackintosh himself, with the following characteristics:

> The first is an isolation from history and tradition. . . . The meaningful can only be in the present. That is why music is the art most popular with war-children. One can understand a piece of music without reference to the past, without reference to anything but the music itself. That is why poetry, the exact opposite of music, is least popular with war-children. They live, the most sensitive of them, in two dimensions instead of three. They can't dig time. . . . ("Letters to Graham Mackintosh, 112)

If Troilus is in some ways beyond the poetic in not even having history as a nightmare from which to awaken, Ulysses with his plans and plots might at times be seen as the figure of Spicer the poet himself. "I was a poet once," he angrily declares in Act II, Scene 2, echoing the refrain of "I was a singer once," which rings throughout Spicer's "A Postscript to the Berkeley Renaissance" (*CP*, 45–46), and Ulysses describes one of his outlandish tactical ploys as "pure poetry in action" (Act I, Scene 3). If Spicer then sometimes casts poetry itself as the mark of an older generation fading into its own irrelevance, on the other hand it's Cressida who often comes closest to Spicer's own poetic concerns. Late in the play she meditates on the ocean, and tries to see it as other characters she mentions have, but fails: "But all I saw was an ocean with pieces breaking off from it in meaningless patterns. . . . Just a cold dark fact that no metaphor could make significant. It didn't even mean to be meaningless" (Act IV, Scene 1). Around ten years later, in *Language*, Spicer would insist "The ocean / Does not mean to be listened to. A drop / Or crash of water. It means / Nothing" (*CP*, 373). In *Troilus*, Spicer's engagement with Chaucer and Shakespeare is mostly oblique, ironic, or very broadly structural, but in at least one instance it is wholly explicit. In Act 3, Scene 4, Troilus's reflection on his "Trojan Cressida" can be seen as a direct response to the famous crux in Shakespeare, where a distraught Troilus strives to distinguish Diomedes's "Cressida" from his own, and suggests in a much-discussed paradox, "This is and is not Cressid" (Act 5, Scene 2). Spicer's version shows that he takes Shakespeare more seriously, or at least more literally, than many of the Bard's commentators.

While Spicer never again embarked on a project remotely like *Troilus*, if we take him at his word in *Admonitions* the play nevertheless pointed the way to composing works that didn't "point nowhere" themselves. It is perhaps not narrative and plot that allowed his subsequent writing to accomplish this, but the very elements that made the play the "mouthful" Spicer derided: speech, dialogue, exchange, debate. *Troilus* immediately precedes a shift to the even more demotic and speech-based tone and diction that would emerge in Boston, as well as to the increasingly dialectical structure of Spicer's work, in which voices fold back upon themselves conversationally and argumentatively. Looking forward in some ways to *The Holy Grail*—another adaptation, in its way—*Troilus* also foretells the poetics of discussion and debate that are among the most distinctive characteristics of Spicer's writing.

Conventions

All titles of poems are Spicer's own, unless noted. The (many) untitled poems are referred to by the first line or a fragment thereof enclosed in quotation marks. Titles of serial poems are printed entirely in italicized capital letters, in contradistinction to the titles of the shorter poems of which these "books" are comprised.

Notebook Sources

Many of the poems published in this volume were found interspersed within bound notebooks that Spicer had dedicated to larger or different projects, or sometimes grouped with loose-leaf drafts. Some feel like out-takes, and others can be read as musings or marginal comments, sometimes almost literally, on the longer pieces within whose pages these poems are found. Here follows a list of these poems, and the note-books where they are located. All of the following material is housed at the Bancroft Library, University of California–Berkeley, BANC 2004/209.

From the *Papers of Oliver Charming* notebooks:
"Orpheus Was A Poet . . ."
Hell
The Waves
"If I had invented homosexuality . . ."
Translator
"Goodnight. I want to kill myself . . ."

From the *After Lorca* notebooks:
Buster Keaton's Shadow
"The boy . . ."
"They are going on a journey . . ."
"Hmm. Tahiti . . ."
"I feel a black incubus . . ."
"It was like making love to my shadow . . ."

Romance Sonámbulo (a partial translation
        from Federico García Lorca)
A Poem Against Dada & The White Rabbit
THE CLOCK JUNGLE

From the *Tower of Babel* notebooks:
  "Ridiculous is a word . . ."
  "Hunters in the great Southwest. . ."
  For Bob
  For Tom
  For Jerry
  "An island is a herd of reindeer . . ."
  "And he said there are trails . . ."
  "Dear Russ"
  Vistas: On Visiting Spinoza's Grave
  Lamp
  Carmen
  Opera
  Mazurka for the Girls Who Brought Me Tranquilizers
  The Birds
  Song For A Raincoat
  Birthday Pool
  Poet
  "Three little waves . . ."
  Hotel
  "No daring shadows . . ."
  The Pipe of Peace

From the *Homage to Creeley* notebooks and drafts:
  "It is impossible to stop. . ."
  Blood and Sand

From the *Lament for the Makers* notebook:
  "Daily waste washed by the tides . . ."
  Shark Island

Stinson
For B. W.
For B. W. II
For B. W. III

From the *Red Wheelbarrow* notebook:
   "It's dark all night . . ."
   "Love has five muscles . . ."
   "Thank you all for your fine funeral . . ."

All of the longer works associated with these notebooks can be found in *My Vocabulary Did This to Me*, with the exception of *The Tower of Babel*, which has been published separately as *Jack Spicer's Detective Novel: The Tower of Babel*, ed. and afterword by Lew Ellingham and Kevin Killian (Hoboken, NJ: Talisman House, 1994).

Abbreviations in the Introduction

CP	Jack Spicer, *My Vocabulary Did This To Me: The Collected Poetry of Jack Spicer*, ed. Peter Gizzi and Kevin Killian (Middletown, CT: Wesleyan University Press, 2008).
H	Jack Spicer, *The House that Jack Built: The Collected Lectures of Jack Spicer*, ed. and afterword Peter Gizzi (Middletown, CT: Wesleyan University Press, 1998).
JSP 2004	"Jack Spicer Papers," BANC MSS 2004/209, Bancroft Library, University of California–Berkeley.
P	Lewis Ellingham and Kevin Killian, *Poet, Be Like God: Jack Spicer and the San Francisco Renaissance* (Hanover, NH: Wesleyan University Press / University Press of New England, 1998).
PJS	Daniel Katz, *The Poetry of Jack Spicer* (Edinburgh: Edinburgh University Press, 2013).

Notes

1 Written in pencil on the back of a still-sealed envelope from the Office of the Recorder, University of Redlands, which was received by Spicer in the Rare Book Department of the Boston Public Library on January 26, 1956 (JSP 2004).

2 This story has been told many times, but it originates in Robin Blaser's essay "The Practice of Outside," first included in his edition of Spicer's *Collected Books*, and now available in his collection of essays, *The Fire*.

3 I don't have room here to provide an adequate overview of Spicer's life and contacts, but there are many resources available for interested readers. If the brilliant biography *Poet, Be Like God* is obviously the most complete, *My Vocabulary Did This To Me* supplements this with an excellent updated chronology which incorporates information not previously available. Much of considerable interest is also to be found in Peter Gizzi's notes and afterword to *The House that Jack Built*, as well as in biographies of Robert Duncan by Ekbert Faas and Lisa Jarnot, and Miriam Nichols's recent biography of Robin Blaser.

4 See *PJS*, 52–78, for more on this.

5 Both these works, published in *CP*, were established by Spicer himself, and a fair copy of the entirety of *Admonitions* had been prepared at least several months before the table of contents for his "Selected" project was compiled.

6 Some manuscripts of still earlier work do exist, but I have chosen not to publish them here. However, four of his poems published in 1941 in *Colonial Voices*, a journal run by the students of Fairfax High School in Los Angeles, which Spicer attended, can be found in *Fulcrum: An Annual of Poetry and Aesthetics* (no. 3, 2004) in a special feature on the Berkeley Renaissance edited by Ben Mazer.

7 The play was previously published under the title *Pentheus and the Dancers* in *Caterpillar* 12 (1970), but the transcription inadvertently omitted the last page of Spicer's typescript; this volume publishes the play in its entirety for the first time.

8 In terms of modernist precedents, Pound of course used a similar myth recounting the failure to recognize Dionysus as the basis for *Canto* II, and Robinson Jeffers, a poet whose work Spicer knew well, retold the Pentheus story in his poem "The Humanist's Tragedy."

9   *Troilus* was previously published in *No: A Journal of the Arts* (issue 3, 2004), edited and introduced by Aaron Kunin, who gave me the textual information above, which had been transmitted in turn to him by Robin Blaser. During the editing Blaser also mentioned to Kunin that Spicer's play was deeply informed by work on Greek religion and culture by W. K. C. Guthrie and also E. R. Dodds, whose class Spicer took when Dodds taught at Berkeley as a visiting professor. Thanks to Aaron Kunin for this information and his invaluable editorial work on *Troilus*.

THE POEMS

BEGINNINGS: *COLLECTED POEMS 1945–1946*

COLLECTED POEMS
1945 1946
Jack Spicer

Berkeley California
1946

TO JOSEPHINE MILES

Within an ever-circular domain
Home of lost orbits and tangential stuff
She snakes her sentences obtuse enough
To arc the angled circuit and escape.

[signed]
Jack Spicer
Christmas 1946

Within the world of little shapes and sounds
Of random pleasures and of vagrant pains
The mind possesses all that it contains
And measures briefly all that there abounds.
If this were all--but something deeper mars
The woof of matter with the warp of dreams
And for a frightened instant time will seem
A dappled horse gone mad among the stars.

THE BRIDGE GAME

> "You're all a pack of cards."
> --Alice in Wonderland

The Bridge
2 Hearts
The Crane of Harts, the King of Hearts
Spades, Spades, Spades
The Bird
2 Spades
The Sam of Spades, the Queen of Spades
Pass, Pass, Pass

Tarot, Tarot, Tarot, Tarot
Pharaoh, Pharaoh, Pharaoh, Pharaoh
Read   Hermes Trismegistus, Hermes Trismegistus
Very   Marco Polo, Khubla's Palace
Fast   "Fortunes told by Mme. Alice."
Pass, Pass, Pass

```
                    Buddha's Wheel
                    Rod and Reel
                    Ace of Cups
                    Holy Grail
                    Bicycle, Bicycle, Bicycle, Bi--
                    THE HANGED MAN
Read with           Alice ! Alice !
an                  Miserere !
imploring           Miserere !
voice               Alice ! Alice !

                    King of Hearts
                    Queen of Spades
Read                Courtesy Bicycle
Slowing             Courtesy Bicycle
Down                Courtesy Bicycle Playing Cards.
```

After the ocean, shattering with equinox
Has cast the last of creatures on its shore,
After the final tidal-wave has turned
And churned remaining rock to sandy vestiges-
Ebbing, it leaves its tide-pools in our skulls.
Amorphous and amphibious, we gasp
And grasp the call and rasp of all recall,
The fishly odor when a mermaid dies.

AT SLIM GORDON'S

Wash up from the sea, stale with the smell of brine,
Puddle-waves and stinking pools of salt;
Tide penetrates the doorways, dwells and seeps.
Torn timber turns to form an ocean floor.
Blunt-bubbled from the sea, blind heads emerge
Bobbing, fine-flecked with phosphorescence, veined
Vaguely, blandly, with the blood of Adam
Deemed, redeemed, but turned to salt.

Among the coffee cups and soup tureens walked beauty,
Casual, but not unconscious of his power,
Carrying dishes mucked with clinging macaroni,
Unbearable in his spasmatic beauty,
Sovereign in Simon's Restaurant and wreathed in power,
The monarch of a kingdom yet unruled.

Now regal at a table in the Starlight Club sits beauty,
Casual but not unconscious of his power,
Kept by a Mr. Blatz who manufactures girdles,
Unbearable in his spasmatic beauty,
Counting with kingly eyes the subjects of his power
Who sleep with Beauty and are unappeased.

THE CHESS GAME

If cylinders ran wild and begat parallelograms,
If odd spheres ran their cold noses against the universe,
Who then could say where the men could move ?
Bishops advancing out of space and time.
Knights cavalierly non-Euclidean.
Rooks flying in black formation faster than the speed of
    light.
These would look down on the brave little pawns
That march in solemn column toward the curve
That leads below the chessboard.
The king is dead and the queen is mad.
Where's Alice ?
Alice should indeed be there
Imprisoned in her four-dimensioned looking-glass.
Dimensional, dementia,
Yes, we are curved now and all the arcs
Are round with envy.
We move counterclockwise toward another Wonderland.
The table upon which we play is cold
Shape-solid but with rapid, rapid
Approach to absolute zero.
Where are the players ?
Do they not laugh at the antics of their men ?
Perhaps they pray:
"Our father, which art in curved and thick space,
Blasphemous is thy name."
White moves.
"Thy chaos come, thy whim be done
In time as it is in space."
Black moves.
"Give us this day our daily doubt
And forgive us our love as we forgive thy hatred."

White moves.
"And lead us not, but deliver, deliver, deliver."
No one moves.

4 A.M.

The many-clanging bell peals loud.
The pulsing, driving sound
Falls groundwards, spent of tone.
Unbound.
I see,
Mind bent around the inner ear,
The long unfeelingness of things
Beyond all sound.

BERKELEY SPRING

I find no quiet here, the rioting
Has curved confusion inward like a ball.
Though all my fractured senses act
As if their insulation were intact
And touch each miracle with much
The selfsame prickles as they would a fact,
I know that now the calendar has greened
And thrown a screen of leaves and branches over all
    the world.

ASH WEDNESDAY

Ashes for us; for Adam, unabashed,
From every fire falls in clinging curls
Of soot and cinder; Falling writhes and whirls
And settles with a whimper on His lashed
And bleeding, blessed flesh; then showers forth
Hot seed which burns its livid Adam-brand
In transit as it sweeps across the land
Flame-frightened from Golgotha towards the North.
Ashes for us; but on His lonely face
Above the Adam-fire there remains
More sorrow than our sorry token trace
Of ashes; on this God-head turn the pains
That twisted from His flesh the bread of grace
And squeezed the wine of glory from His veins.

PALM SUNDAY

He rode into the vineyard on an ass
Reclaiming all the vintage of the land.
The clamoring of those that watched him pass
Grew louder, shriller as he raised his hand
Demanding what he sought to repossess,
His father's fields, the barren, sterile sheaves,
The bitter grapes and fig trees powerless
To harvest anything but wood and leaves.
His face was mild, but those that kept this field
On squatter's rights could not be pacified,
And there was added to that season's yield
One saviour, bound and bled and crucified.

TO THE SEMANTICISTS

Speak softly; definition is deep
But words are deeper,
Unmoving hungry surfaces
Lying like ice-bergs, half submerged
Waiting to feed, to chew the ships and spew
The half-digested sailors from their maw
Back into history.

KARMA

Tickle, tickle little star
Run up and down your orbit through my skin.
My lives, my random lives, are yours.
I'm meshed in stars.
They roar in constellation through my flesh
And every deed becomes a star.
Reborn
Each wish, each wanting wish becomes a star.

CHINOISERIE

Sea-lions bark, betray the rocks,
Define the jagged edges of this night;
Everything echoes.
Contorted conch-shells strew this shore--
My share of that desiring
And that aching, slapping sound of a hundred waves.

A POEM FOR A RESTLESS NIGHT

My love for you rides higher than the tide,
Goes writhing through the current of my dreams
Deeper than sleep.
It bobs and gleams below my brain and seems
To cast its shadows sharper and more steep
Than could be magnified in surfaces.

I saw a thunder-blossomed tree
Extending ripe electric fruit
And there was all eternity
Between its branches and its root
But under it a darkness-thing
Lay struggling on the ground
A moment seeking permanence
A shadow seeking sound.
And from the thunder-blossomed tree
Branch-bending near too far
The random moment's melody
Hung like a star.

BERKELEY SUMMER

The long, cold days of August stretch ahead
A heatless moonlight falls upon my bed.
The sun's in hock, O pawn shop man remember
The unclaimed promise of a warm September.

BERKELEY IN A TIME OF PLAGUE

Plague took us and the land from under us,
Rose like a boil, enclosing us within.
We waited and the blue sky writhed awhile
Becoming black with death.

Plague took us and the chairs from under us,
Stepped cautiously while entering the room,
(We were discussing Yeats) it paused awhile
Then smiled and made us die.

Plague took us, laughed, and reproportioned us,
Swelled us to dizzy unaccustomed size.
We died prodigiously; it hurt awhile
But left a certain quiet in our eyes.

A GIRL'S SONG

Song changes and his unburnt hair
Upon my altar changes;
We have, good strangers, many vaults
To keep the time in, but the songs are mine,
The seals are wax, and both will leak
From heat.
A bird in time is worth of two in any bush.
You can melt brush like wax; and birds in time
Can sing.
They call me bird-girl, parrot girl and worth
The time of any bird; my vault a cage,
My cage a song, my song a seal,
And I can steal an unburnt lock of hair
To weave a window there.

A green wind rose in cones and shook our town.
Bone and timber split and we were drowned in wind.
Down with the sweet, hard greeness we were drawn
And there was left no bone or soul unturned.
The green cone rose and siphoned from the street
The brighter moving objects; carried off
Three brilliant busses; soon the bruising sweet
Green wind will set them down
Where there is neither soul nor bone to drown.

The unrejected bronze lies slowly in my hall.
I call a halt to beauty; let it grow
In polished surface, let its growth be all
The surfaces I know
The groan of growing metal smears the polish short.
My ears will be accustomed; let it pass.
The bulge of growth, too heavy to abort
The monotheism of mass.

I do not see the morning traveller, the phoenix-bird.
The half-drowned mutterings of flame are stilled.
The dawn of monsters, sunless and electric, filled
With all the former sound, the morning sound, is heard.
The song of dawn in birds is gone.
Oh, sing again you phoenix bird,
Sing Christ again, you savior bird.

A NEW TESTAMENT

Old Jesus made a will before he died
And got as witnesses an honest mob
Of good and hungry men; "I'm satisfied
To die," he said, "for dying is my job.
I don't mind doing it to save you guys
From having to endure a second hell.
This one is bad enough, but it's your size.
It fits you, though it blisters pretty well.
So I won't take you with me when I start
Though I can promise you you'll not be damned;
But when I take my flesh off and depart
For Godhead I'd be sorry if I'd lammed
And left you fellows stranded, so to speak,
With nothing but a promise of rebirth.
So, this is legal: "To the poor and meek
I, Jesus, of sound mind, bequeath the earth."

"We had lunch at a marvelous hotel, drank
some more wine, shook ourselves like dogs and
started again in the direction of Sparta."
--Henry Miller

The long wind drives the rain around me now.
What length the wind, and where its roots,
And why it grows, and why it falls,
And how it knots a noose around the air,
Hangs space upon its neck and strangles everywhere:

These are the weather-beaten thoughts with which we start.
We start with nature, draw the sun within the skull,
And have a world to start, a word to write, a world to end,
And then with proper frictions properly applied
We make the groaning start.
But now the wind has stopped, the air has turned.
It will return in time, in time return
When time becomes the distance between cigarettes,
When all the winds are dead and all the clocks are stopped
And there's in reach a climate made of clocks
Where all the climates cross and all the skies
    have stopped.
Oh God, magestic Weather-Man, what part
You play within the wind-wastes of my heart.

But now an ill wind blows the stars across the sky,
Ill wind and dying weather filled with rotting clouds,
No fire in the sky but lightning screams--electric screams,
No water in the sky but steaming rain--but raining streams.
The elements of tragedy, the water-flame, the planet-fire,
The air and grasp of burning gas, are here.
But God, Fair-Weather Friend, who shakes this dying wind?
Who twists these elements to tragedy? Who takes
Death to the fire through my cigarette,
Death of the fever to the air,
Death of the planet to the earth,
Death to the water through my tears.
And God, you great Fair-Weather Friend, these things
    are mixed,
These tears are mixed, this candle-flesh is short.
Death flickers like a candle in the wind--
"Et ego in the last Arcadia" is mixed, is dying, dead.
Fair-Weather Father when an ill-wind blows,
Your light will sharpen also, vanish into wind

And mix like earth and water into mud
And keyed to pitch of fever, vanish into sound,
And light will leap across from every star
To darkness there.

Tell Sparta we have suddenly arrived.
Tell Athens we have left the land we dreamed.
A final landscape is to be contrived.
A final language is to be redeemed.
Under the raspberry-purple sky,
Beneath the liver-spotted sun,
We touch and all the other climates die;
We kiss and all the trains begin to run.

We have heard the wind wobble into Gordon's,
Singing through the bottles like an oyster,
Singing through the tables like an alcove.
We have heard the sorrows of those who are still walking
Melting through our glasses like an ice-cube,
Melting through our cigarettes like fire.
We have listened to the earliest piano
And have played the final number by request.
We have been ended at midnite
By the Board of Equalization.
And have fastened through the fallen night in puddles.
We have forgotten to ask for a savior.

Oh Christ, you pretty Weather-Boy, what part
You play within the waste winds of my heart.
I have walked through the wind and felt a shock in
    every key;

I have squatted beside a casual companion--stranger--looked
   often to his face
And found his every face a shock--and beauty;
And found his every touch a satisfaction--again beauty.

Yes, again beauty, again the shock,
The wind which blows against the night,
The star I wish to fasten on my cigarette.
Yes, always beauty--and if the air is writhing
And the water soundless, and the fire barren,
And time an unbearable quintessence,
If all these elements are weather-borne,
This stranger is my earth, my final sky,
My loss of time.

This book, designed and executed
by hand in Berkeley, California,
is strictly limited to <u>1</u> copy
on American Watercolor M Paper
  and signed by the author.

EARLY POEMS: LOS ANGELES, BERKELEY, MINNEAPOLIS, SAN FRANCISCO

"We bring these slender cylinders of song . . ."

We bring these slender cylinders of song
Instead of opium or frankincense
Because the latter would not last for long
Or stay forever in your memory—hence
We bring you opium of cellulose
And frankincense inscribed in little scratches
And you can take a big or little dose
Or have your memory in scraps and patches

And lest you might forget our joyous eyes
When age has slowed your mind and dulled your face
You'll find below a list of all the guys
Who shelled out money as their last embrace
Of fair Geneva who has made a place
Of beauty under dark and dusty skies.

"There is an inner nervousness in virgins . . ."

There is an inner nervousness in virgins
And a numbness of a kind
The pent attention of the deaf and dumb,
The sensuousness that haunts the blind.
Virginity could summon God before.
Not mine, not mine, my chastities express
The hermit's act, to go and bar the door.

HOSPITAL SCENES I   PENICILLIN

Toward sleep and now the smiler with the hypo moves
Pushing away the tendencies of dream, shelving
The body's compromise with pain—flashlite flexible
And lit within and out the dream.
She will not appease the bed-clothes kingdom. Choose
The real or inner flashlite; choice the same
As every warring morning. Always wrong.
I bear the realer arm; the needle binds. She goes.
What kindness conqueror! and who forgives?
She leaves me viceroy of my inner sleep.

HOSPITAL SCENES II   EVENING VISITORS

Brother, the constipated hours tremble here
When you arrive; I heard the great, sick bells
Strike eight without a groan, without a grunting strain
A sign that doorways are not forced without a sword.
Yes, bring that great, sick sword tomorrow
We will force escape.
All men are brothers but some men are more.

AN ARCADIA FOR DICK BROWN

The limitless and stretching mountains of the damned
Surround Arcadia; they are the hells that rise above the ground
Of this poetic paradise; these hills of parafine are thick;
Their wax is roused to catch the rising dawn.
The scenery is fathomless and deep
As any fragrant ocean caught in sleep.

Terrestrial paradise is isolate.
Chameleons crawl like pilgrims down the hills
But never reach this pit of paradise; the pink
Of salamanders thrashing to the brink,
Thrashing like someone's fingers, clutching and convulsive,
But they stop; reclimb that waxen mountain to the top.

Arcadia is isolate, I said.
Intentioned wildness of a dead
December forest punctuates the pasturings; the pull
Of a rococo wildness aching full of fauns takes shape;
The shepherdry of sleep; the dreaming Edenwards; the feverings;
Real shepherds with imaginary sheep.

Paradise crawl; the salamanders dance
Upon their greasy mountains; all the damned
Perform their daily office, climb and slide
Within the parafine; with every licking lip
They curse the Proserpinish spring; they stress
To make a leaping—rape and rescue it.

A Chinaman much older than the world
Sits quietly among the flocks; his eyes
Are landscape-breaking skies; he dances too.

The Pan, the Wandering Jew, the little dream the analyst forgot,
All these and all Rococo menacings, the key
To this Arcadian chinoiserie.

He tells me fauns are loveless. I have found a faun
Whose beauty is as sudden as the ancestral ache
Of Adam. "Take my sheep," I want to tell him. "Take my sheep.
Make sacrifice of all their rising blood to wake him.
Let my herds be gone
And murdered for this loveless, sleepy faun."

The Chinaman says no. He says no and one eye closes;
Breaks the Dresden landscape closing; breaks the heart
In closing. He says, "Dawn must follow twilight."
He says no. (The salamander twilight dances in the wind.)
He says, "Blood must come from apples." (Eden weeps.)
"You are the killer that your brother keeps.

"You are the Adam of this spring, the Cain
Who asks return for sacrifice. You are the Eve
Who pared the bloody apple to the core
And ate the body of her youngest son.
You are the Lucifer that fell
Into this dark, bucolic hell."

The Chinaman has closed his other eye; the mountains melt. I see
    my faun
Arrived before me like an offering.
He breaks like dawn; asleep, he breaks like dawn.
I shake him. Rising like the sun he wakens
Startling, young, streaming with beauty; tossed
Upon the fragile paradise we lost, he breaks like dawn.

Nijinski swelled like this upon the world; he showed
The plumage of a rose, a petaled faun; the clothes
Of each occasion, every beauty, burst and burned.
He learned that beauty is a sorrow. Leda's dead.
Her egg is addled madness, serpent fruit—
And he's the broken shell, divine and mute.

Now shall I tell my faun that beauty is a sorrow?
Tell my faun that rising flesh is sorrow? Tell my faun
Of Icarus and of the waxen wings dawn melted? Salamanders sing
Their oily hymns to Satan from the hills.
I let him hear their singing. I am Cain,
My brother's lover and his fatal pain.

We rise and all the shapes of hell crowd out to greet us
The enormous blood falls through the veins of landscape far below.
We go as upward as the dawn. The dawning heat,
The fire in my faun, grows like a comet, falls—
And I have dropped my sacrificial lamb
Among the waxy pastures of the damned.

Dear God, real shepherd, curse the setting sun.
Curse all the things in nature that must fall.
Curse those that make them fall, and those that weep.
Curse sheep and curse the wolves that eat the sheep.
Curse those who taste the flesh of beauty bare
And leave the carcass for the world to eat.

MR. J. JOSEPHSON, ON A FRIDAY AFTERNOON

The sun went through the broken bottles on the porch. He saw
The light respond to glass. He knew the whole
Though real was bad reflection; he returned the light,
Retraced the pattern and rebroke the pain that fell from light.
The problem wasn't what there was to be
But what there wasn't—and broken glass
Mirrored another world of broken glass
Toward an infinity of breaking glass.
He squeezed the glass together. The reflections fell
From light through twisted glass, like Lucifer.
His would not fall. "Reject reflected light," he said.
He gave the world his throat to break
And made the glass opaque and real with blood.

ARS POETICA

Arachne was stuck with her shuttle;
And twisted deep like thread upon a spoiled
Sewing machine—poor girl, she's dead—and twisted there,
Bobbins for bones and they make pants and shirts
Of little bits of flesh.
And if you ask Arachne what of garmentry?
What of embroidered blood and seamstress sorcerings?
She'll answer if unraveled carefully,
"Rags, bottles, and old beauty, bones."

"Come watch the love balloon . . ."

Come watch the love balloon, that great
Inflated tautology of angel wings.
(They say it floats somewhere but I have seen
Its stupid flutter like the great sea birds
Who stumble through the city in a storm.)
Its cord goes downwards, watch the dangling men
Upon its drawstrings, watch a sudden wind
Give them a shaking; tangle, change, and bind.
Each wind is fatal. Nothing knows its place.
Beneath that high-flown floater love is like a race
Between the horse and crouching rider; no one wins,
And neither stops till someone wins—or falls.

THE BRIDGE GAME

	The Bridge
	Two Hearts
	The Crane of Hearts, the King of Hearts
North	Spades, Spades, Spades
the	The Bird
part-	Two Spades
ner	The Sam of Spades, The Queen of Spades
Vulnerable	Pass, Pass, Pass
	Tarot, Tarot, Tarot, Tarot
	Pharoh, Pharoh, Pharoh, Pharoh
	Hermes Trismegistus
West	Hermes Trismegistus
the oppo-	Marco Polo, Kublha's Palace
nent vul	FORTUNES TOLD BY MADAM ALICE
nerable.	Pass, Pass, Pass

East   Buddha's Wheel
the oppo-   Rod and Creel
nent vul-   Ace of Cups
nerable   Holy Grail
South, the dealer   Bicycle, Bicycle, Bicycle, Bi—
vulnerable.   The Hanged Man.
                      Alice, Alice, Miserere
                      Miserere, Alice, Alice.
                      The King of Hearts
                      The Queen of Spades
                      Courtesy Bicycle
                      Courtesy Bicycle
                      Courtesy Bicycle Playing Cards.

"Hereafter . . ."

Hereafter
Time and place to be remembered
Time and place by which to measure.
Thereafter, thereupon
Comfort enough.

Backwards, go straddling through infinity
(The animate will sing to me
And things inanimate will stare).
For I shall duck-walk toward the hitherto.
Comfort enough.

Remembered, measured, transferred, hearing sung,
I'll cease upon a peace of nothingness
Comfort enough.

"There is a road somewhere . . ."

There is a road somewhere
It wanders through the rainy night
It marks its passage through the sky with stars
Sometime,
The ticking of my watch assents
Gives rise
To moments, hours, myriads of signs
Inviting entrance through its crystaled face
As through a looking-glass
And something shines toward every pendant eye
A moment perpendicular
A road.

RIDDLE NO. I

The purple skin of pain pulls taut
From this bleak apple wells a tear
Firm with uncertainty and round with fear
I stand congealed in thought
And Jason's journey does not save the Argonaut
The core was here.

RIDDLE NO. II

Come Ozymandias, take us at our word
And fry your sphinx-egg omelette in the sand
The riddle will be rendered on demand
When Oedipus is double-played on third.

"The avenues of flame . . ."

The avenues of flame, paved with what fires
Brighten to blindness
And breaching what bounds, bleaching what bones
Burn me to ice
Plumb-straight from cosmos-center, look, the light
Locus of limpid miles and core of years
A universal carcinoma spreads
Extending fibrous stars.

EUCALYPTUS LEAVES

The tree-tongues which were once so sharp
Are gone from touch or sight
How well they licked the light
That trickled from the sun
And glazed and sharpened one
In June
Now it is winter and the dead are counted
The half-dried sun is sullen.
The tree-tongues all are fallen.
Their lightened sheathes have turned
To brittle rubbish, burned
In the snow.

"A pulse, a quiet lengthening of breath . . ."

A pulse, a quiet lengthening of breath,
A slow advance, and then the senses fall
Fallow, as if a quality of death
Or deathly questioning invaded all
Their ganglia; it is the heavy, dumb
Unbreathing calculus of stars
Made manifest; it is the final sum
As real as breathing was or totals are.
And all the measurements within a leaf
And all the patterns that our pulses give
All throbbing worlds, all qualities of grief
Divide, draw sudden breath and shout, "We live
You live, he lives." I smile to feel your hair
Upon the spot where nerve and bone were bare.

A POEM FOR NINE HOURS

Must I remember this?
This day, the minutes echoing your face
This day where every second tells
Each sudden grace that sweeps your body; all
These calling, sounding, graceful things soon pass
Leaving their trace,
Taking their tolls:
Some moments filled with memory and then
An hour full of bells.

"The screamless voice . . ."

The screamless voice becomes a voiceless scream
The needless streams go flowing out to sea
Growing in soundless strength, their surfaces
Are clotted up with syllabled debris
(I must not mention skulls
I must not mention blood
They are the husks and hulls
Of all the word-tide flood).

THE INHERITANCE: PALM SUNDAY

He rode into the vineyard on an ass
Reclaiming all the vintage of the land.
The stubborn Husbandmen who watched him pass
Cursed silently and spat. He would demand
The crops his father left them to possess,
The dusty grapes, the barren ancient sheaves
Of bitter wheat, the fig trees powerless
To harvest anything but wood and leaves.
His words were soft, but those that kept the field
Struck him with calloused hands, unpacified
And there was added to that season's yield
A precious scarecrow, bound and crucified.

A HERON FOR MRS. ALTROCCHI

Blue-rooted heron standing in the lake
Standing in unguessed song; like me no traveler.
Taking unsinging rest, loose-winged water-bird,
And dumb with music like the lake is dumb.

I stand upon the waterfront, like him no traveler,
Pink-rooted, dangling on my flightless wings.
Aching for flight, for swan-sung voyaging,
I wait that final thrust and take my rest.

They will not hunt us with snares and with arrows.
The flesh of the water-bird is tough and is dumb.
The sound of an arrow, the sight of a hunter
Only remind us of life without wings.

Then let us die, for death alone is motion,
And death alone can make these herons fly.
Though stiff and wingless, we will cross an ocean
On throats too huge for silence when we die.

RE A POEM FOR JOSEPHINE MILES

Sir, to accept the sun is frivolous; we see
By reason of rotation, by a star
That changes with occasion. When it curves
Toward callusing, night-coating, planetry,
And ice-cube knowingness, it's still a star
And alternation's current in its source,
And night's as hot, star-centered, as the day.

BREAKFAST

Dreams are more than nothing and less certain than coffee.
Stains in the saucer, tepid stains of dreams, are left and certain now.
And it is more than nothing one can warm the coffee, warm the dream
And lend violence to the morning cigarette.
Dreams are more than certain.

REALESTATE

I have been sold a shopworn piece of land; a property
Quite soiled and unattractive, torn by many hands
I am beginning to feel
That the agent was not quite REAL.
I have consulted the Better Business Bureau.

BUSFARE

Light travelers like God present a problem

ORGY, PORGY, PUMPERNICKEL, AND PIE

While in an orgiastic frenzy I often read *Harper's* magazine. This tends to give me a clear skin tone. Imagine my surprise when my slightly dissipated eyes saw, directly under Arnold J. Toynbee, the bold capped words, "The New Cult of Sex and Anarchy," by Mildred Brady. Turning nervously to "Personal and Otherwise" I saw the statement which confirmed all my fears. "Mrs. Brady, who lives in Berkeley, describes herself as wife, mama and cook; researcher, writer, and ghost."

It was true then. It had been a ghost we had seen at our tables. It had been a real ghost who jumped out of the pumpernickel bread onto Henry Miller's shoulder that night of the St. Valentine's Day Orgy and turned his beard so white that he had to shave it off. A ghost—we were fairly certain of that then—but now, to know that it were no turnip ghost, no mere Banquo with bloody hands, but a researching ghost, wife, mama, and cook. The odor of brimstone became so clear that I forgot to have an orgasm.

I have written a poem for the occasion.

THE GHOST GOES WEST
or
BEAT ME MAMA, I'M ORGASTICLY POTENT

Orgy, porgy, pumpernickel, and pie
We ignored the girls and we made them cry
We didn't drink milk and we didn't vote
Fried children were our table d'hôte
We smacked our lips and our Bohemia
Became seamier, and seamier
We went to Carmel and built our shacks
And all we thought of was art and s-a-a-a-x

Beat me mama, you researching ghost
My poetry rhymes now, it makes sense almost
You turned me from orgones I'm rereading Wilkie
I find milk more healthy than Christopher Rilke
Oh light bringing spirit you're making me human
You've turned me from Auden to Dewey and Truman
Oh pretty ghostling, my ivory tower
Is open for business, come haunting and glower
At concerts and paintings, if you sense duplicity,
Come anyway ghostling, it's all good publicity.

WHAM, BAM, ...

Marble Rabbit standing firm
Smeared with blood and rabbit-sperm
What inspired hand or eye
Conceived thy fearful sodomy

What age of ice, what chill of years
Could twist thy buttocks cold as tears?
And what duration could inspire
That stolid flame, that freezing fire?

What the quarry? With what drill?
What diamond edge? Or sharper still
What flesh-cut-flesh, what bone-cut-bone
Dislodged your form from aching stone

And when he sees the rabbits come
In bleeding spasms on thy bum
Does your sculptor in his heart
Think that life is worse than art

"We who have wept at the shrine of the bloodless Apollo . . ."

We who have wept at the shrine of the bloodless Apollo
Or have taken the taxi with Hermes for six city blocks
Are famished with beans, broken faith, and numerical blisters
Pythagoras sighs? Let us cover his body with rocks
His incalculable face will perhaps go on singing forever
Let it sing, let it weep. For the phoenix are nesting in flesh
And below us an ocean is giving a wet ultimatum

We must hand out our hunger and angle our bodies on rocks
And on tides and on waters of huge desolation
And die.

"And every boy and girl has a lover . . ."

And every boy and girl has a lover
With bare skin and blue eyes
And hair like wild blackberries.
The rain blows thru the city
Appears, reappears
Like something forgotten.
And the face goes up like a kite
High in the sunshine
And everybody has a face
At the end of his string.
The rain blows back across the city
Crying like a nervous comedian.
And every boy and girl has a lover

"Capone in the springtime . . ."

Capone in the springtime has
Plenty of peach-trees to catch you with
A gun full of grass and a whole arsenal
Filled with roses and toadstools.
Look pal, can all his gunsels get you
If you walk like a river?
If you wear the right clothes trusting God
And Governor Warren?

See the dead gangsters
Walking along Lake Michigan
Like last year's roses
The whole underworld

If I could hear some whisperings . . ."

If I could hear some whisperings among
The ruins in that Babylonish tongue
Which shattered with the tower. If that tower fell
Less wholly or less cunningly what well
Of words and meaning could a digger find
Replacing stone on stone; the bone-yard, Babel
Recombined
Would make the angels moan

"If autumn was a time for love . . ."

If autumn was a time for love
(The sun's still hot but things are dying)
Then I would hold your hands and walk above
The frozen ground. (The birds are flying
Bitterly south.) Oh, lover watch the moon
Cold as a witch. Your lips are dying
Remember all the butterflies in June
Where now the crows are flying.

"This angry maze of bone and blood . . ."

This angry maze of bone and blood, this body
Wanders in cool formal gardens, dry labyrinths
It is a weeping puzzle, God will not let this angry weeping stop
Why? Are we awake in formal gardens pulsing
Blood and bones. Do we sleep? Could turning brain
Shake meaning from these hedges. All the world's awake
Within a maze of sleepers.

A NIGHT IN FOUR PARTS

(first version)

For Mr. L. E., the onlie
begetter of these nightmares.

Part I: GOING TO SLEEP

Stars shake and under the old moon
The cat leaps with casual malice—
Upsetting sleep and timber without sound
Upsetting star and sleeper without sound—
Only the dead weight of the heart's motion
Falling in response.
Without sleep and under the old moon
The cat prowls into cold places—
This is no cat-heart springing without heat.
This is no moon-heart moving without heat.
Only the blood's weight under the heart's alleys
Pressing in response.

Part II: LIGHT SLEEPING

Among
The white angry light of the moon
And the flickings of cattails
It dreams and catches all;
Spawns eye, spawns mouth,
Spawns throat, spawns genitals.
Man is so monstrous naked that the world recoils,
Shrieks like a mandrake
Cries like a cat,
Disappears.

Part III: WET DREAM

Downward it plunges through the walls of flesh;
Heart falls
Through lake and cavern under sleep
Deep like an Orpheus.
A beating mandolin
Plucking the plectrum of the moon upon its strings,
It sings, it sings, it sings.
It sings, "Restore, restore, Eurydice to life.
    Oh, take the husband and return the wife."
It sings still deeper, conjures by its spell
Eurydice, the alley-cat of Hell.
    "Meow, meow, Eurydice's not dead.
    Oh, find a cross-eyed tomcat for my bed."
Too late, too late, it was too late he fell.
The sounds of singing and the sounds of Hell
Become a swarm of angry orange flies
And naked Orpheus, moon-shriveled, dies
And rises leaving lost Eurydice.
Heart flutters upward towards humanity
Jagged and half-awake.

Part IV: WAKING

It wakes and under the new sun
An old self slowly emerges.
This is no moon-self shrinking from the sun
This is no cat-self slinking from the sun—
Only the sober weight of the day's passions
Narrowing response.
Self winds heart-self like a watch, disremembers
The almost-unmechanical, the inhuman.
Chastens itself with water, dresses——
"What was that dream I had, heart-self?
Answer!"
Can't answer.

"The sea is a mirror . . ."

The sea is a mirror to a young microcosm
Reflecting a portrait in tides, making him monstrous
His substance becomes his image; he is reflected, historical
He is the maimed fisherman, the rich king of keepers
His grail is his mind and his mind is an ocean of mirrors
The wounds of the grail throb in the tide
He is divided.
Asleep in the tide he is divided
The present and past and the future are wounds that divide him
His body is stretched on the world and the tree of the world
Bears the magnified flesh of the crucified world of a man
Three questions—but they were not heard in this sea kingdom
Or unasked.
Part his flesh softly all you tides, pity him you sands who were his flesh
He keeps the hallows.

NUNC, IN PULVERE DORMIO

The Prostitute

I used to look down from my window
And watch the sailors passing through
The yellow moon would glow
Over the stones. Then two
Would pause, hesitant as deer, how
Beautiful I was, they were. Oh,
Nunc, ecce, nunc, in pulvere dormio.

The Scholar

I hoped my thoughts would grow
Each anguished year into
Something warm and new
Like a cloak of Persian yellow
To cover my flanks from the cold flow
Of years and smooth hands on my brow
I hoped, I waited, I was cold, and now
Et ecce nunc, in pulvere dormio.

The Birdcatcher

Once I chased birds along the blue
Spaces where small winds sigh and blow
I netted robin, wren, and swallow
Throstle and scarlet virago.
And heard the squeak of dying follow
The noise of captured wings; slow
Regretful, as if all beauty knew
Something would hunt and catch it so.
Et, ecce, nunc in pulvere dormio.

The Zen Master

My students always tried to follow
Their master's twisted path and go
As far with me as nature would allow
Then watch me from below
And learn. But now
They see an empty road and cannot follow
Sed ecce, nunc, in pulvere dormio.

"The world I felt this winter . . ."

The world I felt this winter every hour
Becomes more tense, and now I watch the spring
Suspended like a sweating thundershower
Above a land of cold imagining.
My heart resists. I feel my senses cower
As silent as a bird with wounded wing
While every body, branch, and leaf, and flower
Rumbles with hot and lovely threatening.

Come spring, come thunder, and besiege my heart,
That north whose isobars of guilt and fear
Have kept my weather and the world's apart
And made my body's winter last the year.
Send fertile showers, make my senses smart
And ripen, with the smell of lightning near.

"Look / The king is on the stage . . ."

Look
The king is on the stage
Set upon by other actors, overwhelmed
By a hungry audience.
Oh we are all so glad
When the fancy king is eaten
It makes our hungry hearts rumble
With glad catharsis
Suddenly the stage is as naked
As the body we were born in
And the spotlights spin upon us
And someone sees us.

"This is June . . ."

This is June.
When Jesse James entered by river
Into Hades he gave the charcoal Charon
A large American copper penny.
Death is terrible
It is as if something
Were always burning.
From Memphis to Athens
From Sparta to St. Joe
Wherever the rivers flow
Things die, things die
While burning.

"Flesh fails like words . . ."

Flesh fails like words to translate or to touch
Each other's starkness,
Like files we rasp and rub
Each other's flesh against the darkness
Fling arms as if we wished to weep
Hang mouth on mouth to keep
Ourselves from screaming: Love, love, I love you.

"It was so cold a night . . ."

It was so cold a night. The very stars
Naked and blue, rode the cold air
Crying your name. You were not there.
You were never there when I remembered you
You hurt that night. You scratched like ice,
Like snow against the bone.
Oh, the stars knew
How meaningless and cold, a pointless joke! Nonsense!
Then I heard my voice saying, "Nonsense
Is a kind of magic."
For you returned into my warm room after I had forgotten you
And suddenly in joy I told those stars—
I shared my heart with someone like a piece of bread
And watched him go away.

AT A PARTY

I watched the lovers falling in the dark
Like heavy autumn leaves upon a lake.
They were so very slow it almost seemed
That every color had belonged to them.
Bright shirts and bursting jeans by candlelight
Flickered and fell apart. Then it was late
The bottom of the water had been touched
Love's limit reached, and every color lost.

I waited for you on the balcony.
We trembled like two leaves caught in the sky.
You were so drunk the reeling world stood still.
I was so sober I could see stars fall.
We could not always stay suspended there.
We floated down and touched the lake together.
I noticed that your eyes had lost their color
When we had reached the bottom of the air.

REMEMBERING YOU, I LEAVE THE
MUSIC OF THE INNER ROOM

We were talking. The coffee-cups—empty
Or almost—moistly open down to the last cold dregs—
Staring even separate. Telling the time
Down to the last cold dregs. Our hands almost touching
Almost. But through the space between them
One could have seen the whole jutting restaurant
The door ajar, the ocean even.

"The forward wept . . ."

The forward wept, he saw the bouncing ball
So perfectly. For it was round as any star,
Cold as last October, live
As any jelly-fish. It fell so perfectly.
Horizon hardened rapidly. He felt the floor
Between his legs approach perfection,
Buckle, fall like stones or stairs
Unceasing.

ON FALLING INTO YOUR EYES

No bastard son of sea-froth deified
With all his arrows could twist half the pains
That pinion me as I am swept inside
And sprawl, half drowning, through your inner veins.
Oh, I am doubly cleft, and tides of blood
Pound both my bodies over jutting bone.
Twin currents on a double circuit flood
My bruisèd fragments toward a source unknown.
Oh, eyes of entrance, watch for Judgement Day
When seas give up their dead and arrows drop
Frozen from motion, when the bones and clay
Dissolved within you have a final stop,
Gods die, eyes close, and every several part
Finds rest and wholeness in your swirling heart.

LOST ULYSSES

Telemachus at the telephone,
Penelope pacing up and down,
But never a word from the searching planes,
Never a word in the Lost and Found.

Ships at sea by semaphore
Flash the empty signals back:
Someone picked up, but it wasn't he—
The Secret Police have lost the track.

Bloodhounds, fingerprints, whispers and keys—
The evidence proves he was here, but has gone.
Oh! Never to sail our seas again,
And never to answer our telephones!

"The old moon is still rolling . . ."

The old moon is still rolling
Driving men mad.
Look. How the moon fades.
It has the flesh of a groaning woman
Damp with sweat.
I wish it had ended better,
That we had still been kissing when the stars faded
That a thousand birds had flown between us
As the sun rose
Breaking her light suddenly.
Look. She has a face like a moon
And she inclines it foolishly
On the other side of the world.

Our County Cork Endymion
Disguised as Paddy's pig
Hails Mary with approval
And grunts a little jig.
He feels a bit exotic
Without his auburn wig.

"You are made out of porcelain and black ink . . ."

You are made out of porcelain and black ink,
Frigid and literate
You are an alphabet of plastic stone, Egyptian
Empty like a cipher; screaming
In the warm Egyptian air;
A language chizeled on brick by an industrious nation
That had neither straw nor marble;
You are that sphinx in the hot African sands
With a frozen tail.

"Songs From An Enormous Birdcage . . ."

Songs From An Enormous Birdcage. Peter Tweeter.
Vaseline Press. Browning, Ky.
Herbert Hoover, An Heroic Poem. Phillip Phallus.
On the Farm Press. Palo Alto, Cal.
Regrets From a Blue Policeman. Osbert Tuba.
Gentle Press. Albion, On.

TO A CERTAIN PAINTER

There is a storm at the end of your eyes.
Paint falls through the air like rain, splashing
In and out of patterns. The ground is plunging
Back and forth in shining celluloid colors.

It is God's colored world and at his eye
Shape covers shape and color splashes color
Things move too fast, slop out and start again.
Reality is blowing on the howling wind
Through his kaleidoscope.

If you are a painter with pretty eyes
You can make things stop moving.
You can stop things moving
If you roll your eyes at them.
And you are in a room
And the colors knock upon the roof like rain
But you have hold of the end of the rainbow.
Or you can reach out the window
And catch a falling flash of lightning
And quiet it;
Stroking its jagged strength with easy fingers
As if it were a frightened puppy on your lap.

Big-eyed lover, you seduce what God watches.
You make vision touch you
Gently on the eyes like a kiss.
You rob every storm of its rainbow; every sight
Of its shape and color.
You are looking back at God with your eyes
Through his own kaleidoscope.

Besides, you have pretty eyes.

"I wonder where Orpheus has been . . ."

I wonder where Orpheus has been
Since he was lured out of hell
Upon that fantastic journey.
I wonder where Orpheus is
Now that the soul has taken a streetcar
Out of hell.
The final train that keeps going
At the end of the evening.
Eurydice sobs and
The bars are closing all around the city.
The train was full of the last sailors in the world
At 2:07. It went far too fast out of hell to stop
For earth or heaven.
Where is our Orpheus now?
Does he sing to the grinning conductor
Who eats all the tickets?
Does he sing to the vanishing rails
That bend backwards?
Out of hell there is not much of anything real,
Only continuous motion of lips and of streetcar
Not much of anything real short of dying.

"We were talking . . ."

We were talking
You remember with my hand I traced a pattern on the table
Saying, "This is the third man," and you nodded
"This is the third man who stands between us; robbing
Us, an interpreter, a wave of jelly in the air like ether
In the old physics. A relation

Robbing the universe of all relation
Preventing all relation, robbing us."
You said (and at least he will remember) you said
"Is he really an interloper. We have set a place for him at
Our table.
Can we dine naked? Would not the friction burn us?
Any two at a table with all uninsulated space between them
Would set fire, burn by bone,
Grate skeleton against skeleton.
Anyone against anyone. Burn."
I replied (and surely only he will remember) I said, "Plato
And Aristotle knew him. The third man, the infinite digression,
The shadow cast between men and their shadows. Eliot too,
Almost any explorer."
I wanted to touch you.
I wanted to be a flame that burned between you and your shadow.
I wanted to burn the world off your shadow. To burn you naked
Unshrouded one.
He walked away with us from that moment. Each of us captives. Alone
This was the door that he closed, that Janus-like spectre
This was the door that he closed between us and our shadows
Severed and never to look back again. Locked, fastened, and bolted
Here in the twisted dark, a queer opaque behind-the-mirror world I lie
Watching, talking—above me, pale, pulpy, like ether,
The face of the third man whispering, watching
Oh if there were a final agony to share, some pain still unrelated
        with the world
That gave each fiber tongue
To break my body on the door

"The laughing lady . . ."

The laughing lady greets you as you walk
Down Pleasure Pier. And you can hear her laugh
As far as where the ocean ends or where
Your watch has stopped. She laughs all night.

Beyond the funhouse are the rides and games
Beyond the games the ocean's pulling tides
But in her house the music never stops
The little laughing lady laughs all night.

Ha, ha, ha, ha, she says and moves her lips
As if she laughed it from an ancient grudge
As long as fuse and phonograph will run
The lady's cardboard lips will laugh all night.

"We are too tired to live like lions . . ."

We are too tired to live like lions. We are like stones
Or dead animals washed by tireless acres of remembering water.
The wet sea jingles. It is archaic. It is as if both minotaur
And labyrinth together had become one liquid animal.
Living with waving teeth.
And we sailed to Crete with a black sail
And the sailors cried:
"Let us go to Athens. Let us go to Athens"
And we passed starving jungles, dry and birdless
And the lions in them whimpered, "Sweet,
Sweet Athens. We are too tired to live like lions.
Go, Do not even see us."

The lions were like islands. Each
Bore a wet sea between him and his fellows. Each
Roared only when the water broke upon it
As if it were both rock and animal.
Down the archaic sea
Follow the thread of rocks
Follow the thread of rocks
Down the archaic sea
First Crete
Then sweet,
Sweet Athens.
And I remember
When I was a boy in Los Angeles; almost everyday
In the dry weather of summer
I would go to the hot wet beach
And visit the two old amusement piers
At Ocean Park and Venice.
And go, small in hot itching swimming trunks,
Down the fun zone into Crazy Town,
Designed for amusement
And foolishness.
It was dark, a maze of wooden windings,
Nevertheless there was always
And everywhere
The hot smell of the ocean and the noise of waves cracking
Below the tilting floor.
Even then!
Under the creaking floor
Follow the warp of wood
Follow the warp of wood
Under the creaking floor
First sleep
Then deep
Deep water.

"Whenever I love . . ."

Whenever I love
Whenever I climb from hell
I hear footsteps on the stairs behind me.
Is it only my lover? If I turn,
It and my lover disappear
Betrayed;
If I do not turn,
There is a third between us,
Ravishing us both; we are betrayed together
Hell cuckolds us.
Whenever I ask for love
Whenever I climb into hell
I hear footsteps on the stairs below me.
I know this not a lover. Although it is like smoke
Keeping eye from eye and skin from skin,
It is no ghost. It is hot and personal.
If I bring something out of hell,
This is what I'll bring out of hell.
If I bring nothing out of hell,
I'll leave all beauty there to burn and be torn
Apart by women.
Does it really intrude—It almost protects us
If love were as personal
We would set fire, burn by bone
Grate skeleton against skeleton
Anyone against anyone
Burn. Such waste is surely unnatural
Sing then sing, this tertium gaudens
This lucky Pierre among moony lovers
Only it can be rescued from the black fires
Loneliness, Orpheus, is a passionate natural fact
Like death.

"The new Aeneas . . ."

The new Aeneas and her men I sing
Who, borne on Banking's universal wing
Transport like some great archangelic host
The Coney Island Lares to the coast.
Each time the New Aeneas combs her hair
She rides her cultured broomstick through the air
Unconscious of the quaint applauding claque
Of fairy lovers clinging to her back
That bear her upward like a soft balloon
Between South San Francisco and the moon

"At the sound of Apollo . . ."

At the sound of Apollo
The Titan writhing in my bony loins
Hollers out loud. He is the same
Who split and ate old Dionysus and became
Unwilling prisoner in the pit of every man.
He asks for absolute fire.
He asks I rend my flesh and set him free.
He cannot wait until the drunken women's hands
Will set him free.
Apollo, you never had another lover like this
Oh Helios, he loved the light so much
He chose to die in darkness.

"You thought . . ."

You thought
You were carrying coals to the heart's Newcastle.
Heaping a hot heart with fire.
My heart is not hot; it is wet.
It is soft like an ocean and huge
Too deep to destroy
Get away from the edge of my heart with your lips
Stop trying to burn.
You'll burn to the edge of the beach
Then you'll sizzle and stop
And you'll sputter and sparkle like a snowball in hell
And every delicate ton of your fuel will dissolve
And be lost like a glass of champagne
Fallen into acres of coarse salt water.

DARDENELLA

They said he was nineteen. He had been kissed
So many times his face was frozen closed.
His eyes would watch the lovers walking past,
His throat would sing, and nothing else would move.
We grownups at the bar would watch him sing.
Christ, it was funny with what tired grace
He sang our blues for us. His frozen lips
Would twist and sing the blues out, song by song.
Show us the way to the next whisky bar.
Show us the way to the next pretty boy.
And let the blue anger we feel for us now
Strangle the cat at the pool of our tears.

A TRANSLATION OF GEORGE'S TRANSLATION OF "SPLEEN" FROM "LES FLEURS DU MAL" (DIE BLUMEN DES BÖSEN)

I am a prince in lands gloomy and cold
Passive in riches and aging in youth
Blinded to beauty and deafened to truth
And only with horses and falcons consoled
Who plays without pleasure and dares without fear
And dulled by the seed of the poppy who tries
The sleep of no dream on the couch where he lies,
So richly bedecked it resembles a bier
And courtly ladies with seductive tones
Seeking to lighten their sad monarch's reign
Perfumed and sweet to sight, await in vain
A ragged smile from these perambulant bones.
No bath of blood as sorcerers propose,
To translate life and youth from other men
Can make a vital current pulse again
In vessels where the oozing Lethe flows.

"When your body brushed against me . . ."

When your body brushed against me I remembered
How we used to catch butterflies in our hands
Down in the garden.
We were such patient children
Following them from flower to flower
Waiting and hoping.
With our cupped hands we used to catch them
And they answered us with a soft tickle
For they never stopped flying.
In bed I remembered them and cried for

The touch of their fast wings, the impatience
Of their bright colors
I am too old for such games
But even tonight, now your body has reminded me of butterflies
I lie here awake, pretending.

COFFEE-TIME

Across the coffee cups he said:
"People who act like God—"
Like he were Socrates
Before he bid goodbye to his young men
And lay upon his wooden bench to die.

Young men sipping coffee between wars,
We sat around the coffee cups
Like young Athenians,
Waiting for wisdom to seep into their veins
Like hemlock juice—

Youths awaiting wisdom we knew would disappoint,
We sipped our coffee in a wooden booth,
Awaiting a wisdom that was like a dainty arabesque
On a needle point.

"People who act like God
Are often right," he said,
We looked into our cups for wisdom,
"And often wrong," he added.
Wisdom lay within the coffee cups
The minute of that hour
Like hemlock juice.

LIVES OF THE PHILOSOPHERS: DIOGENES

He spilled his seed upon the marketplace
While all the Greek boys watched. Along the street
The dogs were basking in the August sun,
Scratching their fleas, and panting with the heat.
The brown-thighed boys looked on in discontent
For they had hoped another Socrates
Would pat their heads and talk, and at the end
Confirm their daily wisdom with a kiss.
"Diogenes is Socrates gone mad,"
Their voices shouted, but his sweating face
Was straining towards the sun, blind to the light
That streamed around him through the marketplace.
The boys had left him and the dogs began
To howl in cynic wonder at the heat.

THE TROJAN WARS RENEWED: A CAPITULATION,
OR
THE DUNKIAD

"Sometimes our feelings are so mild they seem like
mere extensions of the English Department."

Invocation

i.

Oh blessed Prudence, our divine protector
Goddess of confident humility
Who helped us suffer through the wrath of Hector,
Paris, and Helen of our faculty,

Give us enough saliva so that we
May chastely kiss them when the meeting closes
For if we bend too far in courtesy
The attitude leaves stains upon our noses.

ii.

Or let us in our tents like bold Achilles
(The oldest sophomore in the Grecian camp)
Pelt the invaders with aesthetic lilies
And spend the battle planning to revamp
Some last year's masque to fight in next year's meeting
When other warrior's ardour has grown damp,
Or else, as fate is cruel and time is fleeting,
To die, a hero, from the writer's cramp.

iii.

So blessed Prudence, bless my prudent verses
Derivative of Eliot and crude,
Temper my temper and uncurse my curses
Let me not let the Trojans think me rude,
Keep open departmental hearts and purses
And let my Trojan pension be renewed
And if my numbers nod, my rhyming bore,
Divert them for me, Prudence—be their whore.

Book I

i.

I do not sing about Achilles' wrath.
Achilles has an even disposition.
He treats the Philistines that cross his path
Like critics on a diplomatic mission.
I sing of Ajax' wrath, that bitter fool,

Whose choler rose to conquer his ambition
Who like the farmyard Sampson—like a mule
Kicked down his grooms and died of malnutrition.

   ii.

Our story starts some days before its action.
Three Trojans met within their palace yard,
Alike united in dissatisfaction
With doings of the Grecian forward guard.
Then Paris rose, and, plotting out the means
That they might use, he spoke, the Safeway bard,
Read in ten thousand grocery magazines
And famed wherever mankind uses lard.

   iii.

He spoke: "Within the shadows of our walls
The noisy Greeks are up to their old tricks.
We that have championed within these halls
The principles of English 106,
A, B, or C have heard their Bacchanale.
If we sound battle 'gainst these heretics,
A thousand ghosts would answer to our calls,
Gayley would swim across the River Styx.

   iv.

"Then let the dead defend us—and the living too.
When we plunge into print our gentle splash
Ripples as far as Partisan Review
And covers us with curses and with cash.
So let us fight together to convince
Or conquer this wild Grecian balderdash.
I like the poems the New Yorker prints—
Shapiro, Auden, Moore, and Ogden Nash.

v.

"I'm not a modern, I'm contemporary,
I understand Stuart Gilbert and James Joyce.
I lecture in a firm impassioned voice,
Never absurd, but never ordinary.
My prose is fragrant, but quite sanitary,
Ancient as milk, but new as gasoline,
Shipped East to the New Yorker magazine,
Homogenized and bottled at their dairy."

vi.

Then Helen spoke, (I fear the syntax used
I cannot translate for she tweaked her thoughts
So hard to make them homely that they bruised
And whirled at one like toy shop Juggernauts.)
She said the Grecians were too self-enthused,
Too closely knit, too limited a clique.
She said she thought their group too interfused
But I suspect she meant—they were too Greek.

vii.

Then Hector spoke . . . But Hector was a friend.
He thought he was a Greek and loved us once,
Drank wine, told jokes, and to the bitter end
Endured our love and laughed at our affronts.
A good big man who'd never condescend
To pose or plot, to slander or pretend,
To hate and hide his hatred with a joke.
He was a friend—we'll not say what he spoke.

viii.

The Trojan three then went about the motion
Of challenging the Grecian force to battle
And hurtled insults with the fierce devotion
Of slaughter house employees killing cattle.
The Grecian bucklers shake, their helmets rattle.
One of the Greeks begins to get the notion
They have not come to pay a formal call.
"They're after us," he screams, "they'll kill us all."

ix.

The Greeks were rounded up from near and far.
Bold Agamemnon gave the call to fight.
His shield was blazoned with a shooting star.
He growled until the foe was gray with fright,
Summoned the Greeks with sounds spectacular.
He gave one awful howl with all his might
Two piercing barks, three yelps, and half a bite —
Then, duty done, turned tail and left the war.

x.

Ulysses too, with slyly piping voice,
Crafty and warlike, shrewd and innocent,
Called on the other Grecians to rejoice
That they had him to help their regiment,
He handed them a handbook, marked the place,
And toward each enemy belligerent
He made one final, philosophic face
Then crept in with Achilles in his tent.

xi.

When fourteen fairies and a few odd women,
And odder men, decide to fight a war,
Their ranks are fluid as a ripe persimmon
And have as squashy an esprit de corps.
To separate the squadrons from menages,
Assess the thoughts of each competitor,
Distinguish purposes from persiflages,
I'll use another book or maybe more.

Invocation

To piss in anger on an anthill shows
No great amount of sense or courtesy
Nor blazing triumph when the puddle grows
And drowns their little lives in poetry.
So let me cease the stream—though Devil knows
My bladder's big enough to moisten three
Or thirty books, or thirty thousand bugs.
I'll stop the flow with prudence or with plugs.

So Terminus, sweet God of second thought,
End soon this war or make its conflicts vast
And magnify the insects that I've fought
Until they look like dragons of the past
And I a chivalrous enthusiast
In haste to save his kingdom from their thrall,
Grant that this second book may be the last,
Keep back my blood, my urine, and my gall.

Book II

    i.

Then Paris suavely stumbled into battle,
Exhaling fumes of golden applejack.
His words made several Grecian corselets rattle.
His breath turned fifty Grecian helmets black.
He carried ripe tomatoes in a sack,
Supplied for nothing from a Safeway store,
Languidly tossed them at the Grecian claque
And to each victim murmured, "You're a bore."

    ii.

Then Ajax answered, "Who would deign refute
A highbrow hack." (His curses came in torrents.)
"A wholesale whore, a retail prostitute,
A tin-can Taine, a grocer's D. H. Lawrence."
Then Paris left the field of the dispute
Exclaiming his opponent was a boor.
He hurried to an Eastern institute
To make a lecture or to take a cure.

    iii.

The battle waned. Achilles in his tent
Sat lost in dreams of paper-backed editions,
He suddenly sat up in wonderment
And rolled his eyes to opposite positions.
A wooden spectre, vague and violent,
Loped backwards at him through the trembling grass
And neighed with a naive embarrassment.
"My God," he cried, "the Trojan horse's ass."

iv.

"Alas," the half-horse sighed and wiped a tear
From just below his tail, "I'm doubly cleft,
My head has gone to college for a year
And I have nothing but my backside left.
(Those pesky Hamadryads ate the rest.)
But I would like to humbly volunteer
To act as mediator, I suggest
You tell the Grecian warriors to ungear."

v.

The half-horse turned and galloped thru the walls
But there he found the Trojans were adverse
To making peace. They sawed off both his balls
And nailed a Trojan banner to his urse.
(He was a good horse til they cut him down,
But all in all they might have used him worse.
I hear that while he visited their town
He won a thousand dollar claiming purse.)

vi.

Even Bill Shakespeare had his troubles finding
A fifth act for an endless Trojan war.
His final curtain left the mortars grinding
And Troilus sobbing torch songs to his whore.
I too will let my heroes go on fighting
While I go yawning towards the exit door
A little foolish butchery's exciting
But I've not patience, bile, nor blood for more.

vii.

So let me beg forgiveness from the foes
I've libeled or I've lauded in these lines,
A wounded warrior at the battle's close
Weaves history in sinister designs,
The damp condition of the shroud he sews
Has made a Trojan ending opportune.
The curtain falls—and rises to disclose
A crippled Ajax singing to the moon.

THE PANTHER - AFTER RILKE

His jungle eyes have grown so tired pacing
His cage that they can only wait and stare.
They seem to see a thousand bars around them—
Before those bars, behind them, empty air.
His body turns and turns in quiet circles
Subduing all its tension in its strides.
It seems a dance of strength around a center
At which, bemused, a captive witness rides.
But even now a door within the eyeball
Slides softly out, then something he can see
Invades the burning stillness of his body
Flames like a moth and ceases there to be.

ALL HALLOWS EVE

Bring on the pumpkin-colored wine.
The ghosts of autumn ask our pardon—
The withered flowers in the garden,
The fruit that frosted on the vine:
Each fickle life that testified
The summer's quick magnificence
Now masks its own indifference
And plays the spook to salve our pride.
They wear bright costumes of the dead
And posture in a clownish way.
The lover that we loved last May
Now wears a gaping pumpkin head.
Our flowers and our lovers all
Implore us from the icy streets
And every painted spook repeats
The gestures of his burial.
Come drink the wine and watch them play
For there is nothing to be said.
No exorcist can drive away
The childish faces of the dead.

MIDNIGHT AT BAREASS BEACH

The surfaces are moving with the sound
Black water makes. As far as I can see
Out from each clinging wave, eternity
Moves back and forth, as black as nothing else.

Cold to the touch, it oozes at my feet
And lies protesting like a dog, then sighs
And slaps again. But what remains out there
Is motionless without comparison.
Naked and brittle as a wave, as I
Run through the water I can hear the sound
Of running echoed back and forth again across the beach—
My flesh.

"The audience was sad to see . . ."

The audience was sad to see
Old Ezra running out of bounds
They saw a smiling football team
He saw the huntsmen and their hounds.

CHRISTMAS EVE: 1952

In our good house we'll light a Christmas fire
And watch each other's faces in the flame.
The very angels will be stricken dumb
To see two lovers using such a mirror.
And when the shepherds knock upon the door
Demanding news of God's nativity,
We'll let them kneel behind our Christmas tree
And watch the fire glitter on its star.

A PRAYER FOR PVT. GRAHAM MACKINTOSH
ON HALLOWEEN

Infernal warlocks dressed in pink
And children wearing masks by night,
Protect my friend from sundry harm
And rest his body in your arms.

Ghosts of eternal silences
And pumpkin-faces wreathed in flame,
Consume the military flesh
Of those who borrow young men's lives.

You white-faced boys that trick or treat
And ring the doorbells of the dead,
Twist out each patriotic bone
Of those that consummate the loan.

And have the nasty little girls
Who steal the seed from dead men's loins
Make pee-pee on their uniforms
And dance on their conscripted flag.

Avenge for him this Hallows Eve
Each moment of captivity.
Let every ghost of liberty
Parade before him in his sleep.

Infernal warlocks dressed in pink
And children wearing masks by night,
Protect my friend from sundry harm
And rest his body in your arms.

EPILOQUE IN ANOTHER LANGUAGE

Ze love I talk for you in poetry
Was in zat strange American
We used to speak.
No romance language zat, mon cher,
Zat was ze heart. (He is a crazy beast
He speak so strange.)
But now, mon cher, we have a better tongue
Ze heart has made no noise
He seldom beat.
When I see you and talk, ze heart, zat beast
Is, how you say
Dead.

"These woods, so fit for emperors . . ."

These woods, so fit for emperors, reveal
A thousand detailed alleys where we feel
Each other waiting.
Believe these royal woods, remember them.
Where we have never been is real.

"As if a Chinese vase . . ."

As if a Chinese vase were filled with blood
Old blood, and set to wait for spring
And someone shattered it, and left the blood—
How can I bear to see your face again
As muffled children playing in the cold
Shove burning embers in the snowman's groin
To make the winter fade, to make things true
How can I bear to see your face again
Oh hero of the heart, oh violent
Exposer of the gap beneath the snow
Oh sun of heart, exposer of the true
How can I bear to see your face again.

IMAGINARY ELEGIES I–IV

(early version)

for Robin Blaser

"All that a man knows
and needs to know is
found in Berkeley."
—William Butler Yeats,
A Vision

Poetry, almost blind like a camera
Is alive in sight only for a second. Click,
Snap goes the eyelid of the eye before movement
Almost as the word happens.
One would not choose to blink or go blind
After the instant. One would not choose
To see the continuous Platonic pattern of birds flying
Long after the stream of birds had dropped or had nested.
Lucky for us that there are natural things like oceans
Which are always around,
Continuous, disciplined subjects
To the moment of sight.
Sea, moon and sun and nothing else is subject.
Other things are less patient and won't rest
Between the intervals of perception. They go about their business
As if we didn't have to see them.
When I praise the sun or any bronze god derived from it
Don't think I wouldn't rather praise the very tall blond boy
Who ate all of my potato-chips at the Red Lizard.
It's just that I won't see him when I open my eyes
And I will see the sun.
Sea, moon and sun are always there when the eyes are open
Insistent as breakfast food.
                                   One can only justify
These cheap eternals by their support of
What is absolutely temporary.
The blond boy, like the birds, although moving,
Has given a sort of fictive presence to this scenery.
He is bathed through the deepest and bluest of waters
Limb upon deep, sweet limb. He is syntactically conjured
Through all of love's possible meanings
Until he is almost alone in this room. Here, and merely alive.

He is bleached by an Apollonian sun
Until he is white as cold, white as my blindness,
An Arctic Circle of absolute dreaming,
Complete with polar bears and Santa Claus and rich with ice.
It is as if we conjure the dead and they speak only
Through our own damned trumpets, through our damned medium:
"I am little Eva, a Negro princess from sunny heaven."
The voice sounds blond and tall.
"I am Aunt Minnie. Love is sweet as moonlight here in heaven."
The voice sounds blond and tall.
"I'm Barnacle Bill. I sank with the Titanic. I rose in salty heaven."
The voice sounds blond, sounds tall, sounds blond and tall.
"Goodbye from us in spiritland, from sweet Platonic spiritland.
You can't see us in spiritland, and we can't see at all."

2.

God must have a big eye to see everything
Which we have lost or forgotten. Men used to say
That all lost objects stay upon the moon
Untouched by any other eye but God's.
The moon is God's big yellow eye remembering
What we have lost or never thought. That's why
The moon looks raw and ghostly in the dark.
It is the camera shots of every instant in the world
Laid bare in terrible yellow cold.
It is the objects that we never saw.
It is the dodos flying through the snow
That flew from Baffinland to Greenland's tip
And did not even see themselves.
The moon is meant for lovers. Lovers lose
Themselves in others. Do not see themselves.

The moon does. The moon does.
The moon is not a yellow camera. It perceives
What wasn't, what undoes, what will not happen.
It's not a sharp and clicking eye of glass and hood. Just old,
Slow infinite exposure of
The negative that cannot happen.
Fear God's old eye for being shot with ice
Instead of blood. Fear its inhuman mirror blankness
Luring lovers.
Fear God's moon for hexing, sticking pins
In forgotten dolls. Fear it for wolves.
For witches, dragons, lunacy, for parlor tricks.

The world is full of watching witches
Bitching the world up. The witchlike virgin god Diana,
Being neither witch nor virgin is the moon's god.
Even her sex changes. She is a black bitch dog.
Look: she has yellow tits. Even her color changes.
But she doesn't exist. When the poem is over,
She is a nice, pretty poet with thick lips and blue eyes
And an elegant wardrobe.
Into the moon she goes.
The world is full of watching bitches
Witching the world up. The witchlike evil goddess Hecate,
Being neither witch nor evil is the moon-god.
Even his sex changes. He is an old black werewolf,
Sharpening his teeth on a berry bush.
But he doesn't exist. When the poem is over,
He is an anxious poet with a few delusions, kind as a rabbit.
Into the moon he goes.
The world is full of witch-hunting bitches
Watching the world upside down. The dragon-slaying hero Sigurd,
Being neither dragon-slayer nor hero is the moon's rival.
Even his sex changes. He is a huge black Walkure,

Looping all over Hell for a lover.
But he doesn't exist. When the poem is over,
He has dug no pit, killed no dragon. He is
Merely the poet at the end of his poem.

Evil somehow exists in the relation
Between the remembered and the forgotten,
Between the moon and the earth of the instant.
Evil somehow exists in the relation
Between what happens and what never happens
Between the poet and God's yellow eye.
Look through the window at the real moon.
See the sky surrounded. Bruised with rays.
But look now, in this room, see the shape-changers,
Wolf, bear, and otter, dragon, dove.
Look now, in this room, see the shape-changers
Flying, crawling, swimming, burning
Vacant with beauty.
Hear them whisper.

3.

God's other eye is good and gold. So bright
The shine blinds. His eye is accurate.
His burnished eye observes the bright and blinding shine
It shines. Now, accurate as swooping birds,
The burnished eye is shining back that light
It saw and shined.
Light feeds on light. God feeds on God. God's goodness is
A black and blinding cannibal with sunny teeth
That only eats itself.
Deny the light. God's golden eye is brazen.
It is clanging brass

Of good intention. It is noisy burning
Clanging brass.
Light is a carrion-crow
Cawing and swooping. Cawing and swooping.
Then, there is a sudden stop.
The day changes.
There is an innocent old sun quite cold in clouds.
The ache of sunshine stops.
God is gone. God is gone.
Nothing was quite as good.
It's getting late. Put on your coat.
It's getting dark. It's getting cold.
Most things happen in twilight
When the sun goes down and the moon hasn't come
And the bats are flying.
Most things happen when God isn't looking,
When God is blinking between good and evil,
And the bats are flying.
Most things happen in twilight when things are easy
And God is blind as a gigantic bat.

The boys stretched out above the swimming pool receive the sun.
Their groins are pressed against the warm cement.
They look as if they dream. As if their bodies dream.
Unblind the dreamers for they ache with sun,
Wake them with twilight. They're like lobsters now
Hot red and private while they dream,
They dream about themselves.
They dream of dreams about themselves.
They dream they dream of dreams about themselves.
Splash them with sunset like a wet bat.
Unblind the dreamers.
                    Poet,
Be like God.

4.

Yes, be like God. I wonder what I thought
When I wrote that. The dreamers sag a bit
As if five years had thickened on their flesh
Or on my eyes.
Splash them with what?
Should I throw rocks at them
To make their naked private bodies bleed?
No. Let them sleep. This much I've learned
In these five years in what I've spent and earned:
Time does not finish a poem.
The dummies in the empty funhouse watch
The tides wash in and out. The thick old moon
Shines through the rotten timbers every night.
This much is clear, they think, the men who made
Us twitch and creak and put the laughter in our throats
Are just as cold as we. The lights are out.

                         The lights are out.
You'll smell the oldest smells—
The smell of salt, of urine, and of sleep
Before you wake. This much I've learned
In these five years in what I've spent and earned:
Time does not finish a poem.
What have I gone to bed with all these years?
What have I taken crying into bed
For love of me?
Only the shadows of the sun and moon
The dreaming boys, their creaking images,
Only myself.
             Is there some rhetoric
To make me think that I have kept a house
While playing dolls? This much I've learned
In these five years in what I've spent and earned:

That two-eyed monster God is still above.
I saw him once when I was young and once
When I was scared with madness, or was scared
And mad because I saw him once. He is the sun
And moon made real with eyes.
He is the photograph of everything at once. The love
That makes the blood run cold.
But he is gone. No realer than old
Poetry. This much I've learned
In these five years in what I've spent and earned:
Time does not finish a poem.
Upon the old amusement pier I watch
The creeping darkness gather in the west.
Above the giant funhouse and the ghosts
I hear the seagulls call. They're going west
Toward some great Catalina of a dream
To where all poems end.
                              But does it end?
The birds believe it's there. Believe the birds.

MANHATTAN AND BOSTON: 1955–1956

MANHATTAN

The horror of this city. Stone piled on stone,
Dollar on dollar, cloud upon cloud!
The little Jewfaced children
Playing in the deep streets.

"White as southern blindness . . ."

White as southern blindness,
The room wakes up
Like a deadly mirror
My hand upon his thigh
I curse and love him.
Tuesday morning.
The crime is not so dear as God's
The mirror
Bends and bows to us
Full and afraid we watch
The light fade.

"When the moon comes out . . ."

When the moon comes out
Then the bells go sour
Then the impenetrable
Paths appear

When the moon comes out
Then sea covers the earth
Then the heart feels
An island in infinite.

Nobody eats oranges
Under the full moon
It is necessary to eat
Fruit that is green and frozen

When the moon comes out
With its hundred even faces
Silver money
Sobs in the pockets

CENTRAL PARK WEST

Along the walks the sweet queens walk their dogs
And dream of love and diamonds as they pass
And I could be a statue or a stone
As they walk by me dreaming of their gods.
Beside their path, an apple's throw away,
I see that old erotic garden where
Our parents breathed the wasteful, loving air
Before the angry gardener changed his will.
The park has no room for that memory.
Its paths are twisted like a scattered sky
Of foreign stars. The spinning queens go by
Within their orbits, leaving me alone.
What cosmic joy. The last companion here
Is Priapus, the gardener's ugly son
Who crouches in the bushes with his shears
And hasn't got the hots for anyone.

"And no one is around to see my tears . . ."

And no one is around to see my tears
But Priapus, the ugly gardener's son,
Who squats among the flowers with his shears
And doesn't have the hots for anyone.

"Easy on squeezing . . ."

Easy on squeezing
Frost off the pumpkin
J. Spicer fecit
Man, but don't break it.

ORPHEUS WAS A POET

Orpheus was a poet who was in love with Eurydice. She appeared in his poems and his dreams and he used her as an image to masturbate by. She was quite beautiful but somewhat indeterminate. Orpheus had created her out of many figures—a dead cousin, a girl he once saw at a birthday party, the body of a boy he had kissed in a Turkish bath, even out of the wind and air of a spring he remembered. Orpheus sang all of his songs to her and, as more and more of his hair seemed to come out with the comb when he combed it, only worried whether she would continue to love him.

One day a perfect stranger came up to Orpheus and began talking to him. He had such an anonymous face that Orpheus knew that he must be a god. "I have kidnapped Eurydice," the stranger said. "You will never see her again."

God or no god, the remark merely amused Orpheus. "Perhaps you don't know," he said politely, "that Eurydice is completely imaginary. So many people who read my poetry think that she is real."

"I have kidnapped Eurydice," the stranger repeated. "You will never see her again. If you don't believe me, look for her."

Orpheus, now angry at the god's foolishness, started to sing one of his best songs about Eurydice. But she wasn't in it. There was just a tangle of images and rhymes where she had been. He started another. The same thing happened. The stanza that enumerated the beauties of Eurydice was now about a red wheelbarrow. The stranger walked quietly away while Orpheus went through each of his songs looking for his lost Eurydice.

The next morning the stranger was back. "Do you believe me now?" he asked.

"No," said Orpheus, "I do not believe you. I know Eurydice is gone, and when you are not around I even forget her name, but I think that she left me because I am growing old. I don't think that you had a thing to do with it."

(Orpheus, being a poet, knew how best to handle gods psychologically. Deny their powers when you face them and keep a close hold on your wallet.)

The god, predictably enough, was furious. "I am Hermes," he shouted. "I am the god of thieves. I have stolen your Eurydice. The fact that you are a piece of decaying meat has nothing to do with it."

Now Orpheus knew the god's name. That was enough. Carefully he worked Hermes into his poetry in the place where—what was her name?, Eurydice—had been before. He could not remember; he had a sense of intolerable loss; but he knew what he must do.

In a few months Hermes again met Orpheus, this time not in disguise. "I want you to stop writing about me in your poems. I am not your lover. I spit on humans. They are neither clever or beautiful enough for me. If you want to write about gods, pick Zeus or Aphrodite or any one of them who gets a kick out of sleeping with natives. I don't want your worship or your poetry."

"Until you give back what you have stolen, I can only write about you," Orpheus said, casting his eyes discretely to the ground.

"I never give back what I have stolen," Hermes said. "It disappears. I couldn't give you Eurydice if I wanted to. So you see, blackmail won't work."

Hermes left him then, quite convinced that Orpheus would stop annoying him. Orpheus, his sense of loss greater than ever, kept on writing poetry about Hermes as a personal lover, stressing now, in addition, the fact that Hermes knew where everything was, that he was, as it were, the museum-keeper of the dreams of man.

The third time Hermes appeared was, of course, crucial. He came carrying a telegram which he handed to Orpheus. The telegram read "EURIDICE IS IN HELL. FIND HER." Hermes had disappeared before Orpheus could thank him.

x   x   x

The corridors were unexpectedly dark. He kept trying to remember her name and what he would sing to Hades to convince him

"I can cure baldness," Hades said.

HELL

Hell. They castrated the cat, then they bought magnetic potholders and an Italian coffee-grinder. Eve wanted a television set in her bedroom and Adam bought volumes of French poetry.

The loss of beauty (hell) is a ritual act
The loss of beauty (hell) is as natural as a rose losing all its petals
The loss of beauty (hell) is not a fit subject for children
Imagine Lucifer
Free,
We dug the ground and grew an apple tree

Adam's childhood was remarkable. Every year he cast off became a little Jesus beside him, as empty of everything as a Jesus crucified or as full of anything as a Jesus resurrected. He called them Cain and Able. At the age of eleven, he pulled Eve out of his penis. She saved him from subjectivity.

What do the goyim know about Hell
We, the original Jews
Know about hell.

THE WAVES

The waves are dark and hungry and as cruel
As little orphans. They cling with baby teeth to things.
Moon-children
Hungry as all outdoors.
The poet or painter composing them
Had better stand far away.
For they can draw the artist up into their own image and in those salt
        square-miles
Undress his roses.

And the wild birds following the ships for their leavings
Cawing at the dead sounds, snatching
Each gutted word thrown in their wake.
Roses? A clam's gut is more appropriate.
Slimy and unyielding, you have to pull it
Like a word in the throat
Out of its own asshole. "Would they care?" I asked
"Care," he said, "The waves all
Have noses like Frenchmen. You could feed a
      Jew ham
Before they'd take a single syllable."
But the teeth of the sea are on the shore
And there they chew roses.
Big roses, young roses, old roses, small roses
Moon-child, you crack those stolen petals like a clam.
Moon child, those gutting teeth
Have eaten roses.

"If I had invented homosexuality . . ."

If I had invented homosexuality
It would be entirely different
Would be incredibly archaic like an Egyptian statue
Or two boys that are pals with each other
Would be
I beg your pardon, Mr. Freud,
Immovably fixed at the crazy level of adolescence.
The sexual ruling classes
Always
Make our bodies posture in their image.

TRANSLATOR

Wet dreamer. Wrestler
with other people's angels

"Goodnight. I want to kill myself . . ."

Goodnight. I want to kill myself.
Goodnight. I want to kill myself.
Goodnight. I wrote a beautiful poem
But goodnight
Barton Barber jumped out of a 20 story window
While his father was buying cigars.
But goodnight.
Donald Bliss drank a bottle of brandy
And then a little bottle of cyanide
Outside the Greek Theater
But goodnight
I have seen enough of you, good night
I have seen that anyone can write a poem.
Hart Crane died so that faggots could write poetry.
And faggots have written poetry
Olson says that he wrote nominative poetry.
Forget it, I said, goodnight.
This is the last trick. I have discovered
How easy it is to write poetry.
How little it counts. How few sighs
At the best are at the end of a poem.
But goodnight, I have learned
How little poetry has to do with anything.

Goodnight. They knocked on my door tonite
And gave me cigarettes
Poetry is gone. Anybody
Can have his door knocked on and be given cigarettes
Anyone can be given a poem

Let me tell you about Barton Barber
Took a Pepsi Cola bottle up his ass
(I was in the next room)
Wrote a poem I tried to quote tonite
(But you two are fucking in the next room)
Goodnight,
I don't want to be big uncle.
Let me tell you about Barton Barber
I don't remember Barton Barber
I don't remember his poem.

Goodnight.
I am not big uncle
Goodnite
Anybody can write a poem.
You can do anything with a poem
With a poem.
Fuck it, anybody
Even Donald Bliss and Barton Barber
Can write a poem.

Goodnight. I want to kill myself.
Goodnight. I want to kill myself.
Goodnight. Tell the Christchild
He has lost his big uncle.

SAN FRANCISCO AND BERKELEY: 1956–1965

FOR KIDS

Boom, boom, boom
Under
No moon.
Henry Clay,
Who
Will
Scream like a gong?

SONNET EXERCISE

How can the lion's jaw chew forth his pride?
The common asphodel without a change
Can fill his mouth and with his teeth abide
Green into death, and find no wordage strange.
So is the poet eating into fame
Who finds his image growing like a weed
And every whore's son shouting out his name
Who scorn the teeth from which his rhymes proceed.
But I have made this sonnet just for you.
My lion's mouth is stopped by argument.
This half-strung bow no forced rhyme can make new
And arrowlike each lion's tooth is spent.
Unreal like rhyme, each lion's jaw grows old
And howls with truth when all its words are told.

BUSTER KEATON'S SHADOW

[Buster Keaton's shadow enters carrying a wheelbarrow-full of footballs. He stands steadily, looking at last Saturday morning without expression.]

The Shadow: It is impossible not to stop.

[The shadow glows in the Saturday morning like a wounded child. All over the world children begin to wake up from whatever dreams they are having.]

The Shadow: I am the other side of Buster Keaton.

[Three philosophical positions enter disguised as dancers. They are The Verifiability Theory of Meaning, The Categorical Imperative, and Occam's Razor. They look as if they are going to cry.]

The Shadow: Good Morning.

[Helen of Troy has been sitting there all the time dressed in a blue nightgown. She picks at a pock mark on her face.]

The Shadow: Do you speak Spanish?

[Helen of Troy screams slightly and resumes picking her scar. The three philosophical positions look on in infinite contempt.]

The Shadow: No one will even talk to me. Where is the football team? I want to listen to the radio.

[Nothing happens. The stage becomes absolutely silent.]

The Shadow: Good Morning. Good Morning. Good Morning. [Buster Keaton, very drunk, walks in from the left and the shadow disappears.]

Buster Keaton: This is the wrong side of the moon.

[The three philosophical positions sing a song. It is not necessary for anyone to listen to it or understand the words. It would probably be best if the stage was empty.]

Buster Keaton [casually opening another bottle]: What I mean is . . .

The Categorical Imperative: Wit is shit.

[They dance]

Buster Keaton [drinking heavily]: I am innocent. Once I looked like a mountain lion. Now I am unloved.

[Helen of Troy slowly tears at the heart of his poetry. She unnerves him by looking about for his shadow. His shadow, unnerved, enters at her summons. She then has a baby.]

Buster Keaton: I don't want to be autobiographical.

Buster Keaton's Shadow: No.

The Verifiability Theory of Meaning: I want to be all of your children.

[Two students throw up a drawbridge. They hand Buster Keaton ale bottles full of shadow. The footballs become alive. They fight with each other to express meaning.]

The Child: 7-14

Buster Keaton: No. This is impossible. You have not expressed what I am really afraid of.

The Child: Go to the hand that is on the other side of your heart. Go to the heart laughing. Go get me a big grave.

Helen of Troy [crying a little]: I am your mother.

Buster Keaton's Shadow: Yes.

Buster Keaton: An artist has no children.

[Time explodes in their faces. It is 2:45, then 3:15, then 4:33, then almost any place in time—drunken and uncalculated.]

Buster Keaton: An artist has no children.

"The boy . . ."

The boy
You will remember
Was masturbating at the ocean
The waves say
"The seed you spill
Will help nothing to achieve nothing
Is nothing
Will
Be nothing

Is wasted
Is as waves surge
At midnite on a black beach."
Crap, though
They will not listen to the sea weave
They prefer rhetoric or a moustache
They prefer rhetoric or John Ryan
Anything but the truth
And as the sand goes
In the breakers
And as the sand goes
In the breakers
Yes
I'll, we'll, you'll / tell nothing.

"They are going on a journey . . ."

They are going on a journey
Look. Those deep blue creatures
Passing us as if they were speed boats made of water sunlight
Look, those fins
Those closed eyes
Admiring each last drop of the ocean
Look (I crawled into bed with sorrow that night
Couldn't touch his fingers. Turned his back
As if he had an ocean of his own
Bang, went the clock
Which meant nothing to either of us
(Look, damn you, look,
Those deep blue creatures.)

"Hmm. Tahiti . . ."

Hmm. Tahiti whom a brother at the bar wanted to get to. Hmm.
Is a series of islands without any policemen
Which
Could self-sustain anyone's loneliness who
Loved islands. Paint
A big blue painting with several palm-trees. Big gray Co-
Conuts dancing with their leaves. Hmm.
How
Fucking lovely.

"I feel a black incubus . . ."

I feel a black incubus crawling
Into my American bed
It is the color the newspapers describe
Of an atomic bomb explosion
Or the color of the full moon
In the night in which I cannot describe my lover.
He is the color of when I close my eyes
Or the little bowl of spit which tells you not to write poetry
Or the loss of hope—or
The single bullet that is going to kill every fucking person in the world
    who is not named Garcia Lorca.

"It was like making love to my shadow . . ."

It was like making love to my shadow
I know who you are, I said
I can make love to you in three voices
None of which have to do with poetry
It was pity, he said
Pity which makes the heart move with
Nothing to do with poetry.
Oh,
No,
I would drop into deepest prose
No, he said
I agree,
I said, like a whale lamp lit in my heart. No,
I said it has
Nothing to do with poetry

Romance Sonámbulo

(partial translation from Federico García Lorca)

Verde, que te quiero verde.
Green wind, green branches
The ship on the sea
And the horse in the hills.
With a shadow at her loins
She dreams about a railing.
Green flesh, green hair

With eyes of cold silver
Verde, que te quiero verde
Under the lying moon
Everything sees her
And she sees nothing

Verde, que te quiero verde
Large stars of frost
Swim with the fish of shadow
That follows the road to sunrise
The fig tree rubs the wind
Like sandpaper with its branches
And the mountain, a cat that steals
Bristles with sour cactus.
But who will come and from where
She follows the railing,
Green flesh, green hair
Dreaming of a bitter sea.

Friend, I want to trade you
My horse for your house
My saddle for your mirror
My knife for your blanket
Friend, I come bleeding
From the ports of the south.

If only I could, child,
This trade would be closed,
But I am no longer I
And my house not my house

A POEM AGAINST DADA & THE WHITE RABBIT

This poem is against Joe Dunn
No one else is able to personify a white rabbit.
This poem is not to teach Joe Dunn not to be a white rabbit
This poem is to teach white rabbits how to personify themselves.
Or, if he had wit to say
What old men in bars had wit to say,
Dada, go personify yourself.

This is a poem against Dada.
It is absolutely accidental (unproved) that I love Graham Mackintosh
That there is no precision in loving Graham Mackintosh
That white rabbits are not Dada.

I will name my imaginary lovers. Graham Mackintosh
Whose head eats worms
Lee Hough whose almost unremembered basketball court is filled
     with heros
(Victims) of the Dada days when I was a citizen of Hollywood
     High School
And the Japanese were busy bombing Pearl Harbor
And Ken dead of a bad heart and the victims
(Heros) of my high school days also pushing thirty two
Walruses
In a sea of bad remembering.

THE CLOCK JUNGLE

Enter
The clock jungle

Green leaves of tick tick
Roots of bong
And, below the multiple hour
Pendulum stars

The black lilies
Of the dead hours
The black lilies
Of the baby hours
All equal:
And the gold of love?

There's an hour so alone
An hour so alone
A cold hour.

Underbrush

Penetrate me
At the mortal hour
Hour of dying
And last kissing
Heavy hour the
Trapped chimes dream
     Cuckoo clock
     But no cuckoo
     Rusty star
     And enormous
     Pale butterflies

Among the brush
Of your breathing
The ariston carillon
Will sound
As when you were young
For here
You have to come in
Heart
For here
Heart

The Whole Landscape

All the confused jungle
Is an immense spider
Which weaves a sonorous web
Upon hope
Upon the poor white virgin
That fucks herself upon hope

The really true sphinx
Is the clock

Oedipus was born in one pupil
Bounded
Limited on the north by a large mirror
And on the south by a cat
Lady Moon is Venus
(Clock face without savor)

Clocks bring us
Winter
Priestly jaybirds
Dead in the Clocks
Robins
Start in summer.

Where the Dream Drowns Itself

Bats are born in clockfaces
And the young bull studies them
Through horn rimmed glasses.

When will be the twilight
Of all the clocks?
When will those white moons
Sink in through the mountain?

Echo of the Clocks

Hear me
In the clearness of time
There was a taming of silence
Of a white
Silence
Frightening ring
Where the stars
Bump against two floating black numbers.

First and Last Meditation

Time
Has the color of night
Of quiet night
Above enormous moons
Eternity
Looks at its watch
And time has slept
Forever in its tower
While we unwound
All the clocks.

Time finally
Has
Horizons.

Edge of the Clock

In your garden
The damned stars open themselves
We are born and we die
Below your horns.

Cold hour!
You put a stone roof
To the other lyric butterflies
And, seated in the blue,
Short wings and limits

One . . . two . . . and three
I sing the hour in the jungle chime
The silence
I spatter with bubbles
And a pendulum of gold
Bears and carries
My face through the air

I ring the hour in the jungle
The pocket watches everybody's watches
Like swarms of flies
Come and go.

In my heart there will chime
For my grandmother
The gold plated clock.

In my heart there will chime
My grandfather's
Gold-plated clock.

—— • • • ——

"Ridiculous is a word . . ."

Ridiculous is a word with three clowns
Repeating that the square root of minus one
Is all over with grease paint
Is As Mysterious
As you remember it from high school
(Warming your toes
Without a single image, lover, or even age to date the word by)
It is as if
An imaginary number went to the mouth
And said "Lover"
Before
I say
You knew what lovers were
Before in fact
Time with its jagged hand
Jacked off
(The square root
Of the square root of minus one)
All over the lower end of what most sons of bitches call beauty.

"Hunters in the great Southwest . . ."

Hunters in the great Southwest
Put bullets in the skulls of rabbits
And
Where the bones are hot great Joshua trees
Dance in the open. Around the campfire
Murdered Indians
And murdered ghosts of Indians
Throw handclasps full of sand

At the spaces. Greasewood
Fallen timber, loads
Of great, golden, greasewood.

FOR BOB

No Negro
Walking in the jungle of his lack of passion
Can believe the beautiful banyan root of dream
See
His lynchers coming at him stark naked
It is terrible to be human, I
Told your voice. It is terrible to be anything anyone wanted you to be.
Make a noise like a sunset. Get lost.
Your black color
Won't frighten the worms you could not have invented.

FOR TOM

I spill whiskey out of the side of my face
Sob at the moon like a beer baron.
What can you see when you begin to close your eyes?
The edge of the moon, Nebraska
The way being 32 settles down into drunken sleep.
No. Prohibition's over
There are rooms
In the finest hotels
Go to bed and sleep. There are coffins & beautiful bodies to give you
Sweet dreams.

FOR JERRY

An economy of words
I saw envisioning your friendship
A drunken Irishman
Hating
The mere thought.
Sure
As the clock goes on to 2:30
We walk
Together hand in hand
In an abyss of beer and misunderstanding.
No, this is not the
End of the poem
Vanish the clock. 2:45, 2:50
Only
We (our thin hands)
Will never make it.

"An island / Is a herd of reindeer . . ."

An island
Is a herd of reindeer.
(I wanted you to understand
But you cannot understand
This poem)
An island
Is a herd of reindeer
(The words
Are icicles dripping water
Into my voice)
Unique

Like a herd of reindeer
No one knows your heart. No one
Knows your heart.
Why (in all that ice)
Does anyone write poetry against
Your silence.
Why aren't you (penguin of the ice)
My lover.

"And he said there are trails . . ."

And he said there are trails rising up each of the mountains
Call us from mountain to mountain
Like sweat on a boy's back.
You do not know, I said
The dull alphabet. The ABCD
Of the dull alphabet blocks every trail
Is a road block
To the hearts desire. Sweat on a boy's back
Merely runs down a boy's back, ends
In a different place than it's beginning.

"Dear Russ . . ."

Dear Russ,

We are about to begin a thirteenth straight day of rain. It was brilliantly warm and people were swimming in Aquatic Park earlier today, but now the sky has become full of black clouds and it will continue to rain for another eternity. I promised you rain last fall, but you didn't stay long enough to let me redeem the promise.

I would like to include a slice of the black-green of the bay in the letter and the noise of the seagulls (who seem to know it's going to rain again) and the smell of the dead bullheads on the pier (they've been running lately and neither seagulls nor cats will eat them) and my love for this beautiful place and for you who are not in this place. But the U.S. Mail does not include boys or seagulls or bullheads or desires.

VISTAS: ON VISITING SPINOZA'S GRAVE

Backed up again against a wall
What does one say?
There is a picture postcard
Of a man (rather surprised) being shot by a firing squad.
Mexican, I guess
Or Spanish
Cupid and Psyche
Have nothing to do with it
Though it is, I guess, Goya.
Archetypes never reecho
Through the animal mind. The dog
That snapped at me when I was delivering Saturday Evening Posts
      in the year 1937
Is now probably as dead as he is.
Who is?
Archetypes never reecho. Let me tell you,
Cupid went to bed too late. Psyche
Would have burned her finger on a butterfly. But
The story is too late. Anyone
Can write a poem nowadays. Anyone
Can steal the shirt off your back. Homer
With his eyes full of sea surge could not even remember
The name of Ulysses.

No. Not lyrical. The lyre
Plunks like
Someone apologising. The archetypes
Are just not true. Cupid
(Whang, whang, whang)
Does not rhyme
Did not hold a candle
Did not burn those lyrical plane trees
Because
(Whang) no one saw through his eyes.

LAMP

Night shades crawl
Like the fingers of the dead
Across the naked bulb.
Night shades crawl
Like the beautiful fingers of the dead
Across the naked bulb.

CARMEN

My heart was a butterfly
With red wings and someoneelse's shoulders.
I cried between two garages
And he started back and forth to meet them.
It was an old game
Between garages is an old game.
Lah la laluh, lah lah lah la laluh.
My old heart is a butterfly
An old butterfly.

OPERA

First the painted backdrop—
The streets of some impossible city
Then the overture—
The touch of the woodwind in the hand
The throat of a cello
Then they sing in fifty bedrooms—
The archetypal lovers:
Curtain, curtain, curtain
Tragedy
Then the backdrop disappears—
There is nothing left but
Music.

MAZURKA FOR THE GIRLS WHO
BROUGHT ME TRANQUILIZERS

In group, out group
In group, out group
Man wearing a beard, 4 ½ collar, and a pair of pajamas.
Out group, in group,
Out group, in group
Woman wearing lipstick, 36 brassiere, drinking gin and marmalade.
Man and woman unique
Try to dance. People
Say that dance is the basic measure of a poem.

THE BIRDS

The underpart of a dove
The skull of a black sparrow
The jaw of a seagull
See them resting in the middle of your pillow
Let them hear your dreams
Let them be your dreams
Let them fly
Back from the regions of understanding.

SONG FOR A RAINCOAT

He will die without breath.
Sailboat. Rigging. Grass grows in the meadow.
There will be a horrible skeleton of a cat.
White. Though the bones are yellow.
He will die without breathing. Oh
Ringless photographer I loved him
Tell me (snip, snap) how his throat feels.

BIRTHDAY POOL

No one else's mind is really interesting
And no one else's body
I know
And how
Many else know this.
No one

Went to Chicago
No one
Wanted to go to Chicago.

POET

He knocks upon our doors un-
Cannily
As if the only test
Were some way of being right
That a poem can give one.
No original grace
He is like an an-
Droid constructed of all our emotions
As if there were some way of being right
A dance
Grim-
Ly determined.

"Three little waves . . ."

Three little waves on the willowy sand
And the tough old kangaroo
Three little waves in the palm of your hand
And your heart goes nang go koo

Sunken palaces and forgetmenots
And the seaweed moon is new
Pale like a skeleton vegetable
And the tough old kangaroo

HOTEL

The house detective
Tells me God is arriving.
Sweeter than sunshine
But signed his name with a capital G
He tipped the bellboy three dollars
And told him that he was going to die

"No daring shadows . . ."

No daring shadows. No (corrupting poetic effect)
Tramping elephant. No
Circuses. No
Salads with brown sugar and vinegar dressing or bright camels
Not even (semi-sixteen year old fagotts
Singing even like the ringmaster)
A merrygoround
With a unicorn
And three sick penises.

THE PIPE OF PEACE

War, said Billy the Kid, is a kind of personal
Wandering
An ability to make loneliness
Not a great sorrow
To bare
The human condition. Shooting
And alone.

And anything you say
                will be held against you
Held
     against you
The pipe
          of peace
What a great gain
When the fire
                    when the fire
Burns.

"Billy came into the bar . . ."

Billy came into the bar and we were all scared.
His mouth was curved into our smile. "I
Am a gang of reckless teenagers," he said
"I am going to shoot you."
George and I had been talking about the San Francisco Giants. Hal
     and Dorrie and Russ had been singing
No, you'
          ve
Made a mistake
I'm not a victim. Try
Your gun on some other body.
They tell me that life here is more alive
That bullets have the sound of the space they've travelled
That bullets
Could cover the space of a whole mountain;
No, I do not believe. Poetry
Has the sound of other people's lips
Try
          some other victim
                    Billy

"This poem has to do . . ."

This poem has to do
With a trip he made to the hospital
With what I thought was his father but Duncan
      says it was his grandmother
It was a proposition.
Those trees (he or she said on the way to the hospital—
      to die there I suppose)
Those fuzzy things
I do not remember the rest of the poem
But remember still the horror
With which I faced the proposition
That the sight grows old
That the heart grows old
That trees can bore one
Even the best of all our senses
                    dying.

HOKKUS

Big, up there
Goddess, they call her
Where in my room do the fish lie
Breathing out of their gills, naked, out of water
Out of any water, God-
Dess where the fish are plunging
Back and forth where there is nothing but sur-
Face.

Past
Remembering
(Torsos stored in a basement) Germane
To an issue.
A big flower
A spot
A see-
D.

Loving you
My poetry said things I don't know.
Now
My poetry tries to heal me.
So im-
Personal, so loving
That poetry can cover both of us like a big
Blank-
Et.

Bitterness
Bitter - ness
People worry more about bitter than they worry about -ness
Worry more about -ness,
Damn you.

It is time to clean my house
Bare walls will attract pictures
Empty shelves paper
It is like a ruined lawn with snow on it
Something besides what has
Been beautiful.

Sure
Eurydice is dead
in hell   or whatever
Black rope she is tied to.
Rimbaud was constructed by forty tinsmiths
Fifty balloonists
No one was ever/able/either.

"In- / Visible zombies . . ."

In-
Visible zombies
East, west, south, north. No
One knows them.
They come from the back of the elbow. The Aus-
Tro Hungarians shot the moon tonight. They
Lost.

"The skull is not the bones . . ."

The skull is not the bones. The Ro-
Mans discovered this. The eighteenth-century classicists
Dropped their hats and cheered
The skill
At making things is not the sure
Body of bones.
The skeleton stays
Says "Mary Murphy sumus.
We grow."

"Lack of oxygen puzzles the air . . ."

Lack of oxygen puzzles the air. They are
Where we have left them:
Brooklyn Bridge or something,
Cloth,
An enchanted squiggle.
Our emotions become uniforms when we talk together. My
Love your
Bonehead
Clothes.

"Down to new beaches . . ."

Down to new beaches where the sea
More carefully than use-
Ual draws wild blue fish apart from its bottom froze-
N (or un-frozen) on the tides where we stand.

I mean, of course, poetry
And
Where the beaches are too long for us
We gather.

"The slobby sea . . ."

The slobby sea where you float in
Has nothing but the edge of the water
I love
Your silence, your weakness, your pain
It is
(For each of us)
As if a single sea bird from the sky landed

LAST HOKKU

I don't like dreams where a right sound
Can put a minor emotion in amber. I mean the
        mirror
Where it is is there and anybody can thickly walk
        into it
I am sick of the right word and the poets
I have tried to teach the right word. There
In the old mirror, non-

Dissolving. Beautiful. I can't mean the

Right word. Trick yourselves, myselves in
Mirror.

JACOB

He had sent his family across the river.
The wives, the heavy oxen—paraphernalia
Of many years of clever living.
The water flowed past them. All that evening
Jacob was wrestling in the arms of a stranger.
It was not unexpected. By midnight
They had explored each other's strength and every hour
       was a tender repetition.
At dawn the angel tried to free himself and Jacob
Held him with one last burst of strength, screaming.
After that there had never been an angel. Lucky Jacob
Limped across the river, thinking of his wives and oxen.

"Mar - tar - dumbs - ville . . ."

Mar - tar - dumbs - ville
The words agglutinate
Just to make Jim smile
Or any oth-

          er
Beat-   Lorca
    nik.
Ron-
    nie.
Personal names are full of worms
Je-
    sus.

"At the back of the age . . ."

At the back of the age
(The breakage)
The swan plunges
Being there in the white water
Alone
Except mere swanishness
They count the numbers 8
7461
My love
For you was/no/more real than those
Numbers.

"I make difficulties . . ."

I make difficulties, you say, make impossible demands
    of belief on people
But my poems make impossible demands
           on me
           of belief
Believe in that they say (it says)
And none of us would argue.

"A hokku is something . . ."

A hokku is something
                                demand-ed
Like love or somebodyelse's fingers
Do you really think I en/joy this
Fifteen syllables and everybodys
Counted.

"No one can rescue anyone from hell . . ."

No one can rescue anyone from hell. Eurydice
Was born that way. And you were born this way.
If you were lucky (which you aren't) Eurydice
Would come and meet you again
With her grave garments open
Showing a rescued body.

"In the smallest corner of words . . ."

In the smallest corner of words
Poetry shouts from
Them together
Bears witness
Words bearing witness
Witness
There
In the smallest corner of words.

"What I miss . . ."

What I miss
Is Mrs. Blake
Farting around in the garden naked, probably not even
      having sex afterwards
But a high hop farther than Angels' Pinnacle
The grief we share cannot be borne alone
There, there must be a garden and high hops
Oh! All that I miss
Is Mrs. Blake.

"Get away zombie . . ."

Get away zombie, I'm going to burn you
What's you doing with his name.
Get away zombie, I'm going to burn you
What's you doing with his name.
Full of whatever holes you are full of
You chair, you table, you painting
Get away zombie, I'm going to burn you
What's you doing with his name.

"Saying love . . ."

Saying love with five thousand puffs and starts of words
Saying love to five thousand people five thousand times
Making love I wish I were able
Making love now you are gone I love you.

"Extend it in words . . ."

Extend it in words and it has even less to do with anything.
    My hand on yr thigh is a sort of blanket
    Or something vaguely to do with sleep
       There is nothing I would not give you
       (There are dead whales
          Floating bellyupward in the middle of the river)
          Except love.

"Hell, / If you have a horror . . ."

Hell,
If you have a horror of dreaming
Kill yourself
All so there is hell
(As Christ said)
When any bird falls dead or blinded by God. In dis-ease.
These
Moral maxims comfort less
Each year.

"No real resting place . . ."

No real resting place for weary head or hill
Billy
Where you sleep the night and don't worry anything
       about waking up in the morning

No real
On hill
No nervous conclusions to poem. Only love
Not even having to be love.
"I don't hate him because he is miserable," we
      say to our best friends
And love
              is hill
Dim but purgatorial. Hill Billy
Is invented creature. Born of pun
Torn from womb
Language.
Yet summon him, them, a whole army of them
      creatures on hill
Billy.

"You have to make moral decisions . . ."

You have to make moral decisions. With your
      hands, your arms. Anything meaning stays in.
You bet wrong you lose your life. They don't
Shoot you.
They bore you with how your life is already lost
      with your con-
Sequence
And let the poem get out of hand
Which tells nothing to everyone. How painful.

"A million carpenters . . ."

A million carpenters work on this single deal
What is truth
Why is silence
Where is the bottom of why
What, what, why
I mean a million carpenters work on this single deal.

"It is as if / Love had wings . . ."

It is as if
Love had wings
And flew out of sight in the sky
Where neither of us could watch it.

HOKKU

Not
Even
Hatred remains
Reminds
Me.
The sparrows flying qui-
Etly over a sky that has-
                        n't even a cloud left in it.

"It is impossible to stop . . ."

It is impossible to stop. This coldness which
Is really winter. Let me say I love you three times
One for each December.
So cold a month I cannot even define
My desire. And it seems limitless. So cold
It is impossible to stop.

BLOOD AND SAND

It is as if the poem moves
Without the poem. I have captured you.
Done all my will. Have done with all
Emotion.

There is something that bothers me about the poem
Not anything real. But a poem. Your body
The noise that nothing makes upon the shore of an ocean
The big without.

It is as if a poem moves
Without your reality. Your not being there
That defines a nice set of arms
Not holding.

Not holding what. An absentness of you.
This bed is there. Defined,
Without the poem.

AN EXERCISE

"God made alligators grey
because they are dangerous
and lizards green because
they are not."
—Ruskin

Mystery Story

The ghost that picked the lock last night
Explained himself in clues
He left a piece of chewing gum exposed
Like claws.

The murder happened last of all
After the death was over
A knocking came inside the door
And the police were clever!

They knew that there would be but one
Final explanation
The chewing gum sang on, sang on
"Himself, himself. Oh, wobbly
Pinnacle of no explanation."

The police themselves explained it
The ghosts that pushed the doors last night
Had rushed in on themselves, themselves
And bolted them too late.

What is the Main Theme of the Poem?

Where is the person that was in the poem you wrote him?
He is out in the field taking drugs through his leg(s) or his arm(s).
What harm
Was there? I could almost
Break a walnut in two with my fingers.

January 25th

Goodnight. The rain rains in
The streets and the edges of our houses,
Our separate houses.
It makes a noise like a cloud of butter or a pipestem
        or a tapestry or something else
Goodnight then
The we
Even
Without the rain falling
Is not really apparent.

The Fifth of November

It needs a human being to summon them;
They, greedy for blood and not words
Grope mindlessly at the trough.
It takes a human being to feed them
One invented by the words he has become heir to
And the little blood flowing, eh
(Who knows what they are?) they watch us.

Playfulness

The whoteeyoo of sorrow, sorrow
"Death to the murderers of Jacques Molay"
And the whole pattern goes into pattern
Love is as strong as your ribs are
Encaged.

Oh encagéd soul grow old
Feel life like a drinking fountain in a park playground
With all the circle of rings there. Grow old.

Limerick

Ebbe Borregaard isn't as bright
As the things that go bump in the night
But they haven't his beard
And isn't it weird
He makes them seem warm and polite

In A Word The Body

In a word the body
Is not its words
As isolated from them as a grapevine.
Hoo! Hoo! Hoo! they say
Do you think that a body only uses words
Do you think that only a body uses words?

Barn Dance

The victim does not hear the sound
Of hatred, sees no enemy;
The quiet voices that are heard around
The barroom and the grocery—

The old man sitting at the stool
The housewife staring at the shelf
He laughs to hear them play the fool
And half believes their words himself
There is a murderer in town

Translation

Magick can't be trafficked
It is as alone as it is because it doesn't exist when people
   are seeing it. The whole Crimean war
Was waged for this purpose.
Getting into history (they always
Got into history) five Chinamen
With red feathers
Eaten into their toenails.

Always in October

Come drink the pumpkin-colored wine
The ghosts of autumn ask our pardon:
The withered flowers in the garden
The fruit that frosted on the vine.

Memorials so beautiful
They play the spook against our pride
(They dance with pride)
To celebrate their burial.

They wear bright costumes of the dead
And posture in a clownish way
The lover that we loved last May
Now wears a gaping pumpkin head

Now, then, and there beyond belief
They dance upon the icy streets
And every painted spook repeats
The gestures of its unbelief.

Congratulations, George Stanley On Becoming An Editor Of C. V. J. Anderson's Beatitude

Forepaws

They are there
As real as eyebrows
About as
Newspapers, Kubla Khan,
Ghosts creeping over them like lice.
For a moment reality stiffens
If this were really a love   poem.

Couplet

Your world of cocks and furnaces does not delight;
Believing in it would keep me up all night.

On Listening To A Game Between The Giants And The Angels In Which Maurice Cigar Was Relief Pitcher

There is nothing wrong with surrealism
That a good
Passion
Wouldn't cure.

Shit-eaters are almost universally in favor of shit-eating

A Comment On The Future of American Poetry

You Can Open That Door Freely

The appearance of sequence
In human life
Spring in San Francisco, for example, or Jim
Alexander going off with a bad copy of my poetry
Human things bumped into.
No light
Appears in the underworld
The songs they are singing go
Twe-eet
Twe-eet
Like birds in the deadlands singing their hearts out
Mur-
      der-
            er.

Homage to Crowley

"Do what thou wilt under the law"
Which is a pretty silly statement unless it means
That all flowers wilt underground
Especially black flowers. The meaning-
Less statements are there. Enough.
To draw a pentagram upon a page
F-
   i-
      v-
         e-
Points
Flowers
All holiness.

With All The Pomp

Like a tuba or a mirror
After you have had it the world comes at you strange
Like something you wore in the company of the dead
Or a poet about to get married: I mean
Facts do not bother teeth gnashing at the leash.

Classical Poem

No wings. Each part moves. There
Are no tomorrows.
By wires and by telegraph, they send messages.
The ground of this is distinct
There are those (in the throat)
The ground catches.

FOR MAJOR GENERAL ABNER DOUBLEDAY INVENTOR OF BASEBALL AND

FIRST AMERICAN PRESIDENT OF THE THEOSOPHICAL SOCIETY

Without a Period at the End

Sorrier for themselves
Those are that aren't there
Dead
      certain.
              The curtain
Of light dazzles all the air
We are free, we are one, we have had
Motion

Quondam et Futurus

Arthur's body is buried out there
Under two stone of rocks
A new aesthetic
What is not willed in a poem
Will rise
Casting off each stone.
King
Once and future
Them
Rocks.

Mary Murphy's Chowder

What it means, of course, is millions of bridges
Built across a world where you would never know it
A sham. Man does not believe these things
The Krazy Kat howls at the edge of the bunker. The world's dead
      and Hitler's going with it. The time's
Ripe.

Concerning the Future of American Poetry II

My grandmother always told me
That when you get in a fight with a dog turd
You only get shit on your fingers.

Scheme

Crap of the ocean
Displayed
On every piece of beach
They have to go on.
Timber with a soft sound of it
Pieces of crab. The
Sea shells.
Yells
In front of the ocean
No.
Disappearing
"No."

Possession

A small French hound
Bound to a time traveler—
The soul in a boat.

Friday or Saturday

After all nothing is very surprising to you if you're locked up with it
You, hypocrite lecture
I don't mean to call you my brother because you aren't
A mere semblance of flesh
Hypocrite lecture, love
Is an idiot daughter of memory
Born of a single womb. Murder
Is what I mean.
Not lampshades
But wristwatch
Or something round the wrist.

Exercise

Is it the word "dream" that causes so much trouble?
Dreams are there like clouds floating endlessly
     in an except for them blue sky.
Over the rim
Is it the word, dream, that causes trouble?
The clouds move in such un-
                significance
The winds blowing there
That
Flag.

—— • • ——

"Daily waste washed by the tides . . ."

Daily waste washed by the tides down
No numbers. Their numb hands
No foghorns. No cock. No thunder.
Brother Zeus, god like we are
Where the dark waters
Run cold to the bone.

SHARK ISLAND

One edge of the sky is a rainbow; the other cloud
There is nothing on this spit of the sea
But sand. Grinding
Of rock.
     Promises
A new day.
     To get out of a poem is no
     more difficult than the choice both edges
     of the sky
Have.

STINSON

At the edge of the known world, we stand amazed
One step and the water would make us wet
The sky fall on us in packets, the moon,
If there was a moon, make tracks for us
In the little ocean that we walked in.

FOR B. W.

Clarify
The light you find
Accidentally on purpose
Your doublewalker goes about with you
His arms
More muscular

FOR B. W. II

I can't teach you anything but style, baby
For anything else you're going to have to walk more than a mile, baby
Croon awhile
Droon awhile
Your man will find
Dreams and walls it never heard of and schemes
To end the hot tongue of the universe in more than one basket.

FOR B. W. III

The fish in the lakes in the hot countries of the North
Float belly-upward as if amazed.
Explain yourself (the 102° degree temperature in Sacramento
Was not fatal to anything but animals)
How gently the wind blows on the sea that by some day
    by overflowing, by rain or piss or mere metaphor
    these waters will be someday among
The winds blow in the big salt water,
Belly-upward. In that wound in grav-
Ity the winds howl.

"It's dark all night . . ."

It's dark all night
Goes into a kind of day
We joke about. The voice from the 22nd row
Says "when or when" or something strange.
You, Heraclitus den leader of our den
It is all at night
There is
If you dream
We joke about
Club leaders say Heraclitus was quiet

"Love has five muscles . . ."

Love has five muscles
The first, I suppose, is the heart because all the blood goes there
The second is the brain where we love absent
The third is the cock or the cunt where we twitch or receive messages
The fourth is the eye for there is no apparent reason for seeing. Saying
      look at him! She is beautiful!
The fifth I do not know about, have
      never used, u-
      nites somehow.

"Thank you all for your fine funeral . . ."

Thank you all for your fine funeral.
The body fits
In the casket like glue.
You, are not the Marxist terrorists, or the aesthetic swine,
     the body fits
Into the casket like glue. You
Are nobody. I am somebody. Funerally
Speaking
I am buried with the rest of you.

"Jesus came to me in a dream . . ."

Jesus came to me in a dream and said
"Wretched person
         you chew more than you eat
Spit the food
Out of your lips before you swallow
Goop. You are dying of bad table-manners."
But the hunger was there.
        And our lips were not content
With the food our bellies hungered for.
And the law. Mr. William Law,
Non-juror, angry moralist, saint.
Mr. William Law who hated the theater
The House of Hanover, and the trappings of the devil.

Died from overeating. Caused the flood too.
Sodomites. Deader than tomorrow's roar.

"Orpheus / Purposes . . ."

Orpheus
Purposes
They lie there in the sun-drenched sea like little whales
Orpheus came to a conclusion. Was kicked out of it
Was everybody's ghost not because of his humanness
      and certainly not because of his music
They swim or float there like the sun
Almost human
About the ship there are thousands of them sporting
Purposes.

AGAINST CORSO

"To present this as military doctrine," Trotsky said, "would be
      formalizing a weakness." Dead poets, one by one
      going to their graves.
You hear them call sometimes like bells: "The enemy is in your own
      country."
Or like a grace note in some banished cathedral, "If
The salt has lost its savour wherefore shall it be salted"
Or camels
Going through the Iron Curtain
Going through rich peoples' eyes.
"The enemy," Sigmund Freud while he was dying in a hundred pound
      a week apartment said, "is in your own country."

SPIDER MUSIC

Spider Music

The spider is awake in the eyebrows of sense
The famous spider famed in song and story
Even the thought of him makes my eyeballs cold. He
     tells one to wait.
That it is his season.
Even his web, which he built, is still at
     the window
Jim, don't we love one another enough
     not to like spiders
To keep their names off the banisters
     of our senses
Impersonal, de-
Personed like our love
We smash their web.

Whom

An anonymous musician
The whole nature of poetry scattered as it is
Its very life I mean to say
It is the anonymous nature of poetry
That I would celebrate if I saw him again
The distant life
The piano.
I mean the names one calls things
Call
The distant piano
As far away as whatever the moon is.
Love.

Greece

Prometheus invented fire which was there anyway.
He then invented a liver which was there to torture him.
A sing-
(And the singer and the song were there in the mountains every night)
A singular lesson.

January

The dead god appears at the window
He is an icemonger
What is sold is short in supply
Everyone knows this winter is longer than the last
The same
Pain.

Gladstone

Old Mortality
Remembered the slogan thrown at him in childhood.
Et ego
Non in Arcadia.
And if the ostrich
Scratches a hole in the African desert
He is digging a nest.

Nikko San

There are sand dunes on the streets of Laredo
Where someone killed a young man with a bullet
Neither of us young, we try to reconstruct ourselves
It is the Japanese code of no emotion and intense emotion
Which the Jews
Call Zen Buddhism

—— • • • ——

FOR HARRIS

All the day you have been arriving
And then, trained like a dog, stop
Just short of the miraculous. The trains
     continue arriving. We have seen
     more trains than in my grandmother's day
Southern Pacific with a train of broken oranges
Tourists
(All the day the trains have been arriving)
To the heart.

FOR HARRIS II

Cradled in what must be the bottom of the world
The sea seeks fathoms faster
Than anything.
No
Side to this ocean extending out, reaching
     down, upwards, sideways, any
     direction you would care to choose.
The black-tailed sharks say, "You
Are not an answer to this question. Ex-
Tending out to its very limits."

Ch'ang Ch'eng

Replace doors when you leave a house
Return and roll up the straw matting
Be courteous and polite to the people and help them
Return all borrowed articles
Replace all damaged articles
Be honest in all transactions with the peasants
Pay for all articles purchased
Be sanitary; establish latrines at a safe distance from people's houses

When the enemy advances, we retreat
When the enemy halts and encamps, we trouble him
When the enemy seeks to avoid battle, we attack
When the enemy retreats, we pursue

Replace doors when you leave a house
Return and roll up the straw matting
Be courteous and polite to the people and help them
Return all borrowed articles
Replace all damaged articles
Be honest in all transactions with the peasants
Pay for all articles purchased
Be sanitary; establish latrines at a safe distance from people's houses.

—Mao

"Be brave to things . . ."

Be brave to things as long as
As long as
As long as the plot thickens
As long as you hold a tiny universe in your
      hand made of stringy oil, cats' hair,
      tobacco, remnants
Of what was once wide.
As it was once as long as, the plot thickens.
      Be brave to thinkers in the night, rusted
      boxes, anything
That has dimension.
As if it were a foot wide
Tall, square, as long as boxes
Were.

"With fifteen cents . . ."

With fifteen cents and that I could get a
      subway ride in New York. My heart
Is completely broken. Only an enemy
Could pick up the pieces.
"Fragments of what," the man asked, "what?"
A disordered devotion towards the real
A death note. With fifteen cents and real
Estate I could ride a subway in New York. No
Poet starved. They died of it.

A NEW POEM

(texts and fragments)

The rope. A beginning
I want to begin with a rope.
Human contact. All I have missed
These meaningless years. All that all have talked to have missed.
A new beginning means that you do not write the same poem
     over again
That you try a new angel
A new angel (Heurtibise am dead and buried. He dead now. You try
     new angel. Write
Some poem.)
Hanging there
With my heart out
My pants ripped. My groin singing
Melodies nobody am never heard of
(Why do them new angels haunt me? Was there angels?) A new
Poem.

_____

The gates of hell are frozen shut. The gates of heaven never open.
     A new
Poem.
Frozen snowgirl Eurydice or Archangel Heurtibise. The doors
     am closed.
Find no more in the wind or a seagull some kind of answer. There
     aren't answers.
Find a wall that is broken into many spaces and a door, a mirror, a few
     chairs. There
Aint no heart in it, Jack.
Tell all your lovers they are bound to miss you. The
                                   A

Doors am closed.
New poem.

_____

It is almost an insult to poetry to continue. Rilke
Am dead now
So am Hart Crane and Shelley
Lament of the makiris
Timor mortis
(They all am dead now)
Conturbat me.
Yeats
Am dead now
With all his spooks and his live wife
That Tom Parkinson interviewed
Homer am dead now
There is no point in continuing. Conturbat
Me.

———————

The paratroopers of poetry
Fly hell
See them drop in a great body
Like moths or giant pandas. Joe Hill
William Shakespeare, Alexander Pope,
Gertrude Stein. Hear them scream
As they hit the edges
Sunya. There is nothing there. No
Female escort, no
Male escort. You are alone
Without even any policemen to try to arrest you.
The loneliness of hell is past belief. Beauty is dead
Sunya. The perception of beauty is dead
Sunya. There are shapes
That walk across the universe. We

———————

Not to be interested in what they tell you.
The poem, the vowel, the original
Grunt
Is outrageous. They tell you
Like checks in a bank. What is magic What
Is dream
What is real (although you do not believe them)
What you dreamed that you said at five o'clock in the morning
      when your only companion was a pillow
      or somebody's shoulder. What
I am trying to tell you is
Not to be interested.

———————

How they will be bored by my love for you. The biographers. The
      monotonous rattle of it through years of poems.

If he can't say goodbye why must he say it again and again like an idiot
      who has found one word to communicate everything
If he whispers I love you to an almost empty bed why can't he do it
      somewhere else except on the pages of these poems
I want his more important loves, his rightful demons.

———————

Effortless
Those loves
Like electricity. Electric
Invisible
But pain hangs on like a dog. The beds we sleep in every night.
    The dull ache of a tooth or a lonely swimmer trapped in the
    night's ocean
And these others are not enough.
Not until the poem bursts into poetry
And the body puts on the glad rags of unreason
And the heart quenches

Pain, I would tell my biographers. The sheer
Pain of being human.
                And when I hold your hand
Or do not hold your hand.
                    This pain.

————————————

Who will tell either of us if anything is true. False angel and true angel
We confront each other
You saw the vowel as scratching on the glass
(The fingers searching a way out from ahead of a mirror)
And I as the tongue saying uh
The only sound it can make without lying.
Who will tell either of us? False and true angel. The grand
    triangle of vowels. How can we possibly

————————————

I met an angel
Who said he was a beatnik
He didn't drink brandy or honey water
Just pure vowels.
Vowels are the pauses between things
Silence is what we fight against, I told him
But his wings
Were paused to beat against the pure air.

—————————

To be loved is well
To be hated by a fool is nicer
I rot where you will rot yourselves,
Lovers or fools: Jack Spicer.

—————————

Go to hell. Orpheus
Did it with his harp. Went
To hell in a wheelbarrow
Searching
Eurydice.
I
Did it
Once or twice
(The dog barked three times) I
Planted a big eucalyptus tree there where there wasn't sorrow.

—————————

Then
What is an angel
It is easy to say that he is a messenger, a postman
Delivering all sorts of important and unimportant letters
Some of which will change your life. Or your death for that matter:
Overdue bills, an unexpected postcard, the kind of thing anybody
     with sense would leave in his mailbox until he could sort
     them out
This is the mailbox, of course
This is my mailbox
This is the angel.

––––––––––––––––

All the way down past the skull
Where the flesh grows on the beach like those thin
Flowers that used to grow in the sand or in the rocks near the sand
     when I was young. Those thin
Flowers. Waxy and fat
(With their own salt water, I guess) imitating
The ocean.
All the way down past the skull. The beach
Admiring the ocean
The flesh
Bunched in ways
That don't admit progress.
If a single flower were able to grow there
With its fleshy leaf and its blossom which was not really a
     blossom but more made of the echo that annoying waves make.
If that flower grew there on those blank rocks
Who would kiss it, pick it, transplant it to grow in any garden? Hell,
The flower that grows near to the sea
hears hell noises, listens
To some loose fragments of sand next to the wave bounces

Is witness to the dead roar.
And I report to you that the thirties are like this
Being years of a man's body they cast their funny flowers on the beach
Being rocks of a man's life.

———————

Disperse each vowel
I, ae, a
No there was no passion like that passion
Queen
For a day
Disperse each sound. I
Did, not want to write this poem. Apples
Are growing sweet and cool at the south of him
Ah, he is a pronoun. He is a pronoun.
At the right of him (writing this poem sun-backwards
Is my shadow).
                    Ah.

———————

There is room for wonder. I am beginning to have a cold.
Can you put everything into a poem
Or do the words resist you? Pine needles
Will be at the edge of the forest. Make
Each vowel sound (each heart) as likely
To burn.

———————

When a poem argues
It argues wrongly
It is not a matter of saying the right word
It is more like a boundary between some places
Some of them real and some of them invented
It is more like my tapestry and my leather jacket that
      fill my room.

———————

The gentleman wants to know
If the word, boulder
Is more wet than dry more sweet than sour more in use than using.
      We rate
The scattering of real things
First on the scale comes good and bad, then, you and I. Then
Sheer chaos
But when the boulder moves
What pebbles (wet and dry, sweet and sour, un-
Imaginable
Are dis-
Lodged from the good mountain?

———————

To forget the landmarks totally
And to forget where you have been, what forests are
        burned up, what creeks are dry, what paths made
        slippery. These
Are important for a poem. You wage
Continual war against finding the path you choose
You have not to know
These landmarks. What
Tree will spring up singing before your eyes.

———————————

The black X and Y of it
The pers-
Onal equation that lasts for a minute like our last match
The coun-
Ter-journalism of it. The share
That two (or fifty people) that are victims of the
        vampire of poetry
                            have
To make heroes or anything else they invent for us.
Sad. The
X and Y of it. And that knife
That you hold in your fingers glitters in my poem
And that direct black fish
That glitters than mine own di-
Rect black fish
In yours.

THE PLAYS

YOUNG GOODMAN BROWN

A Morality Play

CAST OF CHARACTERS
(in order of appearance)

1st Chorus   (three male corpses)
2nd Chorus   (three female corpses)
The Black Man
Young Goodman Brown
Goody Cloyse
Deacon Gookin
The Minister
Faith, Brown's Wife

The scene is a wooded path. There is a rock that looks like a low altar (A) and a tree stump (B). Behind the rock there is a depression (C, upstage) which is not seen or used until the appropriate part of the play. There are flats on either side of it. The 1st CHORUS (xxx) are three male corpses and the 2nd CHORUS (yyy) are three female corpses. All look like corpses and squat perfectly stationary staring out at the audience throughout the whole play. Only one of the three speaks for each chorus.

```
                        (   C   )

Set as
seen from          B          (A)
above         _____
                                                        —Path
              _____
                   xxx                       yyy
```

1st CHORUS *(half-whispering)*: He will be here soon. The Black Man is waiting for him.

2nd CHORUS: It's one of their nights tonite.

1st CHORUS: Yes, but no one has come yet.

2nd CHORUS: It must be that his wife is keeping him. She is standing at the doorway crying, with the pink ribbons bobbing as her face cries.

1st CHORUS: Does she think he's being unfaithful?

2nd CHORUS: They've only been married three months.

1st CHORUS: I hear him coming.

2nd CHORUS: Somebody ought to pray for him.

(THE BLACK MAN has been standing in the center of the stage. He is dressed in black and is a Negro. There are no lights on him and he cannot be seen until BROWN, followed by a spot, enters and almost bumps into him. THE BLACK MAN bows.)

187

BLACK MAN: Young Goodman Brown! You're late you know. I heard the bells in the town strike nine a long time ago.

BROWN: Faith kept me back a while.

BLACK MAN: She was worried? Nice young wives always worry. Don't you worry, Goodman Brown, we have nothing in these woods that would harm either of you.

BROWN *(angrily)*: That's enough.

BLACK MAN: You're right. We've been wasting our time here talking, late as we are. That's no way to get through the woods in a hurry.

(He gestures with the snake-like stick he is carrying.)

You'd better take my stick, Goodman Brown; we have a good long way to walk.

BROWN: The bargain was that I meet you here. Nothing else. I never agreed to go further with you. I have met you here, friend, and now I shall leave you here. I could never do what you would want me to do.

BLACK MAN: That may be so. That may very well be so. But let's walk on a while anyway. We can reason together as we walk. If I don't convince you, then you can walk back those few steps alone. We're still on the very edge of the forest.

(They walk offstage in stylized slowness.)

1st CHORUS: They are going on, into the wood.

2nd CHORUS: They will be back. The edge of the wood is the same as the end of the wood.

1st CHORUS: Yes, the path is always the same no matter where you step into it.

2nd CHORUS: And seems to be the same place.

(BROWN and THE BLACK MAN enter from the same place where Brown entered before.)

BROWN: This is too far already. None of my family have ever walked so far into such a forest.

BLACK MAN *(interrupting)*: And kept such company. Oh, Brown, you make a natural thing so dramatic. I've known your family as well as I've known any family in Massachusetts—and that's no trifle to say, either. I knew your father and your grandfather. They were good men and I helped them. I can remember your grandfather, the one that was constable; I helped him drive that Quaker family out of Salem with a whip; and it was I that brought your father a pitch-pine knot, which I lit at my own fire, to burn up an Indian village with in King Philip's war. Without my help how could men like them have brought order to this wilderness? They were good men and good friends and I've had many pleasant walks with each of them along this path and returned with them merrily after midnight. I'd like to be friends with you for their sake. After all, it's all in the family.

BROWN: Then I have been saved from the damnation of my fathers by the prayers of a good community. The people of Salem pray so well that they can save even such a wretch as—if you aren't lying—I must be. Look back there at the Salem of my friends and their fathers. They are clean. Those men back there, sleeping or praying after an honest Christian day, think of them. Call them my fathers.

BLACK MAN: They are excellent men. One would be proud to call them either friend or father.

(There is silence for a moment.)

BROWN: One thing—

BLACK MAN: What is it, friend?

BROWN: How is it that no breath of this wickedness has reached Salem Village? If the town had heard the slightest rumor of this, they would have rooted my family out. My neighbors will not abide wickedness. They hang witches in Massachusetts.

BLACK MAN: Wickedness or not, I hold good communion among your friends and neighbors. The deacons of many a church have shared wine with me; I have rather an interest in the political affairs of your town and other towns too: Hanging indeed! The majority of the

Great and General Court are firm supporters of my interests. Even the governor and I have a kind of working arrangement.

BROWN: Politics, yes! I can believe that your thumbs may twist politics. It is a tangled web at best even when my neighbors weave it. They have their own ways and perhaps, God help them, their own justification. Those men are nothing close to me. I mean as neighbors men ardently of god like our minister. That good old man loves God with a fury and hates evil with compassion. How could I look in his face again if I went with you. It would be like fire.

(THE BLACK MAN, who has listened politely to BROWN with a grave face, now begins to giggle.)

BLACK MAN *(trying to control himself)*: I'm sorry. *(There is silence.)* Please go on, Goodman Brown, sometimes it's hard for me to maintain a properly dignified attitude towards all this.

BROWN *(with some anger)*: Well, to settle the matter once and for all, there is my wife, Faith. It would break her heart and I'd rather break my own than let hers be broken.

BLACK MAN: I can understand that. We can understand love too, you know. *(Turns around.)* Not for twenty women like the one hobbling down the path there would I let Faith come to harm.

BROWN *(turns around)*: Is there someone coming down the path? It must be one of your damned souls to be here at this time of night. I'd like to see what one looks like.

BLACK MAN *(smiling)*: Really, Goodman Brown, you've seen some of them before.

(The shape of GOODY CLOYSE, badly lighted, can be seen down the path. She is also walking with ritual slowness.)

BROWN: Why, I think it's Goody Cloyse. I wonder what she's doing on the path so late. She shouldn't be going out in the woods at night.

BLACK MAN: Is she a friend of yours?

BROWN: She taught me my catechism. *(Triumphantly.)* You'd better stay away from her. She knows almost as much of the spiritual life as the

Minister and Deacon Gookin do. If you were to touch her, her innocence would burn you to the bone.

BLACK MAN: Nevertheless I think I'll stay on the path and meet her. But perhaps you'd better go over into the shadows where she can't see you. She might not understand what you're doing here.

BROWN *(threatening)*: Stay away from her!

(Nevertheless he slinks over into the shadows. THE BLACK MAN stands still on the path while GOODY CLOYSE approaches. She has her head down and does not see him as she walks toward him. She is muttering indistinctly. When she is close to him he raises his snake-stick and touches her neck with it.)

GOODY CLOYSE: The Devil!

BLACK MAN *(leaning on his stick)*: Then Goody Cloyse knows her old friend.

GOODY CLOYSE: I'd know you anywhere, your worship. With all this dim light and my failing eyes—but you look beautiful tonight, your worship.

BLACK MAN: You've taken a slow way to go to meeting tonight.

GOODY CLOYSE: Some bitch of an unhanged hag stole my broomstick. It was probably that senile old horror, Goody Cory. Your worship does get some of the strangest people at his meetings. I didn't discover it was missing until I was ready to go, all anointed with juice of smallage, and cinquefoil, and wolfbane—

BLACK MAN: Mingled with fine wheat and the fat of a new-born baby.

GOODY CLOYSE *(laughing)*: Ah, your worship knows the recipe. So, as I was saying, since I was all ready for meeting and didn't even have a horse to ride on, I decided to walk. It's a rather hard path to walk at my age but they tell me that there's a nice young man to be taken into communion tonight and I wouldn't want to miss that. But if your worship would like to carry me, we could be there in a twinkling.

BLACK MAN: I'm sorry, my dear, but I'm busy at the moment. Just keep walking and you'll be nearly there.

(He touches her with the stick again and she, after the touch, walks across the stage and exits at a normal rate of speed.)

BROWN (*coming out*): That old woman taught me my catechism.

(*BROWN and THE BLACK MAN are also almost walking at a normal rate of speed. They silently exit together.*)

1st CHORUS: I can remember what a terrible thing it seemed when good turned out to be evil. It seemed as if the whole world was being punished unjustly.

2nd CHORUS: I wonder if that old woman knows what she has done.

1st CHORUS: She has done nothing. It was all done before he took the first step.

(*Enter BROWN and THE BLACK MAN from the usual side.*)

BROWN: Who are those people that were talking there?

BLACK MAN: They are dead people, I think. It's hard for me to tell but I think they are dead people.

BROWN: Dead people!

BLACK MAN: Don't say it that way. Don't be frightened. Meetings like this always attract some weird things. It's just like all sorts of insects flying around a lighted window at night. They can't get in. They just buzz around stupidly. They aren't real like your pious friend Goody Cloyse.

BROWN: Why should I be damned because of her? (*He sits down on a tree-trunk and looks stubborn.*) Friend, my mind is made up. I'm not going to walk another step with you. What if a wretched old bitch chose to go to the devil when I thought she was going to heaven? Does that turn heaven upside down? Should I leave my church and my wife to go after her? (*Points to the audience.*) Take your corpses to meeting with you instead of me.

BLACK MAN (*with a look of sympathy*): You'll think better of this in a little while. Sit here and rest yourself for a few minutes. You've had to struggle to get this far. And when you feel like moving again, here's my stick to help you along.

(*THE BLACK MAN tosses the stick to BROWN who catches it automatically and then throws it down as if it were a snake. THE BLACK MAN exits quickly.*)

BROWN (to Choruses): You, over there, can you hear me?

1st CHORUS: I can hear you better than you can hear me.

BROWN: I cannot stand it here. I am going back.

2nd CHORUS: Go, if you can. Your bed will be warm at home. You have a young wife waiting.

BROWN: I didn't want to come here. What did he want of me? (To the 1st Chorus.) Tell me, what does he want?

1st CHORUS: How do I know what he asks of you. I am not wiser being dead, only colder.

BROWN: It was a close escape. The thought of my wife and my church protected me.

2nd CHORUS: If you see the Minister walking in the morning sun, you can smile at him.

BROWN: Tomorrow when the sun rises I shall have a clear conscience and a knowledge of evil.

1st CHORUS: Go, if you can. You might escape with only pride and weariness.

BROWN: How could I be proud? Yet I suppose I do feel pride when I should be feeling shame and gratitude. I'll feel shame enough tomorrow when I tell the Minister what I almost did. He and Deacon Gookin will pray over me for quite a while, I guess.

2nd CHORUS: I hear somebody coming. You had better hide. It would be terrible if you were discovered now.

(Indistinguishable voices are heard offstage.)

BROWN: Yes, I hear voices. It's funny but they sound like Deacon Gookin and the Minister. It must be my guilty conscience. There certainly aren't any churches around here.

1st CHORUS: You had better hide quickly. They should not find you here before you have taken action.

BROWN: It certainly might be them. They may be on their way to visit some dying man on the other side of the forest. I'll hide and face them tomorrow when the sun is shining.

(As he says this he hides. DEACON GOOKIN and THE MINISTER enter from the left.)

DEACON GOOKIN: It's rather dark here tonight, and the woods look ghastly. Just the right kind of a night for a meeting. Do you know, Reverend Sir, I'd rather miss an ordination dinner than tonight's celebration. They tell me that some of our community are going to be here from Falmouth and beyond, and others from Connecticut and Rhode Island, besides several Indian powwows. Those powwows, in their heathen fashion, know almost as much about this sort of thing as the best of us. Besides, I hear there is a goodly young woman to be taken into the communion.

THE MINISTER: A busy night indeed, Deacon Gookin. But let's hurry along or we'll be late. Nothing can be done, you know, until I get there.

(They hurry off stage. BROWN comes slowly out of hiding.)

1st CHORUS: Did you hear them?

BROWN: I heard them.

2nd CHORUS: It's a warm night. If you were to walk back now into town, you could go back through the familiar door of your house as if you had been walking a dream away. Your wife, Faith, would take you in her arms and would tell you that you had dreamed all these horrors.

BROWN: A man of God like the Minister has been too near to God. He has seen beauty beyond the strength of his soul and it has driven him mad. He has lived with God too intimately and his reason and soul could not stand it. Simple innocence is better, not knowing God too well; if he had had someone like my little Faith to share God with him, this would not have happened.

1st CHORUS: Take your love and go.

BROWN *(looking up at the sky)*: Why, there are still stars up in the sky. I thought the night was too dark for them. With the God of light above and with Faith below, even I can stand firm against the Devil.

(Pause.)

Oh!

2nd CHORUS: Tell me what you see.

BROWN: The wind is blowing the clouds across the stars.

(The voice of a woman wailing but with a sort of joy in her voice can be heard distinctly off stage.)

1ST CHORUS: Is that the wind?

(The voice comes again louder.)

BROWN *(calling in agony)*: Faith! Faith! Faith!

(He rushes off stage in a frenzy. Wind noises, laughter, etc., offstage. In a minute the noises stop and he enters again with a pink ribbon in his hand. He stares at it stupidly.)

BROWN: The wind blew me this ribbon. It is her pink ribbon. *(Quietly.)* My Faith is gone. She's gone.

(Devilish sounds and laughter offstage.)

BROWN *(turning toward the noise)*: You're laughing. Let me laugh too. *(He picks up THE BLACK MAN's stick from where he had dropped it and begins laughing.)* I want to worship too. Where do I go to worship what rules the world? Where is the meeting?

1ST CHORUS: It is here around you.

(The stage is very dark. THE BLACK MAN, who can hardly be seen, begins lighting four large candles on a rock that looks like an altar that has been in the middle of center stage. As he lights the candles the back of the stage, which has been dark and unable to be seen by the audience during the course of the play, is now illuminated by a faint red light. A crowd of people can be seen there but it can never be seen clearly. THE BLACK MAN stands on rock facing audience.)

BLACK MAN: Bring forth the converts!

(The MINISTER leads BROWN to altar from stage left. GOODY CLOYSE leads FAITH from stage right. They stand on each side of THE BLACK MAN.)

Welcome, my children, to the communion of your race. You have discovered in your youth your nature and your destiny. My children, look behind you.

(They turn toward the crowd of people at the rear of the stage. The red light gets brighter and one can almost distinguish faces from the audience.)

This is your blessed community. These are your friends and your fathers. Those are the people you reverenced from youth. You thought them holier than yourselves, and you looked with utter horror at your own sin, contrasting it with them and their lives of righteousness and prayer. When you could not pray you knew that they could. Yet here they all are in my worshipping assembly. Tonight you will be allowed to know their secret actions, their inner lusts. You will see perversion and murder, incest, blasphemy and little knowing insanities, masturbation and various refinements of cruelty. Don't blush, sweet ones, listen! By the sympathy of your human hearts for sin you will be able to smell out all places—whether church or bed-room, the jakehouse or the forest—where crime has been committed, and exult to behold the whole earth one stain of guilt, one mighty blood spot. You will hear the inner thoughts, the fountain of sin bubbling in every man, just as clearly as you can hear his heart beating. Now, my children, look upon each other.

(They look at each other in terror.)

There you stand, my children. Depending upon one another's hearts, you had hoped that virtue was not all a dream. Now you are undeceived. Evil is the nature of mankind. Evil must be your only happiness. Welcome again, my children, to the communion of your race.

(The almost invisible crowd of worshippers repeat "Welcome" in voices of despair and triumph. There is silence and FAITH and BROWN look at each other.)

BROWN *(suddenly)*: Faith, Faith! For God's sake look up to heaven and resist him.

(There is screaming and all the lights on the stage simultaneously go out. FAITH, THE MINISTER, and GOODY CLOYSE exit from stage during darkness. When lights go on, the lighting is as it was at the start of the play. BROWN is on the ground, apparently in a swoon, and THE BLACK MAN is bending over him.)

BLACK MAN (*smiling*): You certainly played hell with the meeting.

(*BROWN looks up numbly and then begins to remember what has happened.*)

BROWN: Is she saved?

BLACK MAN: She, Faith, saved? Of course not. You can't save another person's soul with your own soul. It would be an uneconomic sort of universe that allowed that. You're saved, you know, whatever that may mean.

BROWN: I don't care.

BLACK MAN: I shouldn't think you would care. Do you know what's going to happen when you come back to Salem Village this morning.

BROWN: I'll denounce everybody.

BLACK MAN (*ironically*): To whom? No, when you go back this morning you'll see the Minister taking his morning walk and meditating on his sermon. He'll bless you as he passes. Through the open window of his house you'll see Deacon Gookin praying. You'll see Goody Cloyse teaching the catechism to the little girl who has brought the morning milk. Then you'll come up to your own house, and Faith will run out with her pink ribbons swinging and she'll kiss you in the sight of the whole village.

BROWN: Are you trying to comfort me?

BLACK MAN: Do I look like a comforter? No, for you'll see the evil and the horror gnawing away at each of them. You'll be a sad and sullen man, Young Goodman Brown, and I'll be surprised if they put any marker on your tombstone when you die.

BROWN: What do you want me to do?

BLACK MAN: I doubt if you can do anything.

BROWN (*turning to the 1st CHORUS*): Do you know what I think?

1ST CHORUS: Yes, I know what you think. You think what the dead think.

BROWN: I don't think that there's very much difference between angels —whether they're flying or fallen. I don't think there's very much difference for a man between the pit of hell and the pit of heaven. I think man is very much like a sheep. A sheep loves the good shepherd that sees he is fatly fed and hates the evil butcher that kills him with a clumsy knife. Yet the shepherd and the butcher are in the same business.

(Turns to THE BLACK MAN.*)*

Do you understand my parable, friend?

BLACK MAN *(shrugging)*: I don't go in for parables.

BROWN *(turning to the 2nd* CHORUS*)*: Do you know what I am going to do.

2nd CHORUS: Yes, I know what you are going to do. You are going to do what the dead have already done.

*(*BROWN *takes out a hunting knife.)*

BLACK MAN *(laughing)*: You're not going to try to kill the devil.

BROWN: I'll leave that to God.

(He starts to go offstage and then pauses and comes back for the stick.)

I'll need this.

(He exits.)

BLACK MAN *(to* CHORUSES*)*: Why don't you go away. The meeting is over.

2nd CHORUS: We are dead and we want to see living blood flow.

BLACK MAN: No blood will flow.

2nd CHORUS: Certainly blood will flow. He is cutting out his eyes.

*(*BROWN *comes back on. His eye sockets are bloody. He is using the devil's stick as a blind man's cane, feeling his way along with it.)*

BROWN: Are you here? *(Pokes at* THE BLACK MAN *with the stick.)* Ah, I feel you here. If you were the Minister, you would feel the same. Or even Faith. I can go back to Salem Village now and resume living.

BLACK MAN: Will you escape anything by this?

BROWN: I'll escape seeing them. I will not have to retch at counterfeit innocence or watch the evil bubbling in a beautiful body. Goodbye, friend Devil, I'd shake your hand if I could see it.

(Curtain.)

PENTHEUS AND THE DANCERS

An Adaptation

Sacred to the memory of Pentheus
and to the god that killed him

CAST OF CHARACTERS
(in order of appearance)

Six Maenads:
   Chorus
   Antichorus
   Drummer
   Flutist
   Two Dancers
Teiresias
Cadmus
Pentheus, King of Thebes
Soldier
Stranger
Dionysus
Herdsman
Messenger
Agave, Pentheus's Mother

Outside a gate of Thebes. The gate is in the middle of the stage but can swing open showing a backdrop of the town. The stage is empty when the curtain rises. Six maenads slowly enter from stage right; they are: CHORUS, ANTICHORUS, DRUMMER, FLUTIST, and the two DANCERS. They are dressed in black robes and wear faunskins and ivy. They arrange themselves slowly on the corner of the stage. NB: whenever the maenads are alone in stage action, the lighting narrows down the stage to this corner.

CHORUS: Here we are. Another city. It seems to me that I have spent my life dancing from city to city. *(She goes over and tries the gates.)* They are unlocked. This is the city with the unlocked gates.

Who is walking about inside the gates? Who is walking about on the streets of the city? They had better make way for us. They had better listen through their walls to us, silently and with proper purpose. Listen to the street singers from Asia, citizens of Thebes. *(Flute and drum begin very softly. DANCERS occasionally move. CHORUS returns to place.)* He, in his fortune, who receives this god's mercy will abandon his life for that mercy and will contain it inside himself and the god will surround him. He will wear this god's costume and dance in icy purity upon the mountain. He, in his fortune, who abandons his life to this god's mercy will be his servant and will contain him forever.

(DANCERS are now fully dancing.)

Go, dancers, bring back the god born of god. Carry him on your light feet along the mountains of Asia. Bring back the god born of god. Carry him on your light feet down the highways of Thrace. Bring back the holy child of god. Bring Dionysus home.

ANTICHORUS: He was born here, in this city, aborted by fire; born in the smell of fire and burning flesh, five months in the womb.

It was Zeus then who received him, ripped him from the burning womb of his mother and contained him; it was Zeus that carried him in the coolness of his thighs.

And on the ninth month he was born. He was born without pain from the body of Zeus the father. A horned child and his head garlanded with gentle snakes.

(All the women now turn toward the gate. Some light focuses on it.)

CHORUS: Now join us in our worship, city of the unlocked gate. Join us in our worship, deathplace of Semele. Garland your streets with ivy, disguise yourself with ivy, fatal city.

Branch out, branch out green, fair-fruited creepers. Join us with branches of your oaks and evergreens. Let every tree in your city make a green sacrifice to the god born of god.

Listen, citizens of Semele's birthplace. Strip off your city clothes and assume our god's garments. Put on his dappled faunskin with the hair braided for worship, the stiff crown of leaves, the flowering dress of ritual. Take up the thyrsus and strike the bright air with it. Give worship with the violent wand.

It will not be long before you dance. Our god is coming. It will not be long before you follow your wives and daughters to the mountain and dance. Listen, citizens of the unlocked gate, our god is coming.

(Musicians play.)

ANTICHORUS: Listen to our god's music, citizens of Thebes. Listen to our god's music, citizens of the unlocked gate. He uses the same drum that the Corybantes used in the birthcave of Zeus on Mount Ida, the drum that frightens away the terrors of the night, the drum that deafens all enemies. He uses the same flute that shrills across the long deserts of Asia, the flute that makes the empty spaces blossom with music. He uses the flute that belongs to Rhea, to the great mother. Listen to our music, citizens of Thebes. Listen to our music, citizens of the unlocked gate.

(More and wilder music. Then CHORUS no longer addresses Thebes but turns left towards the mountain.)

CHORUS: Dionysus will welcome the man who falls to the ground dressed in a blotched faunskin, who falls to the ground hunting the wild goat, hunting the delight of warm flesh devoured. Dionysus will welcome the man who falls satisfied to the ground. Dionysus will welcome the thirsty hunter.

The air is full of wine and honey. Dionysus lifts the blazing pine-torch high in the air. Fire trails from it as he runs along and his long hair streams behind him in the wind. He is calling us and we hear him.

Go, dancers. Go, dancers. Like the rivers of Asia that run with gold, sing Dionysus, sing sweet Dionysus. Let your drums sing, Dionysus, Dionysus is the lord of joy. And the flute climbs higher, each note of it climbs higher as you climb the mountain, climbing as you climb the mountain.

In joy then, as a colt with her mare in the pasture, your body leaps and rests. In joy then, you are a dancer.

(There is a sudden silence and the gate slowly opens. TEIRESIAS hobbles out, shortly afterwards to be followed by CADMUS. TEIRESIAS is old and bearded and uses his thyrsus as a blind man's cane. CADMUS is just old. Both are wearing maenad's costumes.)

TEIRESIAS: *(turning back to shout inside the gate)*: Cadmus, Cadmus, come look. I think they are outside the gate. *(He speaks to the maenads that he isn't sure are really there.)* He is Cadmus, son of Agenor. He was the man who founded this city.

(CADMUS comes doddering in.)

CADMUS: Yes, it's them. *(Aside.)* Do you suppose they understand Greek? *(Aloud.)* This is going to be a great occasion. *(Aside.)* I put on all the robes just as you said. You're a wise man, Teiresias, a wise man. *(Aloud.)* This god is going to be a powerful god. Just think, he was Semele's son. In a way, I'm his grandfather. We must see that he has all our hospitality here. It's almost as if a favorite grandchild were coming home.

(Aside.) Where are we supposed to dance? Do you think that we'd better go up to the mountain and dance with the rest of them?

(Aloud.) Explain this to me, Teiresias. You are as old as I am but always were wiser. Tell me where old men are supposed to go to dance. I don't think I'll ever get tired of stamping the earth with this thyrsus. Already I've forgotten that I'm old.

TEIRESIAS: Yes, Cadmus. Neither of us are old and both of us feel like dancing.

CADMUS *(trying to get CHORUS to comment)*: Do you think it would be right to dance on the mountain with them?

TEIRESIAS: It would be right.

CADMUS *(turning)*: I'd better have them get a chariot ready so we can be there quickly.

TEIRESIAS: No, that wouldn't be right. It wouldn't pay the god the same honor.

CADMUS: I'll lead you then, Teiresias. One old man will lead another old man.

TEIRESIAS: Don't worry. The god will lead us both. We will walk without effort.

CADMUS: Isn't anyone else coming? Are we the only men in the city that are willing to dance in the god's honor?

TEIRESIAS: We're the only sane men in the city.

CADMUS: We're waiting too long. I'll take your hand and we'll go.

TEIRESIAS: Take it. A pair of old hands will join together.

(CADMUS takes hand, starts to go, and then looks nervously at CHORUS.)

CADMUS: I'm afraid of the gods. Even when I was a great hero I was always afraid of the gods.

TEIRESIAS: There's no use talking about the gods. We've seen what they can do. We've seen their power since our childhood. No kind of thinking makes them any different. No man's foolish talking weakens them.

They're saying in the city that it's undignified for old men to go dancing, for a man without hair to cover his head with ivy. They say that we're a mockery of the god we are trying to worship. The men who say this are being foolish. The gods do not care who worships them; all humans are the same to them. They do not care whether the dancer is a beautiful youth or a toothless old man. To them all living things are dancers.

(CADMUS has been fidgeting during this speech and now turns TEIRESIAS around smiling.)

CADMUS: I'll give you three guesses who's coming up the road. Come on, Teiresias, you're a prophet. *(TEIRESIAS doesn't answer.)* It's Pentheus. It's Pentheus, my grandson, the new king of Thebes. He's coming to worship with us. We may not be many but we're the most important people of Thebes. The god is really going to have a good homecoming. *(PENTHEUS enters stage left excited and angry.)* He certainly looks upset. Has something happened, Pentheus?

(PENTHEUS ignores them and addresses this to the audience.)

PENTHEUS: I've been hearing strange rumors ever since I left the city. Now I find they're true. Most of the women of the town seem to have left their homes and gone following some wandering magician who's cooked up a new god for them to worship. Somebody just told me that they're all up on the mountain now, dancing around and doing what they call worshiping. The joke of it all is that they say this god with an Asiatic name—Dionsophos or something like that—is really the miscarriage Semele had a few years ago when she was struck by lightning. I've seen the women do strange things in the city but never anything quite as idiotic as this.

So they are dancing there in the dark forest, drunk with wine and god knows what else. You can imagine what happens after the dancing is over. They're so tired from their worship that I imagine the poor things just have to creep into the bushes. There are a lot of bushes up there and I imagine there's a man behind every bush. Worshipers of Dionysus, indeed. Whores for Aphrodite!

I've already caught a few of them and locked them up. The trouble is that all of the women are in on it, even my mother and all her sisters. I'll hunt every one of them down from the mountain before I'm through. We'll see if they do so much dancing when they're wearing chains.

I don't know very much about this magician they're following except that he's from Asia, of course, they always are, and is supposed to be beautiful. He has long flowing perfumed hair and wine-dark eyes, eyes that put women in heat at a glance, and he's always around the dancers, dangling his mysteries of joy before them. I imagine he stays up on the mountain at night too.

If I get him inside these gates, he won't shake his thyrsus anymore or mince with his long hair flowing in the wind—and his wine-dark eyes will close as the blood spurts up from his neck.

This is the gentleman that has them worshiping Semele's abortion. He says that the holy foetus was knitted up in Zeus's thigh afterwards; unburned, of course, in spite of the fact that the fire completely destroyed Semele—destroyed her for her blasphemy as I am going to destroy him for his. He deserves a more hideous death than she had. *(He notices* CADMUS *and* TEIRESIAS.) Good god, what's that? Two old mules dressed as mares. *(He turns and walks over to* CADMUS, *completely ignoring* TEIRESIAS.) Are you going on the stage, grandfather? *(He takes hold of his dress.)* You'd better take off that ivy. It doesn't go well with your complexion. *(*CADMUS *is tapping his thyrsus on the ground in an embarrassed way.)* Don't jiggle that thyrsus at me, grandfather. *(Puts hand on his shoulder.)* You were a hero once. Did you wear ivy then? Remember your position in this town. Come on back home with me. *(Turns on* TEIRESIAS.) I suppose it was you who got him into this. A new god would be fine for you, wouldn't it? More birds, more burnt offerings, more profits. The more gods there are, the better you'd like it. You're supposed to be a priest for Apollo, you know, instead of a pimp for every new god that comes out of Asia. If you weren't so old and feeble, I'd lock you up with the rest of the women. You and that magician, trying to introduce Asiatic corruption into our city, trying to turn our women into prostitutes.

CHORUS *(not moving)*: You seem to have forgotten your respect for the gods and for your family. You were talking with contempt to the Cadmus who sowed a crop of warriors and reaped them long before you were whelped. He is your mother's father. Either say the right thing or be silent.

PENTHEUS *(does not seem to hear what* CHORUS *is saying, but notices the group during the speech. He goes over and ironically inspects the instruments and costumes of all the maenads)*: I see the magician has company. *(As he turns to leave the group he tosses a coin on the drum.)* Here's a nickel, grandma. Now, why don't you girls go off to some other city where they like foreign music better.

TEIRESIAS: Pentheus, listen to me. You don't understand our actions or our motives. You're filled with a passion about things you don't understand and are trying to hide that passion with sneering jokes. And all this you call wisdom.

I had my doubts about the new god too at the start. Here was a god, evidently some local Asiatic god of wine—I didn't know then that he was Semele's son—being imported to Greece and raised to the level of Apollo, I was indignant too, although I know too much about the gods to shout insults at even the least of them—but, when the women started worshiping I determined at least to discourage them. Then I had a dream.

PENTHEUS: You seem to always have dreams when you want to get out of your duty.

TEIRESIAS: Then I had a dream. I don't know whether Apollo sent it or Dionysus himself, but it was one of those dreams that was so clearly magical that I knew I wasn't dreaming it by myself even while I was dreaming.

There was a black jar filled with sand and all the gods were standing around it weeping. I couldn't understand why they were weeping but I knew they were weeping with good reason. Then Zeus appeared carrying with him a white jar of the same size filled with dark purple wine. He poured all of the wine into the black jar that was filled with sand and none of it overflowed. Then ivy leaves began growing out of the black jar and the gods began singing.

PENTHEUS: It sounds like an awful waste of good wine.

TEIRESIAS: That was the dream, Pentheus, a foolishness to mockers but transparent to those who believe in the power of the gods. Now for the sake of Thebes and for the safety of the house of Cadmus, grant me permission to explain the dream to you.

PENTHEUS: I can see there's a long speech coming. I hope it explains why our women should be allowed to go off to the mountain panting like bitches in heat.

TEIRESIAS: Just as in the dream there were two basic and opposite substances in the jars, so there are in the universe—wine and sand—wetness and dryness. These things are basic. They are at the source of everything.

Dryness is first. Just as in the dream the first thing that appeared was the black jar of sand. Dryness is the goddess Demeter—she is the earth and is called by other names and black is her color. She is spread throughout the universe and feeds all things with dry foods.

Wetness is second. Just as in the dream the second thing that appeared was the white jar of wine. Wetness is the god Dionysus—He is everything that is not earth but which mixes with earth and white is his color, the color of the snow on the mountain. He feeds us wetness to match dryness, the moist juice of the grape to match Demeter's bread. He feeds us sleep, he feeds us an ending to the earth's dryness, he feeds us sleep as a sweet medicine for sorrow.

He, being wine, is more than a god. He is poured out on the altars of other gods, poured out, drop by drop, so that the gods will always give happiness to mankind. As it says in one of the Orphic songs, "He is the god who enters the wills of the gods."

And he was stitched into the thigh of Zeus. You laugh at that, don't you? What is the thigh of Zeus but the broad, unburning sky, the sky that is full of white, wet clouds that have the shapes of animals and gods? It was there that Zeus protected Semele's son from the wrath of Hera.

You have implied that I'm being unfaithful to Apollo, the god that I serve in my prophecy. Apollo is not too proud to use the power of Dionysus. To be a priest of Apollo and prophecy a man needs to be mantic. To be mantic a man needs mania, to be seized by the sudden wonder of a god invading him. Dionysus is the god of mania. All gods use him in their prophecy.

Even Mars, the god who guards this city, even he uses Dionysus. What general does not know of a time in the middle of an easy battle when his army suddenly panics, scattering like pigeons before the shadow of a hawk. Dionysus is the god of panic. All the gods use him to create fear.

Listen to me, Pentheus. Don't be so sure that force is the only thing that makes things happen among people. You have a thought and that thought is a passion. Don't be so sure that that passionate thought is giving you wisdom. Receive this god into your land and pour libations for him and wear his garlands on your head.

PENTHEUS *(clapping his hands)*: A good recruiting speech for a whorehouse.

TEIRESIAS: Dionysus has nothing to do with chastity. He doesn't hate it or love it. Those women who are chaste receive purity and remain chaste; those women who are whores receive purity and remain whores. This god can be worshipped through the heart or through the loins. All worship is equally welcome.

This god is like a king. You are glad when the crowds stand at the gates and cheer you. I've never seen you pick an unchaste woman out of the crowd and refuse to let her cheer you. Dionysus is the same.

So Cadmus and I will wreathe our heads with ivy while you mock at us. We will be a toothless grey-haired couple while we dance and you will howl curses at us. We will be undignified and foolish and a shame to Thebes, but we will not be fighting against a god.

You, Pentheus, are so drunk that no wine can sober you; you are so poisoned that you cannot be cured by drugs.

CHORUS: Old man, you are wise. You have shown reverence for Dionysus without dishonoring Apollo.

CADMUS *(putting his hand on PENTHEUS's shoulder)*: You ought to cool down and think about what Teiresias has said to you. Our family has never gained its power by being angry. We've always managed to stay inside the limits of good traditions and not to offend anything that is more powerful than we are. Cool your temper down and think about this thing practically.

What if you don't think he's a god? If people say that he's a god, they will say that Semele is the mother of a god and will give honor to all our family. You're always worrying about the safety of the city. Think how this would strengthen our position.

Actaeon was another grandson of mine. You saw what happened to him when he challenged Artemis. His own hounds tore him apart —and remember that this happened on the same mountain where the new god is dancing.

Be smart, Pentheus. Let me garland your head with ivy. It is a small honor that you have to pay.

PENTHEUS *(as CADMUS tries to put the ivy garland on his head)*: Don't touch me. Go out and be any kind of old fool you want to but don't wipe your hands on me. *(Turns and shakes TEIRESIAS.)* You. You're the one who's hypnotized this old man into all this nonsense. *(Goes through gate shouting.)* Guard! Guard! *(Long pause.)* *(Then words heard from off stage.)* Send a couple of men to Teiresias's house. Tell them to scatter everything they see there. Knock over his birdcages and throw all his fortunetelling equipment in a pile in the middle of the floor. I want to teach him a lesson not to upset the decent order of things in Thebes.

Get a few men together yourself and go out and arrest that stranger from Asia that's been hanging around the city for the last few days, the babyfaced one. Have him chained and bring him back to me for questioning. *(Comes through the gate back on the stage.)* He wants us to dance, does he? I'll make him dance from the end of a rope.

TEIRESIAS: Wicked ridiculous man, you don't even know what you're saying. The anger that you carry inside of you is turning into madness. Cadmus and I will pray to him for you and we will pray to him for the safety of the city of Thebes. *(Turns.)* Hold on to me, Cadmus, and I will hold on to you. *(As they walk slowly off stage.)* I am afraid that Pentheus will mean pain to you and to the generations that follow you. I'm not talking in prophecy now but in my own wisdom. Madness begets madness and begets bitter sorrow. *(Both exit.)*

CHORUS: Holiness, you who are queen of the gods, Holiness, you who fly above the crust of the earth on golden wings, have you heard Pentheus? Have you heard what he said? Have you heard him violate the holiness of Dionysus? Have you heard his violence? *(FLUTE and DRUMS play for a while. Then as the DANCER begins)*: It is through our god that men dance; it is through our god that men worship every god with keen appetite, making themselves shout with the highpitched flute, shout with the drum that beats without ceasing. It is through our god that men smile when they worship. He serves them their holy meal, the broad ivy-hung bowl filled with the cure of all sorrow. And then the dancers rest and drink from the black cup, and then their smiling becomes sleep.

ANTICHORUS: Sorrow is the result of madness. Sorrow is the result of violence. Only silence and cunning will keep each man's house from sorrow. The gods watch. The gods watch both violence and silence.

Intelligence is not true cunning. Thoughts that try to outwit the gods end only in violence. Such thoughts try to see too far and miss what is real and around them. Such, I think, are the ways of madness.

CHORUS: Take us to Cyprus, the small island of Aphrodite. All the Loves are there, all the Loves that hunt the hearts of mortals, on that rainless island bubbling with rivers.

Take us to Pieria, to the cold slope of Olympus; all the Loves are there, all the Loves that rest the hearts of mortals. Dionysus, master, take us there where the Loves are lawful.

ANTICHORUS *(as if she sees the soldier who will be entering at the end of the speech)*: This god loves Peace. He loves her because she is the goddess who gives abundance and lets the young live. To all humans, to the rich and to the hungry, he has given the delight of wine, the delight which is without grief. But he hates the man who will not care for these things—to live the life of blessedness day by day, and the nights without sorrow. It is wisdom to keep the heart and mind away from men of violence. It is wisdom to know and do as the rest of men have known and done.

(SOLDIER enters leading in STRANGER.)

SOLDIER: Here's your wild animal, Pentheus. I'm afraid he's pretty tame. We didn't even have to hunt for him. We just started out and there he was. When we walked forward to catch him, do you suppose he ran away into the bushes or snarled and showed his teeth? Not this one. He put his hand into my hand and let himself be led away like a pussy-cat. I felt pretty foolish saying "Stranger, I capture you in the name of Pentheus, king of Thebes," while all the time he was holding on to my hand.

There's something funny going on in this city though. The dancers that you had jailed are all out of jail and dancing in the streets. They are saying that their master let them out, the one they call god.

And the chains are broken and the bolts of the doors are broken, and no human hand could have shattered them—or at least they're saying this in the city. This stranger either knows some good tricks or he's brought a miracle or two with him. But the rest is your concern.

PENTHEUS: Well, let go of him, you idiot. If he doesn't want to escape there's no use holding on to him. *(Looks the stranger up and down.)* So, stranger, you're quite impressive. You've got an Asiatic babyface. Beautiful, I guess. The kind women go for. Your hair's a little bit too long and you certainly aren't built like a wrestler. *(Taking his arm.)* Your skin is soft and pale as if it had never seen the sun. *(Letting go.)* Quite impressive! *(Completely changing tone, sharply)*: First tell me where you come from, stranger.

STRANGER: I come from Asia.

PENTHEUS: And who sent you here?

STRANGER: Dionysus, son of Zeus.

PENTHEUS: Is there some other Zeus in Asia who is always having new children?

STRANGER: No, this is the same Zeus that you know of. The same Zeus that was the lover of Semele.

PENTHEUS: Was it by day or night that you saw this Dionysus and he asked you to come here—or did he instruct you with an inner voice?

STRANGER: I saw him face to face when he instructed me.

PENTHEUS: What sort of rites do you people have? What are they supposed to do for the worshipers?

STRANGER: You are not allowed to know, and yet it would be worth knowing.

PENTHEUS: That's a pretty obvious trick. I suppose it would work with a woman.

STRANGER: I mean that a man who cannot dance will never be able to dance, and will always need to dance.

PENTHEUS: You say you saw the god face to face. What sort of a god was he?

STRANGER: Of the sort he wanted to be. I had no control over it.

PENTHEUS: You certainly know how to answer without answering.

STRANGER: I don't think you know how to understand my cunning.

PENTHEUS: Is this the first place you've brought these rites to?

STRANGER: All the nations of the world are dancing them.

PENTHEUS: In Greece, I mean. The barbarians do all sorts of idiotic things.

STRANGER: In this case they are wiser.

PENTHEUS: Do you hold your ceremonies at night or by day?

STRANGER: By night mostly. Night helps us remember the god more.

PENTHEUS: And have safer sex in the bushes.

STRANGER: I've heard that men sometimes do evil things in the daylight.

PENTHEUS: You're getting quite a pleasure out of showing your cleverness. I suppose you know you'll be punished.

STRANGER: And you will be punished.

PENTHEUS: How brave this mystery-priest is getting! How well he knows how to threaten!

STRANGER: Tell me what punishment you're going to give *me*.

PENTHEUS: First I'm going to cut off those pretty curls of yours.

STRANGER: They are sacred and cannot be touched. I let them grow for a god.

PENTHEUS: And then I'll have my servants break your thyrsus.

STRANGER: Take it from me yourself. It belongs to a god and has two edges.

PENTHEUS: Then I'll let you cool off in jail for a few years.

STRANGER: My master is a locksmith. He can break chains and open doors. I'll call him.

PENTHEUS: Will he hear you when you're all alone, deep in the prison without any dancers?

STRANGER: He is hearing me now.

PENTHEUS (looking all around, smiling): Where is he?

STRANGER: Here. Where I am. You can't even see him.

PENTHEUS: All I can see is a cheap swindler clothing himself in high-sounding ambiguities. (Calls into gate.) You there, have this man bound and carried away. He has violated the laws of Thebes.

(SOLDIERS enter and stand on either side of STRANGER.)

STRANGER: Do not bind me. I who have control say this to you who are without control.

PENTHEUS: And I who have authority again say—bind him!

STRANGER: You don't know who you are or what you are doing or what your life is.

PENTHEUS: I am Pentheus, son of Agave and Echion, grandson of Cadmus.

STRANGER: Pain.

PENTHEUS (slaps his face): That's enough out of you, my Asiatic beauty. Lock him up in the stables for now. Let him dance among the horse turds if he wants to, or perhaps persuade them to worship him. Orpheus made the trees move with his songs, perhaps this priest can make the horse turds dance. (The FLUTE and DRUMS have started at the slap and have been getting louder and louder.) And those noisy bitches you brought with you from Asia will be sold as slaves. A few whippings and they'll forget all the nonsense that you taught them.

STRANGER: I am ready to go. I do not have to suffer anything I do not choose to suffer. You will. You will be mocked and punished by a god you don't believe.

(Lights on chorus as others exit.)

CHORUS: We are alone outside the gates of a strange city. I do not feel the god anywhere. What if Pentheus is right? What if you are foolish women wandering after a god that is no god? We are alone and the darkness does not answer us, only the whirr of the night-flying hawk and the small sound of a river in the distance.

Dirce, blessed river of Thebes, where Zeus himself washed the embryo of Dionysus, washed the embryo he had rescued from the electric fire, blessed Dirce, healer of Dionysus, hear us.

You were a witness when Zeus said, "Gently, double-born one, enter my thigh, enter my male womb. I will reveal you to Thebes, my doubleborn lover, and she will worship you by that name." You were a witness to this, why do you not proclaim it to Thebes?

Why do you scorn me? Why do you reject me? You told me that the time would come, the time would come as surely as the grape ripens on the vine, when all Thebes would be my witness.

ANTICHORUS: Anger, anger. What anger this earthchild shows, Pentheus, whose father was planted into the ground like a willow, breed of the old dragon. He is a wild monster, he fights against the gods like a giant. He will set me in slavery, chain me where I cannot dance, set me like my master in a dark prison. Son of Zeus, do you see your preachers wrestling against oppression? Come down from the mountains in the full terror of your godhead. Restrain the violence of this man. Restrain the violence of this son of dragons.

CHORUS: Where are you? Where are you? In the tangled brush of what mountains? Where are you dancing now? I can see him on the cold slope of Olympus, dancing in the moonlight, dancing where the songs of Orpheus still hover in the cold night air. That mountain was happy. Any place he dances will be happy.

DIONYSUS *(a voice offstage)*: Listen, I am here.

CHORUS: Where are you? Who is here?

DIONYSUS: Listen. I am here.

ANTICHORUS: Master, master.

CHORUS: Master, master.

(They join him from both sides. He is invisible to the audience. Nothing else can be seen in the darkness.)

DIONYSUS: The earth is shaking.

CHORUS: Soon the house of Pentheus will be falling.

ANTICHORUS: Dionysus is walking in the house of Pentheus.

CHORUS: The marble is cracking. It has fallen. It has fallen.

DIONYSUS: The lightning burns, burns.

CHORUS: Look at the lightning fall from the tomb of Semele. Look at the lightning fall from the god's mother.

ANTICHORUS: Fall to the ground! *(All prostrate themselves.)* Our lord has made high things fall. Our lord has destroyed.

(Lights brighten and STRANGER enters through gate.)

STRANGER: What are you women doing down on the ground? All you've seen is that the god made a single palace fall. Get up and dance if you want to show him how he's impressed you with his power.

CHORUS: You've escaped.

STRANGER: Did you expect less? Don't tell me you didn't think I'd escape.

ANTICHORUS: I was lonely. He put you into such powerful chains. Who would protect me if you weren't with me?

STRANGER: There's no danger. There's never any danger. Those chains! He put them on a bull. *(Laughs.)* You should have seen him. He got me into the stable and then, instead of chaining me, he sweated for a half an hour trying to put the chains on a young bull. He finally succeeded too. He's a strong fellow!

I just sat there watching him and laughing when I heard him laughing. It was about then that the earthquake started, and the god kindled a sheet of fire just to keep things moving. Pentheus rushed around shouting, "Fire, fire!" seeing fire everywhere, I guess, and kept sending his slaves for more water to put it out with.

Then he thought of me again and rushed around with his sword drawn looking for me as if he knew I had escaped. Dionysus, to give him something to do, sent phantoms of me all over the courtyard and Pentheus ran about stabbing the bright air. It was just about then that

216

the earthquake was the heaviest and the main building of the palace collapsed. Pentheus saw it, looked back at the phantoms, and then let his sword fall to the ground.

So I went away leaving him there, but I think you'll hear his footsteps soon and he will come to meet us. After this, what will he say? It doesn't matter. I'll meet him with a calm smile even if he comes with thunder and lightning in his lungs.

PENTHEUS (*rushing out of gate first looks at women and then sees* STRANGER *in midst of them*): How did you get here? Guards! Guards!

STRANGER: You're all out of breath.

PENTHEUS: Did someone let you out of those chains?

STRANGER: Didn't I tell you someone would?

PENTHEUS: Who did? Try answering my questions directly for a change.

STRANGER: The god that makes the grape grow.

PENTHEUS: The god that gives our women an excuse to make whores of themselves.

STRANGER: The god who gives joy to women and to such men as believe him.

PENTHEUS: Bah. Dionysus, whoever he is, is better than that. You're just using him as an excuse for your own twisted lusts.

STRANGER: He needs no excuse from you. He is here now.

PENTHEUS: He is, huh? (*Goes to gate and yells.*) Close off all the gates to the city.

STRANGER: Don't you think gods know how to climb walls?

PENTHEUS: Calm and sane. Calm and sane. Except at the times when you should have sanity and calmness.

STRANGER: When I most need to be then I am most sane.

(HERDSMAN *enters left.*)

STRANGER: If you pay attention to what he's about to tell you you will understand true sanity. Listen to him for a moment. I'll be waiting for you. (*He walks away into the half shadows.*)

HERDSMAN: Pentheus, master, lord of Thebes. I have just come from the mountain. It's still snowing there.

PENTHEUS: Well, go on. What's happening on the mountain?

HERDSMAN: The women have been wandering like wild mares on the mountain. Almost every day we see their white legs flashing in the snow. I came here to tell you . . . Is it all right for me to tell you perfectly frankly what I saw sir? I don't want you to be angry at me.

PENTHEUS: Tell everything. That babyfaced faker over there is the one I'm going to be angry at.

HERDSMAN: I was climbing up from the foothills a little after sunrise. The cattle were climbing with me, looking for pasture among the rocks. I came upon the women then, resting their heads on the needles of the pine forest. Three bands of them scattered over the pine forest, sleeping there naked and alone.

I called softly to the other herdsmen so they could see the sight—for we had never seen the women sleeping before and they joined me and we stood there watching at the edge of a clump of pines.

Then your mother sprang up from among them and called them to waken, for she had heard the noise our cattle were making in the early morning sun. And they jumped up as if they had never been asleep, all of them, young girls, wives, and old women.

First they let their hair fall loose down over their shoulders and then they put on their faun-hides. Then thousands of snakes came out from the rocks and into the wet meadows and let the women coil them around their garments. The snakes showed no terror. I saw one of them lick the cheek of the young girl that held him like a puppy.

Some whose breasts were still full held fauns or wolf-cubs in their arms and let them suck eagerly on the white milk.

As the sun began to drive the shadows from the forest they gathered oak leaves and tendrils of ivy and made themselves garlands of them. One woman took her thyrsus and struck a dry boulder—water spurted from it in a clear stream. Another twisted her thyrsus into the black earth and the god sent up a blazing fountain of wine. Milk oozed from the ground wherever they scratched it and honey dropped from the tip of each thyrsus. If you'd been with me, King Pentheus, you would have been completely convinced of the power of this god.

All of us who had been watching were completely bewildered by what we had seen and decided that we'd better leave. Up the mountain we saw other herdsmen and told them about it. One of them, who had lived in the city for a while and knew more about politics than we did, told us that it was our duty to take your mother away from the rest of the women, and that, if we brought her back to you, it might please you and you might reward us. At the time this sounded right and so we went back and hid in the brush and watched the dancers gathering.

By now they had started to call upon the god. They called him Iaccus, lord of the screaming throat. They called on him together, all in one voice. And the mountains and the wild beasts screamed with them—and there was nothing on earth that did not move.

In the middle of all this Agave happened to dance by me and I saw my chance to catch her without any fuss. I grabbed at her and caught her arm as she came by. She twisted herself like a snake and broke my grip without even losing the rhythm of the dance. Then the fat was really in the fire. She called to the other dancers all the way down the forest, "Look," she cried, "Look, my sword-toothed bitches, we are being hunted by men. Let's show them how sharp a bitch's tooth is."

Well, that did it. All of us broke our cover and ran as fast as we could. But they didn't seem to want to catch us. They went after our cattle instead. I've never seen wolves do worse things than they did. I saw one tear the swollen udders off a heifer and then claw her in half through the belly. It looked like a slaughterhouse—guts and blood and splinters of bone strewn out among the pine cones. They even got the bulls. One minute they were standing with their horns lowered looking proud and stupid—and the next minute they'd been dragged down to the ground and their skin was being torn off by the hands of young girls.

Then, like birds that are flying so fast that they cannot stop, the women rushed toward the small villages in the foothills, places where those families live who grow wheat near the river, and they threw everything down—houses, equipment, the barns, where the grain was stored. They carried children from their homes and trampled the wheat in their fields. All that they stole they balanced on their shoulders, bone-crushing weights, and still they kept dancing. They carried fire upon their hair and it did not burn them, and, when the men from the villages gathered to attack them and drive them off, no sword could wound them but their ivy thyrsoi cut their enemies like real swords.

Finally they returned to the forest they had started from and the streams of milk and rich wine were still flowing from the ground. They washed the blood from their hands in the mountain river and the snakes wiped clean with their tongues the little drops that had spattered their cheeks.

Sir, I think you'd better set up a worship for this god in the city. He works greater miracles than I've ever seen. I think that perhaps the reason he's so powerful is because he's the god that makes wine flow. Wine is the most powerful thing in the world. If there's no wine, there's no love or any other pleasure.

CHORUS: I do not want to speak words of disrespect before a king and yet the words must be spoken—Dionysus is the equal of the greatest gods.

PENTHEUS (ignoring CHORUS): I don't blame you for being impressed by the tricks and the fury. You're a simple man. (Almost pleading.) We can't have things like this going on in our city. The flummery and hysteria gives rise to more flummery and hysteria just like flame feeds on flame. If this doesn't stop, travellers from the rest of Greece will pass our city by with knowing smiles and say, "Thebes used to be a powerful city before its citizens were driven crazy by an Asiatic god." I'm going to have to act quickly without any time for real planning.

Go to the Electrian gates. Tell the corporal of the guard to call out the regular troops, every soldier that is sworn to protect Thebes. The only way to fight these dancers is fight them as if they were a foreign enemy, which they are in a way as long as this Asiatic madman keeps them hypnotized. I think our swords will be stronger than the swords of the men of the foothills. Things have come to a pretty pass when a gang of women can frighten grown men into running away from them.

STRANGER *(coming over close to* PENTHEUS*)*: You haven't paid any attention to what I've told you, Pentheus. You've treated me with violence but I'm still giving you advice that it's desperately necessary for you to accept. Don't fight against a god, Pentheus. *(Pentheus who has turned away from him turns back angrily to interrupt him.)* Be quiet! This is your last chance. Dionysus will not allow you to drive his dancers from the screaming mountain.

PENTHEUS: Don't preach at me, you Asiatic wart-hog. You're out of jail. Isn't that enough for you? Are you trying to talk your way back into it?

STRANGER: You should sacrifice to him instead of kicking the ground in anger. Hah, a man fighting a god.

PENTHEUS: I'll sacrifice to him all right. I'll give him all the sacrifice he's entitled to. I'll cut the throats of a hundred of those screaming whores on his altar.

STRANGER: It will be rather embarrassing when your great army with all its swords and spears and bronze shields starts retreating before a few women waving sticks at them.

PENTHEUS: This foreigner is certainly an exhausting opponent to have. In chains or out of them, he can't keep his tongue quiet.

STRANGER: Sir, the whole thing can be settled very easily.

PENTHEUS: How? By my becoming the slave of my slaves?

STRANGER: I'm trying to save you by means of my powers.

PENTHEUS: You've already made a pact with the dancers. You're one of them.

STRANGER: The only pact I've made is with the god himself.

PENTHEUS *(goes to gate, shouts in)*: Bring my armor. *(STRANGER comes behind him. PENTHEUS turns.)* Keep quiet.

(STRANGER screams softly and piercingly and touches him.)

STRANGER: Would you like to see them lying out there in the mountain forest?

PENTHEUS: I certainly would. I'd give somebody a great deal of gold if I could manage that.

STRANGER: You seem to have a sudden love for them.

PENTHEUS: I hate the sight of drunken women.

STRANGER: And yet you would like to see something that you hate.

PENTHEUS: I certainly would like to hide behind the pines and watch them.

STRANGER: Even if you go secretly they'll discover you.

PENTHEUS: Then I'll go openly. That's a good suggestion.

STRANGER: Would you like me to help you get there?

PENTHEUS (grabbing STRANGER's hand): Yes. (Lets go.) Well, there's no real hurry.

STRANGER: You'll have to put on a linen dress.

PENTHEUS: Am I to be a woman?

STRANGER: They'd kill you if they thought you were a man.

PENTHEUS: That's true. Yes, that's a good suggestion. You've been a great deal of help to me all along.

STRANGER: Dionysus has told me what to do.

PENTHEUS: What had we better do first?

STRANGER: I'll take you into the palace and dress you.

PENTHEUS: In a woman's dress? I'd be ashamed to.

STRANGER: It doesn't have to be you that goes to spy on them. You could send somebody else.

PENTHEUS: What kind of dress would it be?

STRANGER: Long robes and a band around your hair, a faun skin draped across your shoulders—and a thyrsus, of course.

PENTHEUS: I can't wear a woman's dress.

STRANGER: If you attack the dancers openly, you'll cause bloodshed.

PENTHEUS: That's right. I ought to find out how strong they are before I send my troops against them.

STRANGER: Much wiser than hunting down violence with violence.

PENTHEUS: How will I get through Thebes without people seeing me?

STRANGER: I will lead you through deserted streets.

PENTHEUS: Anything is better than to be mocked by those dancers. We'll go into the palace and . . . I'll decide there what I want to do.

STRANGER: Whatever you decide, I'll be ready for you.

PENTHEUS: I'll go in now. When I come out I'll either be dressed in full armor or ready to go with you. *(Exits.)*

STRANGER *(to DANCERS)*: Women, our animal is in the trap. He is ready to die on the screaming mountain. Dionysus, the next move is yours. You are nearer to him than we are.

If we are to have vengeance, give him panic. Pull him apart with not quite insane fears and desires. He must choose to dress as a woman, wear clothes he would never wear with unfrenzied senses.

I want him to be laughed at, led through the crowded streets dressed as a maiden, through the very city where he made threats against our god.

I will go into the palace and dress him myself with the robes he is going out to meet death in. I want him to know Dionysus, the god who is terror and joy.

(MUSICIANS have started playing during the last of this. DANCERS join. STRANGER watches for a moment and then exits.)

CHORUS: Has the time come when I can dance barefoot on the mountain, flinging my head back in the clean, misty air?—Like a faun leaping in the green joy of the meadow far from terror, far from the heavy breathing ring of watchers, the woven nets of the hunters, and the hunters have shouted at their dogs and called them back, then the faun, almost breathless with running, dances like a storm cloud in the wet meadow, rejoicing in places empty of men and in the life that rustles the shadowy hair of the forest.

What is wisdom? And what is the power of holding your enemy in your hand, a power given to you by a god? That which is beautiful shall be loved forever.

ANTICHORUS: Restless and inevitable is the power of the gods; punishing those who are hardminded and without wisdom, those who will not worship. The gods, in their cunning, run on unyielding legs of time, slowly pursuing, slowly devouring their guilty victims.

It is never right to go beyond the limits of mankind, either in thought or action. It is safer to believe that power only lies with the gods and with whatever is a god and that these limits will bind us forever.

What is wisdom? And what is the power of holding your enemy in your hand, a power given to you by a god. That which is beautiful shall be loved forever.

CHORUS: A man is happy when he has finished working. A man is happy when he finds money or when he receives power. A man hopes and a thousand men may have a thousand hopes—some bring rewards and some don't. But a man is happy when he is happy in the heat of the moment.

What is wisdom? And what is the power of holding your enemy in your hand, a power given to you by a god. That which is beautiful shall be loved forever.

(STRANGER enters calling offstage through the gate to PENTHEUS.)

STRANGER: You, Pentheus, anxious to see something it is forbidden to see, hurrying toward something it is not necessary to hurry toward, come out and join me by the gates. Let us see how you look as a woman. Let us see how you will look to your mother when she kills you. *(PENTHEUS enters in costume.)* Hail, daughter of Cadmus!

PENTHEUS: But now I seem to see two suns and a double city under their flickering light. *(Turns to STRANGER.)* And you, stranger, you seem to walk before me like a bull. There are horns in your head. Were you an animal all the time? Is that your real shape?

STRANGER: The god is with us. He was once our enemy but he is now our friend. You see what you should see.

PENTHEUS: How do I look? Do I look as beautiful as my sister? Do I walk with the dignity of my mother?

STRANGER: You look like both of them. I'm afraid that lock of hair isn't quite in place.

PENTHEUS: I was dancing in the palace. I must have loosened it.

STRANGER: I'll fix it for you. Lean your head back. That's what I'm here for—to dress you perfectly.

PENTHEUS: Yes. You are the one to dress me perfectly. I am made over to you now.

STRANGER: And the belt on the dress is too loose. Look how uneven it is around the ankles.

PENTHEUS: Only on the right side. The left side is perfect. *(He looks back over his shoulder at both legs one by one—bending his knees in a womanly way.)*

STRANGER *(straightening the dress)*: You'll see what a good friend I really am when you see how purely the dancers behave up there in spite of what you expected.

PENTHEUS: Which hand do I hold the thyrsus in—the right or the left? *(Demonstrating as if before a mirror.)*

STRANGER: You raise it in your right in rhythm with your right foot. *(PENTHEUS tries it awkwardly.)* Your mind has changed.

PENTHEUS: Could I carry that mountain on my shoulders if I wanted to?

STRANGER: If you wanted to, you could. A few hours ago your spirit wasn't healthy. Now it is as it should be.

PENTHEUS: What would be the best way to get it down on my shoulders? Should I pry it up or should I kneel down and tear the mountain out with my arms?

STRANGER: You'd destroy all the shrines of Pan on the mountain if you did something like that. You wouldn't want to hurt a little god would you?

PENTHEUS: You're right. Anyway, women oughtn't to be conquered through strength. I'll hide among the pine trees.

STRANGER: Almost any hiding place is a good one for a man who is watching the dancers secretly.

PENTHEUS: Um. I wonder what they're doing now. I wonder if they're making love in the bushes.

STRANGER: Do you want to watch them making love? Well, perhaps you'll catch them at it, unless you're caught first.

PENTHEUS: Take me there by the public highway. I want all the country-side to watch me while I go on this errand.

STRANGER: You are doing this for your city. You alone. You have a contest to engage in that you were destined for. I'll follow you and give you safe conduct there. But other hands will bring you home.

PENTHEUS: My mother?

STRANGER: All men will see you.

PENTHEUS: I won't mind being seen.

STRANGER: You will be carried home—

PENTHEUS: You're pampering me.

STRANGER: In your mother's arms.

PENTHEUS: You're doing too much for me.

STRANGER: As much as I promised.

PENTHEUS (*smiling childishly*): Well, I'm off to claim my reward. (*Bounces off.*)

STRANGER: Strange you are, strange and terrible, and you will suffer strangeness and terror when you get there; and you will receive a cleansing from terror, a cleansing from strangeness.

Stretch out your hands for him, Agave. Stretch out your hands, nieces and sisters of his, daughters of Cadmus. I bring this boy to a great contest, a contest where the victory will be with god, the god of the screamers and the dancers, god. (*Silent in awe and then slowly turns to the* CHORUS.) It's happening. (*Exits.*)

CHORUS: Run, swift bitch-hounds of madness, run to the mountain, run howling where the daughters of Cadmus hold their worship. Enter into their hearts as swiftly as a breath of black air, consume their hearts with madness against the man wearing woman's clothes, the man who is watching their madness.

Then his mother will see him watching from some high place. "Look!" she cries, "What is that thing watching us, that thing with yellow eyes staring from the pinetop. Look at it, there. Look at the child of horror crouching there."

Then let Justice come openly, let Justice come with a sword in her hand, openly and without mercy. Let Justice stab the throat of the lawless man, the godless man, the man born of monsters.

ANTICHORUS: Oh, Dionysus, when a man denies you and your mother, when a man tries to force the gates that cannot be forced, setting his mind against sanity, for him death is the issue of all his purposes, violent against what never can be conquered; but the man who asks no questions about things that belong to the gods, his is a painless life.

I do not envy the wisdom of the violent. It is a delight for me to hunt other things, dancing for the gods as they appear before me, worshiping the gods through the short nights and days of my life.

Then let Justice come openly, let Justice come with a sword in her hand, openly and without mercy; let Justice stab the throat of the lawless man, the godless man, the man born of monsters.

Let yourself be seen as a bull, let yourself be seen as a snake with many heads. Let yourself be seen as a flaming lion. O, beast-god, show yourself smiling before this hunter, show yourself as he hunts among your animals, appear before him savagely smiling.

(MUSICIANS play and DANCERS dance a dance to make the curse come true. Then MESSENGER enters and walks to gate. With arms folded and back to audience.)

MESSENGER: Family of Cadmus, earthborn and known throughout the world for happiness, now even a slave weeps for you.

(CHORUS comes over and taps him on the shoulder. He turns.)

CHORUS: What is this news you're announcing?
MESSENGER: Pentheus is dead.

(The WOMEN scream in joy the same way that the STRANGER had screamed at PENTHEUS.)

CHORUS (face upward): God, you have shown yourself powerful.
MESSENGER: What's the matter with you, woman? Are you happy over my master's death?
CHORUS: I was a stranger in your city. Now your master is dead and my master has triumphed. No one will throw me in chains now or try to silence me.

MESSENGER: Do you think Thebes has no men left in it?

CHORUS: Thebes has nothing to do with me. Dionysus is my city.

MESSENGER: Oh, I don't suppose I blame you, and yet it isn't a beautiful thing to see women rejoicing over a violent death or the suffering of a city and a family.

CHORUS: Tell me, how did he die?

MESSENGER: I went along with him and the stranger as a sort of body guard. I met them on the road about a mile outside the gates. It was a beautiful day and we walked the easiest way to the mountain, down through the two villages that were raided by the wild women and up through the foothills, crossing the river at the wooden bridge.

We rested and waited in a meadow full of tall grass and wild barley, moving only slightly and saying nothing. Above us there was a small stream edged with pine trees which trickled down from the rocks. Along it we began to see the wild women, peaceful now and doing the chores of their daily living. One was repairing a thyrsus that had lost some ivy leaves from its tip, another was washing a faun-skin, two or three others were combing their hair and singing hymns of Dionysus in antiphony.

Poor Pentheus, who didn't seem able to see the women, finally whispered, "Stranger, I can't see these creatures from where I am. If I could only get to the top of one of those high pine trees over there, I could see everything."

Then I saw a miracle. There was a giant pine tree about fifty feet from us whose tip seemed to stab the blue sky itself; he seized that tip and bent it down, down, down towards the black earth as the bow bends for an arrow.

Then he took hold of Pentheus, with his hands around his waist and carried him and placed him gently on a branch of the bent tree. Then he let the tree snap back again and it rose slowly into the air with my master riding on its back, half asleep.

When the tree stopped and I could distinguish him crouching there, the stranger was gone and there was a voice from the air crying, "Women, I bring you a man that has mocked you. Punish him."

As the voice was saying this there was a glare like fire between the air and the earth, and afterwards the forest was quiet as if the air had gone still and you couldn't hear a leaf move or a bird cry.

The women, there were more of them now, looked questioningly around, like cattle who have heard an uncertain noise in the distance. Again the voice thundered—and this time they must have recognized their god, for they seemed more like birds, beating their arms and legs with incredible swiftness and flocking towards the meadow. They were all there, his mother, his sisters, all of the women, leaping over dry rocks, coming from everywhere along the banks of the stream.

Then a few of them located the tiny figure high up in the pine tree and began to throw rocks at it, climbing up to higher ground to make the distance of their aim shorter. Others began clawing the bark from the pine tree with their bare hands and a few more standing up the stream tried to hurl their thyrsoi at him like javelins. But there he sat, too high for them to touch him, poor fellow, hopelessly trapped.

Finally some tried to set the green wood of the pine on fire while others drew branches from a shattered oak and used them as levers against the tangled roots of the tree, but they effected nothing.

Then Agave said, "Come, worshipers, let us stand in a circle around the tree and start it swaying back and forth. We can shake this creature down, we can shake down this creature that has been watching us from the branches."

And they put a thousand hands against the pine and it swayed and tottered—and down from his branch, down to the needle-covered earth fell Pentheus. Screaming for he knew he was going to die.

His mother began the slaying and fell on him. Weakly he tried to pull the false hair from his head so his mother could recognize him. While she was clawing at his face, he pulled one of her hands to his cheek and said, "Mother, look at me. I am Pentheus, your son. You bore me from your womb. Let someone else kill me."

But she was like a madwoman and her mouth frothed and her eyes stared at nothing. She seized the arm he had touched her with, and, standing with her foot hard against his ribs, she wrenched it from its socket. The god made her able to do this without effort.

And, on the other side, his sister was tearing at his flesh with her fingernails—and the rest of the women gathered around him and began to join in on the sacred work, they shouting and he screaming as long as he was able to scream.

After a while it was over and they began amusing themselves with his body. One lady lifted an arm high into the air and waved it like a thyrsus. Another was trying to toss a leg, which still had a hunting-boot on it, into the crotch of a nearby oaktree. His ribs had been broken open and they were playing with the fragments. Every hand in that forest had blood on it.

His body lies scattered now among the stones, in the tall grass of the meadow, and in the underbrush that rises above it.—And his head. His mother seized that, yelling like someone quite overcome with victory, and transfixed it on the point of her thyrsus. And now she is carrying it through the forest, exulting as it if were the trophy of some great animal, and telling all around her that she and her god had been mighty hunters and had won a super-human prize.—The prize, I think, will be deadly sorrow for her share in the contest.

I don't want to stay here any longer. She'll be coming here and I don't want to see her. There's nothing I can do about this, I guess —just leave you women to your triumph. *(He exits.)*

(DANCERS and MUSICIANS begin.)

CHORUS: I will sing a song for the death of Pentheus. I will sing a song for the death of the dragon child. He put on our clothes and they could not contain him. He raised our thyrsus and it was a thyrsus of poison. I will sing a song for the death of Pentheus. He followed a bull into the mountains.

Oh, sister worshiper, you have made a song that we can sing for-ever, you have made a song that will give you deadly sorrow forever, it is a victory that will be remembered forever. Sing the song, Agave, with your hands gloved in the blood of your child. *(CHORUS stops the*

DANCERS and MUSICIANS with her hand.) I think I see her coming. She's stumbling as if she's carrying a great burden. *(AGAVE enters.)* Come and dance with us, Agave.

(AGAVE is carrying the head of PENTHEUS. She lifts it high.)

AGAVE: Look at this, sisters from Asia.

CHORUS: Why are you calling us?

AGAVE: I have brought a curly-headed thing from the mountain, a trophy blessed by Dionysus.

CHORUS: I see it. You are one of us now.

AGAVE: I didn't have to set a trap for him, I caught him out in the open, with my bare hands.

CHORUS: In what lonely canyon?

AGAVE: On the mountain.

CHORUS: The mountain.

AGAVE: Where I killed him.

CHORUS: Who killed him?

AGAVE: I had the honor.

CHORUS: Blessed Agave.

AGAVE: They call me that now.

CHORUS: Who helped you kill him?

AGAVE: Cadmus—. *(She is beginning to run down.)*

CHORUS: Cadmus?

AGAVE: Cadmus's daughters helped me prepare him.

CHORUS: But you caught him?

AGAVE: Yes, it was a lucky day for hunting.

CHORUS: Blessed Agave.

AGAVE: You will share in the feast with us tonight.

CHORUS: I am not hungry.

AGAVE: The animal is young. See the hair on his cheeks is as soft as a young bull's.

CHORUS *(examining the head)*: Yes, his hair makes him look like a wild beast.

AGAVE: Dionysus was the huntsman. He guided the beast into my hands.

CHORUS: Yes, our lord is a hunter.

AGAVE: You are proud of me?

CHORUS: I am proud of you.

AGAVE: And Cadmus.

CHORUS: Will be proud of his daughter.

AGAVE: And also—. *(Pauses.)*

CHORUS: Pentheus, your son.

AGAVE: Will be proud of his mother.

CHORUS: For she is carrying a trophy.

AGAVE: The head of a mountain lion.

CHORUS: A brave trophy.

AGAVE: And bravely obtained.

CHORUS: Do you delight in what you have obtained?

AGAVE: I delight in what I have hunted and in the god that helped me hunt it. This day will be remembered.

CHORUS: Then show your trophy to the Thebans; let them rejoice for you and our master.

AGAVE *(yelling into the gates)*: Come out of the gates, men of Thebes. See the trophy that I have here. See the beast we daughters of Cadmus have hunted down. Break your spiked javelins, burn your cunning traps. They will no longer be needed while we are hunters. We, the daughters of Cadmus, killed this creature with our sharp white hands, we caught him and tore him apart with our hands.

Where is my father? I want him to see this. Where is Pentheus? *(To CHORUS.)* He is my son. He will want to mount this head above the doorway of his palace; it is the head of a fine mountain lion caught when it was young and proud. Cadmus, Pentheus, where are you? Come out and see this.

(CADMUS enters from stage left followed by two servants carrying a bloodstained sack. AGAVE at the gate doesn't see him.)

CADMUS: Follow me, servants, carrying this impossibly sad burden, the last flesh of Pentheus, collected here and there in the forest before the wolves and birds could get to it. *(To ANTICHORUS.)* I learned what my daughter had done when I got back to town from the dancing, leading old Teiresias cheerfully through the city gate. They told me then and I turned the long way back to the mountain.

Two of my daughters were still there, dancing and screaming. Not as they used to but more solemnly and intensely—as if their mouths were filled with acid-tasting sorrow. I left them there.

They told me I would find Agave here, dancing before the gates of the city. And I see she is here.

AGAVE *(seeing* CADMUS*)*: Father, look! Look what I have done. I caught this with my bare hands. *(She presses the head on him.)* Take this father. Put this gift of your daughter above the doorway of your house. I meant to give it to my son for his palace but he hasn't come to see his mother's triumph. Take it, father, you deserve it more. You fathered the daughters who were able to hunt this. *(*CADMUS *doesn't touch the head.* AGAVE *puts it on the ground.)* Have your friends to a feast and show them this. Your deeds of valor have been multiplied in your children.

CADMUS: Deadly sorrow. Not to be looked at. Did you know what you killed? Did you know the sacrifice you were making to the god? *(She looks bewildered.)* Yes, we have invited all Thebes for a feast—sowing portions of deadly sorrow and shame for all our family. The god has destroyed my family, with justice and beyond justice. The god who is supposed to be the son of my daughter, to be my own grandchild.

AGAVE: Father, you're an old fool. Don't you understand what I'm giving you? I wish Pentheus were here and could see this trophy. But he probably wouldn't be interested either. He isn't much of a hunter. He'd rather fight against the gods than go out hunting like other young men do. I wish you'd say something to him about that, father. *(To servants.)* Will some of you please go out and call my son so he can see his mother's triumph.

CADMUS: Oh, if you would never waken into grief, never again see your actions clearly. If this madness could only last forever—you would not be fortunate, but your dreams would escape misfortune.

AGAVE: What is there that is not bravely done? What cause is there for deadly sorrow?

CADMUS: Daughter, look up at the sky.

AGAVE: All right, I'm looking at it. *(Looks for a while.)*

CADMUS: Does it seem the same or is it beginning to look different to you?

AGAVE: It does seem brighter and more like a sky should look.

CADMUS: Are you feeling calmer now?

AGAVE: I don't know what you mean, but . . . my senses seem to be clearer . . . something has changed in my mind.

CADMUS: Can you understand me now when I talk to you?

AGAVE: I don't remember what we were talking about.

CADMUS: Do you remember the name of the man you married?

AGAVE: Certainly. His name was Echion. He was one of the sons of the dragon. He died a few years ago. But . . .

CADMUS: Did you bear him a son?

AGAVE: Of course I did. Pentheus. You must have seen him recently. How can you forget his name?

CADMUS: Whose face are you holding in your hands?

AGAVE: A mountain lion. They tell me it was a mountain lion.

CADMUS: Come. Just look at it. It will only take a moment just to look at it.

AGAVE *(looking)*: What is it? What is this thing?

CADMUS: Keep your eyes on it. Look at it closely.

AGAVE: I see. It has a face of deadly sorrow.

CADMUS: Is it still a mountain lion?

AGAVE: No. I am holding the head of Pentheus.

CADMUS: You have been carrying him for a long time.

AGAVE: Who killed him? How did it get into my hands?

CADMUS: You killed him. You and your sisters.

AGAVE: Where did he die? What has been happening? Where did he die?

CADMUS: Up on the same mountain where the hounds tore Actaeon to pieces.

AGAVE: What was he doing there? Why did he go up on the mountain?

CADMUS: He went up there to insult the god you were worshiping.

AGAVE: I was worshiping? What was I doing there?

CADMUS: The women of the city were insane and you were among them.

AGAVE: Yes, now I understand. Dionysus wanted to destroy us.

CADMUS: He had his reasons.

AGAVE: May I see my son's body now?

CADMUS: I have it here.

AGAVE: Is it in bad condition?

CADMUS: You'd better wait a while before you look at it.

AGAVE: Is it broken?

CADMUS: There's nothing to be done. Sit here and rest a moment.

AGAVE: Did Pentheus go mad too? *(She sits.)*

CADMUS: He was like you, unable to worship a god he ought to worship. You have to call that madness.

He was the only male in my whole house, the last hope of my family. Now there is nothing but ruin.

He was the breath of my house. Oh, child, it was you, my daughter's son, that held my place together and was a terror to the city, who protected an old man from the insults of old age, who kept my house together and me in it.

But now, any stranger may insult me on the streets of the city, any whim of the rabble may drive me into exile. I am dishonored, an old man who could not build a house that would last his lifetime.

Oh, child, child that I will still love most of all, never again will you touch my beard and call me grandfather, put your hand on my shoulder and say, "Who wrongs you, sir, who dishonors you? Tell me who wrongs you and I'll punish him."

But now. Oh, everything's gone. I am an old man who was once a hero watching what the gods have done and believing with all my heart in their filthy power.

AGAVE *(pointing to sack)*: Is this my son's body?

CADMUS: Most of it.

AGAVE: I'll take it in my arms for a moment. It was once a baby that I told lies to and sung to. I held him in my arms then like this. Then it was a boy with the down just beginning to grow on his face, blushing often. *(She looks down at the bloodstains.)*

CADMUS: Stop it, Agave.

AGAVE: Then he was a man in the terrible fury of manhood. I didn't know him very well, then. It wasn't the same somehow. Now, he's in my arms again and I can carry him—. *(She suddenly throws the sack down.)* Him, it. A sack of jumbled flesh.

CADMUS: None of us are much more than that, Agave. Even when we are alive.

AGAVE: Now is about the time for a god to come in and tell us the moral. To come and strut about and blame us for the weaknesses that we can't help and for the strengths that annoy them. In a minute Dionysus will appear from a creaking machine and tell us about justice and sanity and what we did that made the gods offended.

CADMUS: Agave—

AGAVE: Shut up! How could that bitch-god punish me more, that god who has no children and hates mothers. Do you hear me, Dionysus? Come down, bitch-god, come down from your machine! *(She pauses, waiting.)* He'd rather leave me with the body of my son. *(She goes over and picks up the head.)* This head, I wonder if it can sing.

CADMUS: Has Dionysus sent you mad again?

AGAVE: The head of Orpheus sings and prophesies. *(Pats the head.)* Sing, son. Sing and prophesy. Like the head of Orpheus. Dionysus killed him too.

(DIONYSUS emerges from machine. Any device may be used but his appearance must be sudden, mechanized, and a bit ridiculous. He is the STRANGER wearing a beard.)

DIONYSUS: It will not speak, madam. Your son was an ordinary sacrifice, as likely to prophesy as the wheat which is cut down in the fields.

He was neither able to accept my spirit nor able to contain it when it was forced upon him. He has been broken like a clay cup breaks when hot wine is poured into it. You've broken cups like that yourself. They don't prophesy.

There is nothing worthy of pity in a man who is unable to contain his god. He will never prophesy, and will be neither praised nor remembered. Nor will you, madam, although you have cracked and not broken.

Go into exile now, Cadmus, taking your whole family with you. There is no room in Thebes now for you and your family, murderers and children of murderers.

I put a curse on all those who are unable to receive me. I put a curse on all those who are unable to contain me.

(Lights dim and DIONYSUS *and* CHORUS *disappear from stage.)*

AGAVE: I couldn't speak, although I wanted to shout curses at him.

CADMUS: Did you understand what he was talking about?

AGAVE: I think I did. I think he means that a man has to learn how to dance with a god inside him. Anyway he's wrong about one thing. Pentheus will be remembered.

THE END

Golden Gate Y.M.C.A.
San Francisco
Aug. 25, 1954

TROILUS

> *Trojans and Greeks are fighting on the bare stage when the curtain rises:* PRIAM *vs.* AGAMEMNON, AENEAS *vs.* ULYSSES, ACHILLES *vs.* HECTOR, MENELAUS *vs.* PARIS, *and* TROILUS *vs.* DIOMEDE. ZEUS *enters and snaps his fingers. They stop suddenly and go like sleepwalkers to opposite sides of the stage and sit down.* ZEUS *is dressed in a black frock-coat and string tie.*

ZEUS *(addressing audience)*: Before we start I'd better introduce myself since I'm the most important person in the play. I'm Zeus, the god of all other gods. Men sometimes call me the lord of the cloudless sky and sometimes they call me lord of the thunder-tortured sky. I'm the same person. You'd better get that in mind or you won't understand the play. You can usually tell who I am by looking at my eyes. When my eyes are blue they are the absolute blue of a sky reflecting itself back and forth again into an ocean. When you look into them then you can see nothing but distance endlessly repeating itself. This is more or less my normal mood. But sometimes my eyes are merely a black surface flecked with yellow, almost the color of fire. When you look into them then you can see nothing but light. It is for those eyes that men call me lord of the dead.

But, I imagine some of you are thinking, isn't this a play about love and war? What do eyes like those have to do with love and war? The point is, I'm the lord of everything in between too, the lord of the dirty joke, of the shaggy-heart story. It all comes to the same thing, but I wouldn't expect human beings to understand that.

Well, that's enough about me and my beautiful eyes. Now to the play itself. One thing you'd better get out of your mind at the start is all this nonsense about the Trojan horse and the fall of Troy. The Trojan war has been going on for the last three thousand years and it hasn't stopped yet. All the stories you've heard about the destruction of Troy are just daydreams Ulysses invented to keep himself sane. You've probably dreamed like that yourselves, waiting for a war to come to an end. *(Slightly embarrassed.)* One thing, though—the people in the play don't seem to know how long the war has lasted. They have the idea that it's only been going on for nine years or so. I don't know why. Human beings don't have a very good time-sense.

There are various kinds of love in this play—none of them very dignified—and I don't think you'll have much difficulty understanding them. But you may have a little trouble understanding the war. Oh, I know, you've all followed wars in your newspapers and know how thrilling it is to watch a young man stick a sword or a bayonet into the belly of another young man—but the military skills involved here are a little bit different from those you people use. To help you out I've decided to show you some of the warriors in person and tell you a little about their weaknesses and capabilities.

I'll start with the visitors first. Agamemnon here *(ZEUS goes over and leads AGAMEMNON from his chair to the front of the stage. AGAMEMNON, as do all the Trojans and Greeks in the prologue, walks like a sleepwalker. All are dressed in costumes of the sort American colleges would use if sword-fighting to the death were an intercollegiate sport. The Greek uniform is blue and gold, and the Trojan red and white.)* is what you might call the captain of the Greeks. You can see he's getting a bit fat *(ZEUS pats fleshy places)* and out of condition. He doesn't do much fighting anymore. He's a good captain though, mainly because he doesn't have too much strength or intelligence or imagination, so the other Greeks rather despise him and follow his orders without jealousy. *(Leads AGAMEMNON back and brings out ULYSSES.)* Ulysses here was the pleasantest surprise I had. He didn't want to come to the war at all and when he was finally sent here he moped around in his tent for the first year writing poetry about exile and the unimportance of heroism and how he missed Penelope. Then something happened. I think he must have discovered that war has a kind of poetry of its own. He suddenly became a savage, clever fighter and the best strategist the Greeks have. *(Leads ULYSSES back and leads out ACHILLES.)* This is Achilles, the best fighter on the Greek side and probably the best fighter in the war. You can see the size of his muscles. *(Pats them.)* He's quick as a cat too, amazingly good reflexes.

The only trouble with him is that he doesn't have what you people call "team spirit." He's more an individual performer—the kind of a person who would like to wander around the world fighting his own battles like Hercules and Theseus did. But that's the only thing wrong with him. He's very valuable. I don't think the war could go on without him. *(Leads* ACHILLES *back and leads out* MENELAUS.*)* You can see that Menelaus here isn't in any better physical condition than his brother. He's usually out of breath five minutes after he starts fighting. But Menelaus fights every day and usually does a good quiet job of it. In a sense it's his war. The Greeks are fighting the Trojans for his wife, and Menelaus feels his position pretty deeply. He's not a very exciting fighter though—or a very exciting person. *(Leads* MENELAUS *back and leads out* DIOMEDE.*)* And finally there's Diomede. He's the youngest of the top Greek fighters—the war had been going on for four years before he joined it. He's almost as good a fighter as Achilles and, in a way, he's almost the more valuable of the two because he really enjoys the war and Achilles doesn't. Diomede even fights the gods. He cut Aphrodite once when she got in his way when he was trying to fight Aeneas. Made her bleed. He wasn't punished for it either. We all rather respected his enthusiasm. *(Leads* DIOMEDE *back, leads out* PRIAM.*)* Now for the Trojans. This is Priam, their captain. You can see by looking at him that he hasn't fought in any war for twenty years or so. He's captain because war for the Trojans is rather a family affair. Three of these people *(pointing)* are his sons and the other is his nephew. This all gives a definite cohesiveness to the Trojan strategy but does make it seem a little provincial. *(Leads* PRIAM *back and leads out* AENEAS.*)* We'll start with Priam's nephew first. This is Aeneas. He's a fine, steady fighter and does most of the commanding on the field. He had a goddess for a mother—Aphrodite—and she takes a very active interest in his welfare, sometimes an embarrassingly active interest. She's always around trying to help him when she thinks he's in danger, like that time with Diomede, but she doesn't understand war very well and usually only succeeds in making Aeneas nervous. After all, what soldier would want an invisible mother following him around all the time? Aeneas does very well, considering everything. *(Leads back AENEAS and leads out PARIS.)* Paris is Priam's oldest son. Look at that physique! He has the natural build of a fighter. You'd think that he'd be the most active Trojan on the battlefield, being the cause of the war and all that and being so capable of fighting well. He isn't at all. He's reacted to his position in the opposite way that Menelaus reacted to his. He talks about the ultimate aims and causes of the war far more often than he fights in it and he's usually just in the way on the battle-field. He can fight well—and he sometimes does when he's forced to—but, on the whole, he's been very disappointing. *(Leads PARIS back and leads out HECTOR.)* Hector, of course, is the best of the Trojans. He's strong and steady and has that extra something that champions have. He doesn't enjoy war, doesn't even like it, but his conscience won't let him do anything less than his best. You could say that he lacks something, the unexpected perhaps, but as a day-to-day fighter he's superb. *(Leads back HECTOR and leads out TROILUS.)* This is the last of Priam's sons. His name is Troilus. He's a newcomer to the war. He's only been fighting for a year. But, on the other hand, he has one tremendous advantage over the others—he grew up with the war and can't really remember what peace was like. This makes him a strong and unpredictable fighter. He doesn't think the same way the older men think. All the others have lived in peace as well as war. They're amphibious. But Troilus is—. Well, you'll see what Troilus is. *(Leads TROILUS back.)* That's the lot. You'll see other people, of course, as the play goes on, but the rest of them are more concerned with love than with war, and you'll understand that part without my telling you. Don't expect anything really important to happen—they're only human beings after all—but watch the strong, passionate way that they react to the little things that matter to them—life, death, and love. Don't laugh too loudly when they do something awkward or foolish or feel too sorry for them when they scream and cry. They're really happy in their own way. They're nice boys and you'll like them.

(ZEUS snaps his fingers again and they start fighting in the same pairs as before. ZEUS looks on for a moment, then leaves and the curtain goes down.)

ACT I, Scene 1

> *Room with table and chairs like a Board of Directors' room. Map of Troy and adjoining territory on the wall.* ACHILLES *is standing and* PATROCLUS *is sitting on the table. Curtain goes up in the middle of conversation.*

PATROCLUS: . . . nine years. Nine damned years. You were nineteen and I was sixteen when it started. That's—what is it—a third of your life, more than a third of mine.

ACHILLES: You don't have to keep telling me that. They're not going to argue me out of it this time. I've finally got an excuse to quit fighting and none of those bastards are going to argue me out of it.

PATROCLUS: That's not the point I was trying to make. Suppose everything works. Suppose this silly war collapses when you refuse to fight. What do we have then?

ACHILLES: I'll have Breiseis and a home to go back to. *(Puts hand on PATROCLUS's shoulder.)* You will too, Patroclus.

PATROCLUS: Do you remember all our plans back when the war was just starting—back when you were nineteen?

ACHILLES: I thought you promised me you wouldn't bring that up again.

PATROCLUS: I'm not talking about the loving—Well, I guess in a way I am. When we were holding hands on the beach waiting for the ship to come and we said that the war would be over in a month or so and then we'd take a ship through the straits and hunt the golden fleece and fight the queen of the Amazons and then maybe find an entrance into hell and go down in it and rescue somebody like Theseus and Peirithous did. Do you remember that?

ACHILLES: I remember.

PATROCLUS: And do you remember what time of year it was?

ACHILLES: It was early spring. I remember.

PATROCLUS: You remember after nine years of war, nine years of idiotic sword play and not even a dead rose in the mud to tell you what time of the year it is. Well. Do you think we could hunt the golden fleece now even if we still loved each other?

ACHILLES: Or descend into hell.

PATROCLUS: That might be easier.

ACHILLES: I know. Sometimes when I begin to wake up in the morning, I don't remember the bed I'm in and it's nine or ten years ago and there's going to be green grass and pine trees that grow all the way down to the ocean and something beautiful is going to happen; then I start to move and suddenly I lose all those years in a second and it's now and I'm twenty-eight and thirty pounds heavier and I'm almost ready to marry and settle down.

PATROCLUS (*moved, touches* ACHILLES's *shoulder briefly with his hand*): Okay —What do you suppose they'll say to you in the staff meeting?

ACHILLES: Oh, Agamemnon will start out by making a speech about unity. He always does. And then Nestor will make some wise and sensible remarks about loyalty and say that in his day young men didn't refuse to help avenge their dead companions because they were sulking over losing a woman. And then I'll interrupt him and ask if precisely why the dead companions were dead wasn't because Agamemnon's brother was sulking over losing a woman, and Menelaus will glare at me and Agamemnon will explain patiently about the difference between one kind of honor and another.

PATROCLUS: But not offering to give back Breiseis.

ACHILLES: He can't. That's the beauty of it. He's made it a matter of prestige and he's stuck with it. Anyway, then will come Ulysses who's the only one who understands what I'm doing. He's brighter than I am and I'm not sure what tack he'll take.

PATROCLUS: He'll probably tell the truth for a change and simply point out that if you stop fighting on this excuse, other people will stop fighting on other excuses and the whole war will fall apart. He'd love to see Agamemnon forced to give up Breiseis to you. He'd have Agamemnon's job in six months if that happened.

ACHILLES: Don't you think Ulysses wants the war to end?

PATROCLUS: Why should he? He's old and ugly.

ACHILLES: Well, when Ulysses gets through with whatever he has to say, I'll get up and state my demand again. They'll refuse. I'll walk out and they'll have a nice long meeting and a nice long war without me. If only none of the gods are watching and decide to stop me—.

PATROCLUS: The gods. You're always worrying about them. Has anyone ever seen a god?

ACHILLES: You know you have.

PATROCLUS: Something like it. But nothing like the kind of gods everyone's always worried about—a set of supercelestial idiots playing on both sides of a war that doesn't belong to them.

ACHILLES: Whatever they are, you can't fight them.

PATROCLUS: Exactly. And they can't fight you. They're more like abstract qualities—hatred, power, darkness, beauty—stuff like that.

ACHILLES: Show me how to run away from an abstract quality and I'll sleep in your arms forever.

(Door opens and THERSITES enters. He is extremely ugly. He carries a tray with a pitcher of wine, a pitcher of water, and some glasses. Sets tray down and pushes PATROCLUS off the table.)

THERSITES: Get your fat Greek ass off the table, pretty boy. Men are coming in.

PATROCLUS *(takes THERSITES by both arms and dances him around)*: We're going to leave the war, Thersites.

THERSITES: Nobody leaves this war but the corpses. *(He disengages himself and starts setting out the pitchers and the glasses.)* What's the clever plan this time?

PATROCLUS: The same one. This is the final meeting. Agamemnon can't afford to lose face and give back Breiseis, and Achilles has a perfectly honorable excuse to leave the war if he doesn't give her back.

THERSITES: And you, I suppose, have an honorable excuse to leave the war because you're Achilles' former fancy-boy?

PATROCLUS: It's honorable enough for me. Aren't you glad that we're going to diddle Agamemnon, Thersites?

THERSITES: I'll be glad if all the Greeks and all the Trojans and all the gods who are diddling the both of them would die of leprosy. That would make me glad. *(THERSITES finishes his table setting with this speech.)*

ACHILLES: You'd better get out of here, Patroclus. Agamemnon and the rest will be coming in.

PATROCLUS *(bouncing to the head of the Council table and imitating AGAMEMNON)*: Gentlemen, it seems to me that we often fail to realize how important unity is for the final achievement of victory. Leadership is something organic like the . . . *(THERSITES has opened the door and started to exit during this. He turns back in the doorway.)*

THERSITES: You'd better get out. I see them coming down the path.

PATROCLUS *(walks toward the door, stops, and pats ACHILLES on the shoulder)*: Good luck, kid! *(Exits.)*

(ACHILLES takes a seat at the table and, in a moment, the door opens and AGAMEMNON, NESTOR, ULYSSES, MENELAUS, and DIOMEDE walk in. AGAMEMNON immediately goes to the Council chair, but the others, except MENELAUS, say hello to ACHILLES. ULYSSES deliberately sits down next to ACHILLES.)

AGAMEMNON *(clearing his throat)*: Gentlemen, it seems to me that we often fail to realize how important unity is for the achievement of victory. Leadership is something organic like the . . .

(Curtain has been slowly going down from AGAMEMNON's first word and hits bottom here.)

> *Later that day.* PARIS *and* AENEAS *are sitting half-dressed on a bench in what looks vaguely like a locker-room. An open door stage right leads to the showers. Pieces of military equipment are spread around in disarray.*

PARIS: Not much fighting today.

AENEAS: No one to fight with. None of their big boys were there. I guess they were having another one of their conferences. Those bastards sure love to talk.

PARIS: Achilles hasn't been out for over a week.

AENEAS: Maybe he's sick. *(Turns suspiciously.)* You're not trying to start one of your peace rumors again? For God's sake, it's only been three months since the last one.

PARIS: I'm not saying the Greeks are breaking up. I simply say it's significant that Achilles hasn't been out on the battlefield in over a week.

AENEAS: Bullshit!

PARIS: Look, it stands to reason that the whole lot of them must be sick of the war and sick of each other by now. One good quarrel between Agamemnon and Achilles would finish everything off. After all, they've been here nine years and they aren't any farther than the day they started.

AENEAS: Neither are we.

PARIS: Damn it, it's just a matter of time.

AENEAS: There I agree with you. If the war goes on just a few years longer, Helen will die of old age and there'll be nothing left to fight about.

PARIS *(slamming his helmet on the floor)*: Can't you get it through your thick skull that Helen is just an excuse? Do you and everyone else in this goddamn town have to go around shouting Greek propaganda? No one's fighting about Helen. We're fighting about commerce and so are they. If I hadn't run away with Helen, they'd have claimed that father stole Agamemnon's umbrella or something and started a war about that. They want to destroy us and Helen's only a convenient excuse.

AENEAS: All right. Let's not argue about it. I think I'm tireder with arguing about Helen than I am with the war itself. It doesn't matter. After a year or so of a war no one ever remembers what really started it, if they ever did know—or care. *(Trying to change the subject.)* So you really think something funny has happened with Achilles?

PARIS *(refusing to change the subject)*: Helen cares. How do you think she feels when people blame her for all this? How do you think she feels when mothers who have lost sons in the war cross to the other side of the street when they see her on the sidewalk? How do you think she feels when people make jokes about her—jokes about how she drinks blood and . . .

(Just at the end of AENEAS's speech TROILUS has come in from the showers. He has only a towel tied around his waist. He is very young. He has been listening until PARIS sees him and stops.)

TROILUS: Hi! *(There is a pause.)* Go on talking about Helen if you want to.

AENEAS: What do you think about Helen, Troilus?

TROILUS: Well, she was hatched from the egg of Nemesis and I had to call her Auntie Helen when I was a kid. Hell, I don't know what I think about her. She's not in my generation.

AENEAS: Do you think she caused the war?

TROILUS: Her fatal beauty and so forth? No.

AENEAS: What did then?

TROILUS: I did, by being born so close to it. What was she like before the war started, Paris?

PARIS: What?

TROILUS: I mean I was such a little kid when you came here with her, mother would never let me ask any questions and nobody ever wants to talk about anything but the war anymore. I know you ran away with her and all that, but, I mean, how did it happen? You know, how?

PARIS: How did I happen to fall in love with her?

TROILUS: All that. I mean what was it like when you first saw her and so forth? *(He is moving while he says this and has placed one foot in a rather deep pool of blood. He raises his bare foot and looks at it.)* What in hell's name is this?

AENEAS: I'm afraid that's where they put Deiphobus yesterday.

TROILUS: Someone should clean up after us. *(Finds a rag and starts methodically wiping the blood from his foot and then from between his toes.)* Go on, Paris. I'm not being funny. I really want to know.

PARIS: It was a long time ago but I remember it better than yesterday. I'd been on a long tour of Greece—partly for fun and partly to arrange trading rights for father. I'd stay a week in one palace and then a week in the next one, traveling up the coast. I'd been traveling almost a year that way when I met Helen. I'd already heard all those stories about her, about how beautiful she was, how all the Greek princes had been after her. They had been too, I guess. Ulysses only married Penelope because she was Helen's cousin. I can remember so well. Late at night at almost any place I visited the men would start talking around the fire about Helen. How she was hatched from the egg of Nemesis, or, they didn't bother being consistent, how she'd come from her mother's womb in an egg four months after her mother had been raped by a swan. Zeus, of course, was the swan. Then there was another story they used to tell about how she really wasn't living with Menelaus at all, that the Helen there was merely a clever imitation of the real Helen that Menelaus had a Cretan craftsman make and that the real Helen was in Egypt and was being worshipped as a goddess in a temple full of snakes. The stories would get even wilder later in the evening after everyone had had a lot to drink—the old men talking about the tragedy she would cause and the young men talking about her beauty. But the point is—everybody talked about her. So you can imagine what I was looking forward to seeing when I got to Menelaus's palace. A sort of a combination of Aphrodite and a whirlwind. The servants told me that Menelaus was away for a few days but that Helen was out in the garden. I found her there sitting on a bench in the sunshine. I was so disappointed that I was almost rude—. She was smaller than I thought she would be and her nose was peeling from sunburn. I'd seen thousands of women more beautiful than she was. We talked and had a nice, comfortable conversation—the same one that I'd had with the wives of a half a dozen Greek princes. The crops, the weather, the fashions in Egypt, things like that. When it was all over I'd forgotten that she was Helen, and had even forgotten my disappointment. It was just another social situation. I was a young foreign celebrity and she was the lady of the palace trying to entertain me until her husband came home. I dreamed about her that night and the next, but it wasn't until the third day that I realized that I'd been in love with her from the moment I saw her. Even now, when I look at her after I've been gone for a few hours and she's not as beautiful as I remember her being, I love her as violently as I did when I first discovered that I loved her at all.

TROILUS: But when did you first decide to fall in love with her?

PARIS: I didn't.

TROILUS: Oh, well, you just don't remember. I mean you can be burning up to sleep with somebody or tremendously tender about someone's beautiful way of being alive, but there's a point where you decide— where you say "I'll let myself fall in love." Once you say that, it's too late, you can't change your mind again. But there's that point where you consciously let go and let the rest follow. I guess that must have happened to you on the third day.

PARIS: It didn't happen at all. I didn't have anything to do with being in love. I don't think she did either.

TROILUS: But people don't fall in love by accident. People die by accident but they don't fall in love by accident. Now if you'd been talking about your death, I'd believe you. Death doesn't need anyone's consent.

AENEAS: It isn't lucky to talk that way Troilus. My mother . . .

TROILUS: Your mother. Oh, your mother's listening! May arrow-shooting Aphrodite—or is that somebody else?—forgive me and all that. (To PARIS.) I don't think you understand what I mean. All I mean is that they give you a chance about falling in love and they don't give you any chance about dying.

PARIS: You don't know what you're talking about.

TROILUS: Look, there was a time, say in that third day, when you looked at Helen and triple-winged Eros was on the wing and Aphrodite was looking on, hot as a lizard in the sunshine, but all the same you had to say to yourself, "I love her" before you really did, and if you hadn't agreed at that moment, all the gods short of death couldn't have forced you to love her.

AENEAS: Shut up, you asshole. My mother's around listening to everything.

TROILUS *(to PARIS)*: It's true, isn't it?

PARIS: No. *(PARIS and AENEAS now suddenly seem to change personality. It is as if someone partly, only partly, had taken them over.)* Let me put it this way, Troilus. Is there some girl around that if, say, your theory is true, you might have that moment of deciding whether or not you want to fall in love with her?

TROILUS: There are several, I guess.

PARIS: Well, pick one of them so we can have an example.

TROILUS: Cressida will do. I don't know her very well but she's one of the two or three women in the town that everybody talks about. That ought to make it a better analogy.

AENEAS: Calchas's daughter?

TROILUS: Yes.

PARIS: I take it that you have no intention of falling in love with her.

TROILUS: Not the slightest. The only thing I'm in love with is this war.

PARIS: Well, just imagine for a moment that you are looking at her, that you suddenly know, know on the word of Aphrodite, that Troilus and Cressida can be known through history as a pair of lovers, known with the fame, with more than the fame of Philemon and Baucis or Jason and Medea.

TROILUS: Or Paris and Helen.

PARIS: Or Paris and Helen. That whether tragic or happy, that whether short or long, your love will be shouted through other centuries by other lovers, that every tear you shed, every kiss you give her will be remembered somewhere by some poet and that you'll be able to remember this while you're crying or kissing, that when you touch her it will be history, that when she rumples your hair it will be history. Imagine this, Troilus!

TROILUS: I'm imagining.

PARIS *(smiling triumphantly)*: And aren't you in love with her now without having consented to anything?

TROILUS: Good lord, no! I hate history.

PARIS: You don't want to be immortal?

TROILUS: History make me immortal? *(To AENEAS.)* I beg your mother's pardon again, but the king of hell doesn't allow anybody to bring history into the land of the dead, not even goddesses. It's a contraband material there and Cressida and I could wait an eternity in that darkness before we heard a single whisper about ourselves or about our kisses. History! I wouldn't give a single drop of blood to become a part of history.

PARIS: You're too young to understand.

TROILUS: Your war keeps me young. I know all you people like to hear poets talking about huge heroes rescuing golden apricots and sowing Gorgon's teeth and so forth, but I like a war like this one that goes on every day in the same place—and if I ever went to Thebes or Colchis, there'd be a war there too and someone would be besieging us. I like music. You don't have to believe anything to hear it.

PARIS: Music without words?

TROILUS: Music without anything. Music without history. Music without Cressida. Music without Troilus. I imagine that the land of the dead is filled with music. But go on with your temptations. Make me love Cressida without wanting to.

PARIS: I . . .

AENEAS: Paris has been going about this in the wrong way. He doesn't understand the way your mind works, Troilus. Look at her this way. You know how people have been muttering against her ever since her father went over to the Greeks. They say that treason is what has kept the Greeks going so long and that Cressida is one of the traitors. You've heard them talk. You know that it's just a matter of time before public opinion will force us to expel Cressida from the town—or worse.

TROILUS: Yes, I've heard them talk. Better to make a mistake about an individual than to risk our nation and its destiny. Nine years of treason or you can't break an egg without making an omelette.

AENEAS: All right, think of her that way, Troilus. Not just as Cressida but as the symbol of somebody who's being pushed around by idiots. See in your mind a mob of super-patriots getting ready to tear her apart just because she had the wrong father. See yourself rescue her . . .

TROILUS: Not me. Every day on the battlefield the Greeks try to tear me apart because I had the wrong father and nobody sees me as a big symbol of injustice. Your Cressida is even less tempting than Paris's. I know you people do a lot of strange things on account of indignation, I suppose you could even fall in love on account of it. But I couldn't.

AENEAS: You're constantly indignant.

TROILUS: Honestly, Aeneas, I don't think I've ever been indignant in my life. I'm angry and hurt all the time but I'm never indignant. Getting upset because people are persecuting other people is like getting upset because it rains in the winter, or because people get killed in the war.

AENEAS: Then you'd let the mob take her?

TROILUS: I sure as hell wouldn't fall in love with her because they were trying to.

PARIS: It isn't going to work, Aeneas. I think he picked Cressida because he knew he couldn't fall in love with her. She isn't a real woman.

TROILUS: What on earth do you mean by that?

PARIS: There's a smell of death about her. Oh, I know, I know, they say the same thing about Helen—but that's because people are fools and only look at the surfaces of things. Helen could cause the death of ten thousand men or even murder them herself and she'd still smell of life —life that's lived too hard, that costs too much maybe, but still life. Cressida! She'll never probably cause the death of a single man, but she smells of death. She isn't a real woman, she's more like an ocean. Whole nations of men could drown in her and she'd still be unmoved.

TROILUS: That doesn't sound like you talking, Paris.

PARIS: Have you seen it in her eyes?

TROILUS: They say that the Styx is a river but I've always thought that it was an ocean. Sometimes at night I can hear it splashing miles and miles below Troy—you know, just like the ocean sounds from the tower when the wind is right.

PARIS: That's why she was such a bad choice, Troilus. Pick another woman and we can make you love her.

TROILUS: You see death in her eyes?

PARIS: Death, yes. Not anybody dying. Death itself.

TROILUS: Maybe you've succeeded after all. I'm going to take another shower and wash this blood off my feet. *(Exits into showers.)*

PARIS *(after a moment)*: We shouldn't have teased the kid that way.

AENEAS: I don't think we did. I'm afraid it was my mother talking.

(Curtain.)

ACT I, Scene 3

> *The same place as Scene 1, three quarters of an hour later.* NESTOR, ULYSSES, *and* DIOMEDE *in casual poses around the table. Empty glasses show where the others have been.*

ULYSSES: It ought to stall things for a bit anyway until we can think of something to do about it.

DIOMEDE: I'm surprised that Agamemnon agreed.

ULYSSES: He wasn't going to until he saw how Achilles reacted. He was all set to play the heavy leader role—"Go and be damned"—and how Achilles would have loved to go—but Achilles had to open his mouth and accuse me of trickery when I asked for a postponement. Agamemnon may not be bright, but he knew enough to agree to anything that would annoy Achilles that way. And Achilles had to agree too because he can't leave the war with honor unless he's the offended party. It was all very nice.

NESTOR: All we have to do now is work out some compromise they'll both agree to.

DIOMEDE: That's all. Hell, it would be easier to find peace terms both sides of the war would agree to.

ULYSSES: There's one big difference—this is on a smaller scale than the war is. Just one unimportant thing could change everything. For example, suppose Breiseis had an accident, fell off a rock or something and got her head smashed in. Achilles and Agamemnon couldn't very well fight over her corpse, could they?

NESTOR: That would be pretty risky. Agamemnon's been keeping a guard around her.

ULYSSES: I was just giving an example. Besides, what makes you think that Agamemnon would be unhappy if Breiseis had an accident? If it came to a matter of facesaving, I mean. He isn't really any more interested in Breiseis than Achilles is.

DIOMEDE: Don't you have any plans that are a little less bloody?

NESTOR: You know, I remember one time when Jason was trying to leave Medea and . . .

ULYSSES *(interrupting)*: Oh, I have several other plans. That one is only for emergencies. The first thing we have to do is to build up somebody's reputation so that Achilles will be afraid that we can replace him without any trouble. We need a new hero. *(DIOMEDE begins to look interested.)* I was thinking of Ajax.

DIOMEDE: Ajax!

ULYSSES: It can't be any of us. It's got to be somebody that's relatively unknown, somebody who hasn't any record.

DIOMEDE: And what are you going to do to make Ajax into a hero? Find him a magic sword to fight with?

ULYSSES: It's simpler than that. You know that Ajax is Hector's cousin? And you know how fond of dramatic gestures Hector is in the middle of a fight? If Ajax challenges Hector to single combat and can keep going for a while until Hector gets bored and feels like a dramatic gesture, Hector is very likely to stop fighting and say something like, "I can't kill a blood relative. Let's call it a draw." It would help his reputation and he wouldn't care if he was building up Ajax at the same time. And Achilles—Achilles would be pretty jealous wouldn't he?

DIOMEDE: But what if Hector doesn't say that?

ULYSSES: We try something else. We haven't lost anything.

DIOMEDE: Except Ajax.

ULYSSES: Except Ajax.

NESTOR: Are you going to tell Ajax about the plan?

ULYSSES: Hardly. We'll make Ajax Achilles's temporary replacement on the staff and the staff will draw lots to see who does single combat with Hector. Ajax will win.

NESTOR: It might work. It seems to me that you're gambling with pretty long odds. A plan as complicated as that, with so many factors to it. Something's bound to go wrong.

ULYSSES: Oh, we won't just rely on that. I have a plan for putting pressure on Agamemnon too. I think we can work out some strategic withdrawals (although we'll have to be pretty careful with them) so that it will look like the Trojans have beaten us all the way back to the boats. The line we're holding now isn't a very good one anyway and we won't lose much by letting them through. But we can make it *look* dangerous. Then we can go to Agamemnon and scare him into giving back Breiseis to Achilles.

DIOMEDE: I just don't understand you, Ulysses. If you spent half as much time figuring out a plan to settle the war that you're spending on settling this two-bit fight between Agamemnon and Achilles, you could find a compromise that would satisfy us and the Trojans and we could all go home. I could understand it if you felt about the war the way I do. I don't particularly care if this war ever comes to an end. I like to fight and in this war they occasionally even let me fight against the gods without anybody blasting me with lightning. I'm quite happy if things go on this way for quite a while and Nestor . . .

NESTOR: This is my last war. But you haven't any reason for not wanting to end it, Ulysses.

ULYSSES: Of course I want the war to end. But I want it to end properly. I've wasted nine years of poetry on this war and I'm not going to have it ruined with a sloppy ending. Imagine if after nine years of fighting, if after nine years of strategy and decisions, nine years of trying to break into Troy, that suddenly everything was settled. We go away and leave Troy still standing. We go away admitting that we've wasted nine years of everything—my poetry, his youth, your age—everything. The Trojans stay on their mudhill thinking of the years we've wasted on them and they've wasted on us—waving us goodbye maybe. You can't compromise a war anymore than you can compromise a poem. Not a real war anyway.

DIOMEDE: Do you mean that we would look foolish if the war ended with no one being defeated?

ULYSSES: Worse than that. The war would look foolish.

NESTOR: It's my opinion that the war will end when the gods want it to end and not a day sooner. Wars don't last this long by themselves —not nine years. In all my life I've never seen a war that lasted nine years.

ULYSSES: There's no use worrying about what the gods are doing. That's something you can't control. If I could, I'd use the gods themselves to break Troy into pieces. But I'd use an earthquake too, or lightning, if I could.

DIOMEDE: You ought to have been a god yourself, Ulysses. That would have solved your problem.

(ULYSSES walks over to a map on the wall. The others look like they know what's coming.)

ULYSSES: There's one other thing I want to discuss with you. You two are the only people in the army who keep open minds about unorthodox strategy. I have a tactical idea . . .

DIOMEDE: Not birds again!

ULYSSES: No, but I still don't think that idea had a fair test. If we had had enough birds some of them would have been bound to set fires in places where the Trojans couldn't have put them out. And the rags should have been tied to their feet, not around their bodies—that interfered with their flying—and we should have soaked the rags in something more inflammable than oil.

DIOMEDE: As it was the Trojans were eating roast pigeon for weeks.

ULYSSES: I admit I may have gone a bit overboard on the scheme, but the idea of burning birds—it was pure poetry in action.

DIOMEDE *(bringing him back to the subject)*: But this new idea doesn't have any birds in it.

ULYSSES: No. It's quite simple and practical. I think even as unimaginative a person as Agamemnon will concede that it's practical. But I thought I'd try it out on you two first before I brought it up to the General Council meeting to sort of work the bugs out of it.

DIOMEDE: As long as there aren't any birds in it.

ULYSSES *(pointing to the map)*: You see here where the bank of the river slants almost straight up. There's never any fighting there because there's no good place to attack the wall from it. But it's less than half a mile from the wall. Nobody's ever around there. A hundred men could camp there for months and nobody would see them.

NESTOR: So?

ULYSSES: A tunnel, of course! We can't get over the wall, or through the wall. There's only one thing left. We go under the wall. It would only take a couple of months for a hundred men to dig the tunnel all the way through. When it's finished, we could use half of our forces to fight outside the gate and the other half could go through the tunnel and take the city behind their backs. Well, wouldn't it work?

DIOMEDE: Two months, you say.

ULYSSES: About that. I've asked some of our engineers.

DIOMEDE: And with a hundred men working on it you think that you could keep the tunnel a secret for two months? The Trojans wouldn't even need spies. The first foot-soldier they captured would sell the information to them before he took off his helmet.

ULYSSES: We could keep it a secret from our men.

DIOMEDE: And supply the diggers? And replace the ones that got sick? Whatever you did, when we started to attack, someone would be at the other end of the hole with a club in his hand taking care of us one by one as we came out. It would be like shooting fish in a barrel.

ULYSSES: There is that danger, isn't there? But you agree that the plan's a good one except for that one weakness?

DIOMEDE: More or less.

ULYSSES: I'll simply have to find a way around it. Maybe fresh troops utterly unconnected—well, I have something to think about.

NESTOR: I think it's time for dinner. *(He and DIOMEDE get up to leave. ULYSSES stands by the map.)* Aren't you coming?

ULYSSES: I have to write a letter first. I'll be along in a few minutes.

(NESTOR and DIOMEDE exit. ULYSSES sits down and starts writing. While he does this a recording of his voice is played on a loudspeaker.)

ULYSSES'S VOICE: Dear Penelope, I have written this letter so often (varying it slightly every time because I cannot bear to believe, although I know, that you are unlikely to receive each particular letter I am writing) so often that you must have received this letter and replied to it God knows how many times yourself. Some day I will receive your letter and be able to write a new one of my own.

The war goes on—a thousand miles and nine sour years away from Ithaca. I go on playing the clever general, using up my poetry as a fuel for my cleverness as a freezing man burns up all his property to keep himself warm. You, of course, have become a ghost and Ithaca a mythical kingdom—but you are a dear ghost and Ithaca is a mythical kingdom toward which I can afford to hope someday to sail.

So this letter, as usual, ends with hope and I, the writer, struggle to finish the last sentence of the letter knowing that I am a liar, knowing that I have no faith in you and no hope for the fut . . . *(ULYSSES stops in the middle of the word and starts erasing the paragraph—there is a scratching noise on the loudspeaker while this goes on. The voice goes on again when he finishes erasing.)*

So this letter, as usual, ends with hope. It is the least that we can afford to give each other. Yours, Ulysses.

(Curtain.)

ACT I, Scene 4

> *The following morning. The Trojan locker room.* TROILUS *is choosing a sword from the sword-rack and* PANDARUS *is checking his bow.*

PANDARUS: I still don't understand why you never mentioned her before.

TROILUS: I didn't know. I didn't know. It sounds like a stupid adolescent sexual fantasy, but I'm in love with Cressida. I'm suddenly in love with Cressida. *(He starts slashing around with his sword.)*

PANDARUS: Calm down a minute. What do you mean you didn't know?

TROILUS: It only makes me sound stupider. I'd been with Aeneas and Paris and we were talking about love and Cressida was mentioned. I didn't know her. I mean I'd seen her passing by a few times and talked to her once but—anyway, this started me thinking about her. And then I had a dream about her last night. This is pretty embarrassing. *(He waits for* PANDARUS *to comment but* PANDARUS *doesn't.)* There was a strange looking person dressed all in black, some absurd costume, and I knew right away he was a god.

PANDARUS: What god was it?

TROILUS: That's what I wanted to know, even before I wanted to know what it wanted with me. So I asked all the names of the gods in alphabetical order—you know—are you Apollo, are you Aphrodite, and so forth—only I mentioned Hades first because I always sacrifice to Hades—it really annoys my father—anyway the god kept answering, "No, I'm just a god." So then the god took me by the hand and suddenly I was in a place I'd dreamed about lots of times before— it's a flat place, all gray, and there are a lot of flat stones scattered on the ground and they're gray too. Usually when I have this dream the stones start moving slowly in a circle and the sky starts closing in and I wake up screaming. But, instead of that, there was Cressida. Now—and this is the hard thing to understand—she was more than just Cressida, she was like the pieces and fragments of everything I had wanted in my life all put together. Do you understand what I mean?

PANDARUS: You mean the qualities you had wanted from life?

TROILUS: No, the things. The things I'd wanted. The kite my father wouldn't buy me when I was five years old, getting my mother to come into my room to talk to me when I'd had a bad dream, being able to run as fast as the kid I'd admired in school—those were pieces and she fitted them together in herself. *(He slams his sword down.)* It wasn't a sex dream. I mean I didn't touch her but I could have touched her and it didn't matter whether I touched her or not. You don't mind my talking about her this way?

PANDARUS: She's only my niece. That's not a very close relationship.

TROILUS: Anyway, I know that I'm in love with her.

PANDARUS: Since you woke up in the morning.

TROILUS: Since I woke up in the morning.

PANDARUS: What do you want me to do?

TROILUS: Arrange for me to meet her. Have a dinner or something and invite us both. Give me advice about her. Even just talk about her. I want to hear everything about her.

PANDARUS: Look, Troilus, this puts me in a funny position. If it had been any of the rest of your family that asked me for something like this, I'd have just been amused at being in the position where one of those snobs had to ask me for a dinner invitation. I'd have gone through with the whole thing just for comedy and to see what would happen. But you've always been decent to me. I like you.

TROILUS: I don't understand what you're trying to say.

PANDARUS: I don't mean there's anything wrong with Cressida. She's a nice girl and intelligent too. I don't like her very well, but I don't like anyone in my family. If you just wanted to seduce her, that would be fine. I'd be delighted to help you. What I'm trying to get at is that this sounds serious and I don't want to get stuck as the third party in something serious. I don't want the responsibility. I don't trust gods dressed in black that won't tell you their name and I don't want to get mixed up with the dreams they cause.

TROILUS *(goes over and puts his hand on PANDARUS's shoulder)*: Please, Pandarus.

PANDARUS *(after a pause)*: I suppose it's too late to say no. I'll arrange the dinner and I'll talk to you about her. Now go away and let me get this damned bow tested.

(PRIAM walks into the locker-room closely followed by HECTOR.)

TROILUS *(in a mocking voice)*: Father, what are *you* doing here? Are you going to put on some armor?

PRIAM: Deiphobus is dead.

TROILUS: That's too bad.

PRIAM *(to HECTOR)*: I told you he'd act this way. *(To TROILUS.)* You can't be decent even at a time like this. He was your brother.

TROILUS: Hadn't you better hurry up and get mother pregnant again. We'll be running out of brothers.

(PANDARUS is trying to exit unnoticed.)

PRIAM *(seeing him)*: No, stay. Let every common soldier in Troy see the respect Troilus has for his father and his family.

TROILUS: It's a big family, father. One soldier more or less doesn't matter.

PRIAM: You talk to him, Hector. I can't stand to hear any more of his clever comments. *(Exits.)*

HECTOR: I don't see why you're so hard on father, Troilus. He's an old man and it's very easy to hurt his feelings.

TROILUS *(mocking)*: Poor Deiphobus!

HECTOR: You always seem to blame father for the war. If the war's anybody's fault it's Paris's, but you're good friends with him.

TROILUS: I don't get angry at anybody for causing a war or keeping it going. I just hate anybody who enjoys a war without fighting in it. When's the funeral?

HECTOR: Tomorrow afternoon.

TROILUS: I know you don't understand me, Hector, and I'm glad you don't preach at me. Come on back over here, Pandarus, the hurricane is over. *(PANDARUS, who has been making himself inconspicuous at the back of the room, comes over to join them.)*

HECTOR *(rather stiffly)*: Hello, Pandarus. *(To TROILUS.)* I've got to go now and calm father down. For God's sake, Troilus, don't bait him at the funeral.

TROILUS: I'll be a monster of filial devotion. *(HECTOR exits.)* How about having that dinner tomorrow evening, Pandarus?

PANDARUS: After the funeral?

TROILUS: It's as good a time as any. *(Goes up to PANDARUS, who has just finished adjusting his equipment and practically rushes him out of the door.)* Come on, Pandarus, let's go out and kill some people.

(Curtain.)

ACT II, Scene 1

> PANDARUS, TROILUS, *and* CRESSIDA *seated at the dinner table in PAN-DARUS's small bachelor apartment.* TROILUS *is seated in the middle and* PANDARUS *and* CRESSIDA *at either end. It is the evening of the next day.*

CRESSIDA: Pass the salt please. *(TROILUS passes salt.)*

PANDARUS: It was one of the best funerals we ever had. Didn't you think so, Cressida?

CRESSIDA: It was a good funeral.

PANDARUS: The priest they have to replace Calchas seems to be quite satisfactory. He's some sort of Phrygian isn't he, Troilus?

TROILUS *(afraid that* CRESSIDA *is embarrassed at the mention of her father)*: I don't know where father got him from. Father's been getting very fussy about religious matters lately—following the priests around and getting in their way when they're trying to sacrifice and telling them the right way to perform every ceremony. "Young man," he'll say, "that isn't the way we do it here. The blood is supposed to flow counterclockwise when you sacrifice to Artemis." *(He pauses, and then to* CRESSIDA*)*: I hate my father.

CRESSIDA: I hate my father too.

TROILUS: Good. I mean not because of all this business about the Greeks but because he's your father.

PANDARUS: I don't even remember my father, but I'm willing to hate him to keep you two company. He was your mother's father, Cressida.

CRESSIDA: Yes.

TROILUS: Why do you hate your father, Cressida?

CRESSIDA: Because he's ridiculous and because he's fussy about things. For years he was making long-winded speeches at home about how offensive the war was to the gods and how the Trojans should get rid of Helen. But he always made the speeches at home.

PANDARUS: And then one day he deserted to the Greeks.

CRESSIDA: It wasn't quite that way. The Greeks just happened to be there. He doesn't believe in their side either.

PANDARUS: Why does he stay with them then?

CRESSIDA: He has to stay somewhere. Father's an idealist.

TROILUS: So is mine.

CRESSIDA: Aren't you going to ask me now what I think about the war, whether I agree with my father?

TROILUS: You don't think about the war, Cressida. No one thinks about it. People sometimes talk about it, but that's as far as it goes.

CRESSIDA: I don't think about anything.

PANDARUS: You must get awfully bored.

CRESSIDA: I do, uncle. Awfully bored.

TROILUS: They ought to let the women fight too. They pretend that women are causing their wars but they don't let them fight in them.

PANDARUS: Would you like to fight in a war, Cressida?

CRESSIDA: It would be better than thinking.

TROILUS: It would be marvelous. You, Helen, and mother all out there in armor. And Andromache slashing at Achilles with an ax. I'll bet the Greeks would be jealous.

(They have all finished eating by this time.)

PANDARUS: I'd better get rid of these dishes or I'll have them on the table for the next week. You two amuse yourselves.

(He starts clearing off and goes into the kitchen with the first stack of dishes. TROILUS and CRESSIDA look at each other. There is silence.)

CRESSIDA *(shouting into the kitchen)*: Oh, Pandarus, I didn't tell you. I got a letter from father today.

PANDARUS *(coming out of the kitchen quickly)*: From Calchas?

CRESSIDA: Yes. There was an exchange of some foot-soldiers and they handed over the letter with the prisoners. *(PANDARUS has by this time cleared away the rest of the dishes and is closing the door back into the kitchen.)* He wants me to come and live with him.

(PANDARUS stops and stands in the doorway with the dishes in his hand.)

PANDARUS: To go over to the Greeks?

CRESSIDA: He didn't put it that way—to be a loyal daughter and to show everybody that I, at least, respect his integrity.

TROILUS: You're not going, are you?

CRESSIDA: No. If he'd merely said that he wanted to see me and that one side was as good as another, I'd have packed my bags and slipped through the gate as soon as I received the letter. But, of course, he didn't. He wouldn't be there in the first place if he could say something like that. *(PANDARUS goes into the kitchen, closing the door. There is the sound of running water in the sink. To TROILUS.)* You'd feel that way wouldn't you?

TROILUS: I don't see any point in changing the side you start with. You won't leave Troy, will you?

CRESSIDA *(looking around)*: Uncle has a nice apartment, doesn't he?

TROILUS: Is this the first time you've been here?

CRESSIDA: Yes. Uncle never paid much attention to father and me.

TROILUS: Have some more wine. *(He starts pouring it into her glass.)* It's a beautiful apartment, the pictures . . . *(He has been pouring wine into a full glass. He notices it spilling onto the table and tries to stop it and in doing so upsets all the wine from the glass onto CRESSIDA's lap. She takes a napkin and starts wiping the wine from her dress.)* I love you, Cressida.

CRESSIDA: You love me.

TROILUS: Do you love me?

CRESSIDA: I think so. *(At this moment PANDARUS comes in from the kitchen.)* Uncle, there's been an accident.

(Curtain.)

ACT II, Scene 2

Four days later. A barbed-wire fence crosses the stage. ACHILLES and PATROCLUS behind the fence are sitting on campstools facing the audience. Attached to the fence is a sign saying, "END OF NEU-TRAL ZONE. EVERYTHING PAST THIS FENCE IS GREEK TERRITORY." Someone has chalked in "temporarily" between the last two words. ACHILLES and PATROCLUS are eating a picnic lunch of fried chicken and are drinking wine. ULYSSES enters on the other side of the fence from stage right. ACHILLES and PATROCLUS are wearing brightly colored bathing trunks while ULYSSES is in full military dress.

ULYSSES *(very angry)*: What are you two doing here?

PATROCLUS: Eating an excellent lunch and enjoying the sunshine. Have an olive. *(He extends an olive through the barbed wire. ULYSSES ignores it.)*

ULYSSES: I might have known you'd try something like this.

ACHILLES: Like what? Look, I promised not to attend the fight but I didn't say that I'd stay cooped up in my tent on a nice sunny day like this. And being so close to the fighting grounds I knew that I'd get news of the fight as soon as it happened. Is it over yet?

ULYSSES: It's just started. You two can't stay here. There are Trojans wandering around the neutral zone.

PATROCLUS: You mean some of them aren't interested in watching Hector battle for his life against—Ajax? You ought to put on better fights, darling. You're losing your touch.

ULYSSES *(to ACHILLES, ignoring PATROCLUS):* If one of the Trojans sees you, they'll know something's wrong.

ACHILLES: Oh, if any of them ask, I intend to tell them. I'll say, "Well boys, I'm sorry there isn't a better fight for you to watch, but Agamemnon decided that he'd rather keep Breiseis than keep me. And if you want my autograph you'd better ask for it now because I don't think I'll be around much longer."

ULYSSES: We've practically persuaded Agamemnon to agree to give her back. You're spoiling everything. You promised to wait a week.

ACHILLES: There are two days left of the week and I intend to wait them.

ULYSSES: Everything will be all right. I'll work out everything. But you see, if the Trojans find out about this . . .

ACHILLES: It will be your own fault. If you'd gotten someone better to fight Hector, the Trojans would be *watching* the show instead of wandering around.

ULYSSES: That's not my fault. I didn't particularly want Ajax. He just happened to draw the lot.

PATROCLUS: Tell us another story as funny as that one, Ulysses.

ULYSSES: What do you mean?

ACHILLES: Don't let him go into his act, Patroclus. Look, we know and you know that we know that you arranged this whole deal. I don't get the point of it yet and I'm willing to believe that it doesn't have anything to do with me and Agamemnon. I'm willing to believe it if you can show me that you arranged it so you could pick somebody's pocket while the fight was going on or because Ajax has mentioned you in his will or any other reason, provided the reason is sufficiently complicated and dishonest. But just don't tell me that *you* didn't choose Ajax.

ULYSSES: We can talk about that later. The point is—will you two please get out of here before some Trojan sees you?

PATROCLUS (*looking offstage to the right*): It's too late. There's one coming now. (*Stands up and waves.*) Hi!

(*In about twenty seconds* TROILUS *enters from right on neutral zone side. He had obviously not intended to come over until* PATROCLUS *waved at him and is rather puzzled.*)

TROILUS: Hi!

ACHILLES: How's the fighting going?

TROILUS: Oh, Hector's pretty slow today. They're just slashing around at each other. Nothing much has happened. (*Pause.*) You're Achilles, aren't you?

PATROCLUS *(extending a hand through the barbed wire)*: Yes, and I'm Patro-clus and the old gentleman there who's glowering at you is Ulysses. What's your name?

TROILUS *(shaking hands)*: I'm Troilus. *(ACHILLES rises and shakes hands through the wire too. TROILUS turns to ULYSSES, who glares at him.)* Look, am I in the wrong place or something?

PATROCLUS: You just stumbled on a military secret. Have a drumstick!

(TROILUS accepts one through the fence and starts eating it.)

TROILUS *(between mouthfuls)*: I'm afraid I'm not very good at military secrets. *(Turns to ULYSSES, politely trying to change the subject)*: You're the one who thought of the pigeons, aren't you?

ACHILLES: See how famous you are, Ulysses?

TROILUS: It was the only thing in the war that I ever admired. It was a beautiful idea.

ULYSSES: You wouldn't have thought it was a beautiful idea if it had burned all you damned Trojans up in your filthy city.

TROILUS: Yes, I would. I mean *(makes a sign against evil omen)* Zeus pro-tect me, I don't want to die by fire, but think what I will die by—my own stupidity. All of us will. That's how people die in a war. The day comes when you forget to keep your guard up, when you stumble over a stone when somebody's attacking. That sort of thing. And you die from stupidity—your own stupidity. But to die on account of somebody's cleverness. That would be dying.

ACHILLES: You sound like you think the war is going to last forever.

TROILUS: Doesn't everybody?

PATROCLUS: Not the people who intend to leave it.

ULYSSES *(quickly, to stop this dangerous subject)*: Did the birds do much damage?

TROILUS: No, unfortunately. People just laughed at them. They can't un-derstand dying except in their own dull way. I used to try to think of a trick like the birds to use against you people. You know like raising a herd of mountain lions and letting them out of their cages suddenly when you start attacking. But there isn't much like that that you can do when you're on the inside of a city. Wouldn't it be nice if we could change around every five years or so—you take the inside and we get a chance to try the outside?

ULYSSES *(to* ACHILLES *and* PATROCLUS—*not sure if he's being kidded but trying to pump some information)*: Sounds like the Trojans are sick of the war, doesn't it?

PATROCLUS: Not as sick of it as we are.

TROILUS: Sick from it, most of them. Pretty sick. They try to tell you that it's no worse than a bad cold. Fortunately for me, I was born with it and so I have a natural immunity. But you don't like my idea of changing sides every five years? Haven't you ever wondered what it would be like to be inside a city?

ULYSSES: I've lived inside bigger cities than Troy.

TROILUS: I thought so. You look like a man who had lived inside cities. Why don't you come over to our side? Anybody who has lived in a city is a Trojan at heart.

ACHILLES: Do you think I'm a Trojan at heart?

TROILUS: You're Achilles. You're not at heart. *(There is a pause.* TROILUS *throws away the remains of his drumstick and wipes his mouth.)* By the way, how is Calchas getting along?

ULYSSES: So that's what you came here to find out? Tell the Trojan General Staff that Calchas is very happy and more certain than ever that the Greeks are going to win.

TROILUS: That's me. Troilus Priamides, boy spy. Listen, I came here by accident, and I stayed here because I like and respect you, and all you do is stand here and talk like my father while these two giggle. Why do you have to pretend to be a fool?

ULYSSES: Why did you ask about Calchas then?

TROILUS: Because I know his daughter. *(Less angry.)* Do you people use him as a priest too?

ULYSSES: Of course we do.

PATROCLUS: When he lets us.

TROILUS: Then you people have the same gods we have? I mean you're not like the Egyptians or anything like that, are you?

ULYSSES: The same gods. We've shared our gods with you for this war.

TROILUS: That's the way I like to hear you talk. Now you don't sound like my father. And Calchas really says that the gods tell him the Greeks are going to win?

ACHILLES: Tell him the truth, Ulysses. If you don't, we will.

TROILUS: Oh look, if it's a secret and so forth, I don't want to know. It will just start the Trojans arguing about why you told me and whether to believe it. *(To ULYSSES.)* Who's your favorite god?

ULYSSES: What?

TROILUS: Your favorite god. The one you make sacrifices to.

ULYSSES: It's too warm an afternoon for this kind of humor.

TROILUS: No, I'm serious. I mean it isn't a military secret too, is it? The thing is I think I'd understand you better if I knew who your favorite god was.

ULYSSES: Do you mean the favorite god of the Greeks or just my personal favorite god?

TROILUS: Yours, of course. I mean if the Greeks had all agreed on a favorite god, they'd have beaten us long ago.

ULYSSES: I suppose it's Pallas Athene.

TROILUS: Cold wisdom.

ULYSSES: She's more than that. She's the kind of wisdom that balances everything I see and feel until there's a kind of a dance around my senses.

PATROCLUS: Ulysses is talking poetry.

ULYSSES *(angrily)*: I was a poet once. Anyway, I pray to her.

PATROCLUS: Was she your goddess when you were still writing poetry or did she come to you afterwards, after the war started?

ULYSSES: I suppose you think that poetry doesn't have anything to do with war, that it's something made of whipped cream and kisses.

(PATROCLUS smiles and drinks an imaginary toast.)

TROILUS: What about you, Achilles?

ACHILLES: Hera. Definitely Hera. After nine years of war I can only believe in someone like her. Outraged virtue, jealousy, mother-shrilling anger, qualities like that. Maybe I'll find a pleasanter goddess to worship after the war.

TROILUS: And you, Patroclus?

PATROCLUS: It used to be Aphrodite but now I'm sick of the whole lot of them. I have an imaginary Egyptian god that I pray to. He has the head of a crocodile, the genitals of a stallion, and the heart of a cat.

TROILUS: Aren't you afraid to say something like that? I mean the gods are always taking human shape. Suppose I was one of the gods pretending to be Troilus?

PATROCLUS: Which one?

TROILUS: Hades, the king of hell.

PATROCLUS: Have another piece of fried chicken.

ULYSSES: Why Hades? I can't think of anything more improbable offhand than the lord of the dead masquerading as a wisecracking Trojan youngster.

TROILUS: You're not being very logical. Just because he's the lord of the dead doesn't mean that he's a corpse himself. I think that my shape would be a good one for him.

PATROCLUS: It's a good shape.

TROILUS: Yes, it's a good shape. All perfectly constructed of flesh and bones and blood. Who would make a better king of the dead than a youngster made of flesh and bones and blood? And all of the dead men older than him—and without shape.

ACHILLES: Well, if you're a god, you have a message for us. What's your message, Hades?

TROILUS: Why should there be a message? I . . . *(At this point DIOMEDE comes running in.)*

DIOMEDE *(out of breath)*: It's a draw.

ACHILLES: What do you mean a draw?

DIOMEDE: They both decided to quit. They'd been fighting evenly for about ten minutes and then Hector suddenly put down his sword and said, "I can't fight a relative and you can't either, can you, cousin Ajax?" and Ajax after a moment said no he guessed he couldn't, and so they stopped fighting and decided it was a draw.

ACHILLES *(suspiciously to ULYSSES)*: You don't look very surprised.

ULYSSES: Ajax is a good man.

TROILUS: Hector wasn't feeling very well this morning. He was in one of his moods.

DIOMEDE: Who's this?

ULYSSES: This is Hades, lord of the dead—alias Prince Troilus.

TROILUS: We've fought against each other but we haven't been formally introduced.

DIOMEDE *(extending hand)*: Diomede.

TROILUS: I'd better get back if it's over.

ACHILLES: You haven't told us your message yet, Hades.

PATROCLUS: The message is that Ulysses has successfully pulled off another swindle. He's going to diddle you back into the war with this trumped-up draw.

DIOMEDE: What's this Hades business?

ULYSSES: A joke. *(Extending hand.)* Goodbye, Troilus. I'm sorry I was so abrupt with you at first.

DIOMEDE: I'll walk back with you. I'm going to have to help Ajax with his gear.

TROILUS *(walking off with DIOMEDE)*: Goodbye fellows! *(To DIOMEDE as they exit)*: Who's your favorite god?

ACHILLES: Suppose he really was Hades.

ULYSSES: You certainly tried to give him every bit of information you could.

ACHILLES: Balls! He wasn't even interested enough to ask why I wasn't fighting.

ULYSSES: That was the suspicious part of it. It wasn't natural. Anybody but a spy would have asked you.

ACHILLES: A god wouldn't. Anyway, why wouldn't a spy have asked me?

ULYSSES: He would have assumed that this whole setup was a fake, a put-up job. I would have if I'd been a Trojan spy stumbling on it. We're damn lucky he was a spy.

PATROCLUS: You're both crazy. He's a nice youngster who just doesn't

care about military secrets. And if you think, Ulysses, that this trick
with Ajax . . .

*(At this moment a dead eagle falls from above down on the stage between ACHIL-
LES and PATROCLUS. PATROCLUS starts to take it but ACHILLES snatches it and
turns it over carefully in his hands.)*

ACHILLES: No arrow in it. Just dead. *(Passes it over the barbed wire to ULYS-
SES.)* Look at it. *(ULYSSES looks at it.)* You can't say *that* doesn't mean
something. I wish I could be sure who he really was and what he
wanted.

(Curtain.)

ACT II, Scene 3

> *The next day. CALCHAS's tent. The walls are lined with books. There
> are a number of bad plaster reproductions of statues of the gods
> and a stuffed owl. CALCHAS's costume looks a little like that of an
> English clergyman. He is seated at his desk as ACHILLES enters from
> stage right.*

ACHILLES: Are you busy, sir? *(CALCHAS puts down his book and looks up.)* I'm
Achilles. I want to ask your advice about something.
CALCHAS: There's no need to be so formal, son. Call me Calchas. So
you're Achilles? Sit down on that chair over there.
ACHILLES: You're sure you're not busy?
CALCHAS: What would I be busy with? I'm delighted to have someone
come and *ask* me for advice. Most of you people come to tell me what
I should be saying.
ACHILLES: I'm not a very religious person.
CALCHAS: No.
ACHILLES *(not wanting to beat around the bush any longer)*: I've been told
that the gods will stop me from leaving the war. Would they stop me?
I mean if I decided to stop being a hero . . .

CALCHAS: A hero's conscience would stop him from not being a hero even before the gods could. An apple can't suddenly decide to be an olive, and a hero can't suddenly decide to be an ordinary human being. You want to leave the war?

ACHILLES: I have a perfect right to leave the war. Agamemnon refuses to give back Breiseis and I have a perfect right to leave the war to save my honor.

CALCHAS: Then what are you worried about?

ACHILLES: You've heard what Ulysses is like. He doesn't want me to go. First he maneuvered a delay of a week to find a compromise and now he's arranged it so Ajax has gotten a drawn from Hector in a fixed fight.

CALCHAS: What does *that* have to do with whether you leave the war?

ACHILLES: I don't know whether I'm allowed to leave until I save my reputation. Hector and I have never fought, you know.

CALCHAS: If that's all, you don't have anything to worry about. You would be even more of a hero if you left the war to save your honor when you knew that leaving it would hurt your reputation.

ACHILLES: Yes, but would the gods see it that way?

CALCHAS: Of course they would. The only thing the gods are concerned with is seeing that people behave according to their natures—that apples don't try to become olives.

ACHILLES: Are you sure that's all?

CALCHAS: You Greeks are so damnably superstitious. You can't seem to understand that the gods behave rationally and according to the laws of the universe. Ajax is nothing to worry about. On the other hand you'd better be sure that your Breiseis isn't merely an excuse for not fighting. If you leave before every real hope of compromise is exhausted, you will be violating your nature and the gods won't like it.

ACHILLES *(angrily)*: Ulysses put you up to saying that.

CALCHAS: Calm yourself, son. Nobody put me up to anything. It's up to you to decide when hope for a compromise is exhausted, not up to Ulysses.

ACHILLES: And how do I decide that?

CALCHAS: By using your mind and your conscience.

ACHILLES: In other words, anything I want to do is all right?

CALCHAS: No, anything that you are able to do. *(He rises to show that the interview is over.)*

ACHILLES: There's one more thing. *(Embarrassed.)* How does one go about making a sacrifice to Hades?

CALCHAS *(angrily, but as if he has said this many times before)*: Listen, I cannot communicate with the dead and I wouldn't if I could. *(CALCHAS had been about to sit down but he rises again during this speech.)*

ACHILLES: Oh, I don't want anything like that. It's just that something strange happened yesterday and I—well, it doesn't ever hurt to sacrifice to a god. They all like being worshipped, don't they?

CALCHAS: Hades is the god of the dead. He makes laws for the dead and is worshipped by the dead. He doesn't have anything to do with you. *(He sits again less angry.)* You see there are some parts of our religion that don't fit very well into the modern world. They belong to old customs and old superstitions. Men wanted to have a god for everything then—even for things that humans shouldn't bother with. I don't mean that Hades doesn't exist—but it's perfectly foolish to sacrifice to him.

ACHILLES: But it wouldn't hurt.

CALCHAS: It might hurt. It might be the first step to something worse. Look, do you know why I got so angry? Just three years ago in Troy I was asked that same question. Three kids, they couldn't have been more than fourteen or fifteen, had beaten up an old man on the street, almost killed him. And they didn't have any reason for it. They didn't rob him; they didn't even know him. They all came from good families and one of them—well, he came from a very good family. It was that one who had gotten the other two to do it—the one from the very good family—and so the authorities sent him to me. Before I could say anything to him he asked me how he could sacrifice to Hades, the same question you asked.

ACHILLES: Did he tell you why they had beaten up the old man?

CALCHAS: He said that they wanted to do an unselfish action. An unselfish

277

action! He kept pretending that I sympathized with his motives, that I wanted to compliment him.

ACHILLES: Who was he?

CALCHAS: He has the same right to secrecy you do. Everyone who talks to me does. But that doesn't matter. The point I'm making is that a question like yours is a dangerous symptom. You should worship the gods of life, Achilles, and not pay attention to . . .

(At this point there is a knock on the door and ULYSSES *enters before* CALCHAS *can say anything.)*

ULYSSES: Are you busy, Calchas? *(Seeing* ACHILLES.*)* Oh!

ACHILLES: I was just leaving. *(Shaking hands with* CALCHAS.*)* Thank you, Calchas. I think I understand your story.

CALCHAS: Goodbye, son. *(*ACHILLES *exits. To* ULYSSES *in a hostile voice)*: What do you want?

ULYSSES: What sort of advice did you give him?

CALCHAS: Haven't you learned yet that you can't bully me?

ULYSSES: Sometimes I think that the Trojans sent you here. You come to us all full of talk about how we represent the right side and that the gods have told you that the Greeks will win the war. So then what do you do? You sit here playing the oracle, making damn sure that we won't win it.

CALCHAS: What do you want me to do? I've told you that I'm less certain now. I'm not sure that either side is the right one.

ULYSSES: But you sit here in our camp, eating our food.

CALCHAS: Send me back to Troy or have me killed as a spy. You don't have to feed me.

ULYSSES: You know you're safe there. We'd look like fools if we let you go or if we killed you.

CALCHAS: You didn't come here to bluster and make stale threats at me again. What did you come here for?

ULYSSES: To bribe you.

CALCHAS: Really!

ULYSSES: The Council wants to know why you've requested that they exchange Antenor for your daughter Cressida.

CALCHAS: You've come here representing the Council?

ULYSSES: Yes.

CALCHAS: Tell the Council that I made the reason perfectly clear in my note. It is wrong and unnatural for an unmarried daughter to be separated from her father.

ULYSSES: No. You don't understand. Why do you want us to exchange a valuable prisoner like Antenor for her? The Trojans would let her go if she asked. She has no military value.

CALCHAS: It's impossible.

ULYSSES: But why?

CALCHAS: She's under other people's influence.

ULYSSES: You mean you've asked her and she doesn't want to go?

CALCHAS: She's easily influenced. The Trojans have poisoned her mind against me. They've persuaded her that I'm a traitor.

ULYSSES: And you want us to force her to go?

CALCHAS: I wonder why I always feel dishonest when I talk to you. I'm not trying to force anyone to do anything. It's simply a matter of what's right. You know yourself that it's against all decency for an unmarried daughter to be separated from her father. Anything could happen to her in Troy. There's no one to take care of her there.

ULYSSES: You mean she's not old enough to be trusted?

CALCHAS: You know what I mean. I'm giving your side a chance to perform a simple act of justice and piety. Even if it cost you five prisoners it would be worth it.

ULYSSES: And we'll win the war by doing acts of piety?

CALCHAS: You've tried everything else.

ULYSSES: And you'll announce that we're going to win the war after we've performed this act of piety for you?

CALCHAS: I'll do nothing of the sort. Damn it, can't you get it through your head that I'm neither a liar or a fool. I'm not for sale.

ULYSSES: But the gods are?

CALCHAS: What do you mean?

ULYSSES: You seem to be saying that the gods can be bribed by simple acts of piety but that you can't. (CALCHAS *starts to say something.*) Oh, shut up! You'll get what you want. The Council has already voted it. Now you'll have both your conscience and your daughter to keep you company.

(ULYSSES *exits slamming the door.* CALCHAS, *alone on the stage, fidgets at his desk for a moment and then goes over to the plaster bust of Apollo and kneels before it in silent prayer. Curtain.*)

ACT II, Scene 4

> *The same evening. The top of one of the Trojan towers. Darkness and a little moonlight can be seen through the window-like openings. There is a pile of small rocks on the floor—evidently being used for some kind of repairs. The stage is empty as the curtain rises. A door from the stairs on stage right opens and* CRESSIDA *and* TROILUS *enter, a little out of breath. Behind them is a figure dressed in black wearing a black mask with holes only for the eyes.* TROILUS *and* CRESSIDA *do not see this figure during the scene and the figure in turn is never hostile or encouraging. Unless there is a stage direction to the contrary, it merely repeats their actions.*

CRESSIDA: All those stairs.

TROILUS: But look out there now. You can see the ocean glowing in the darkness. (*He takes her to the window.*)

CRESSIDA (*looking out*): And the Greek campfires.

TROILUS: And the moon. (*They are silent for a moment.*) Which of them do you want? I'll give you anything that's out there in the darkness.

CRESSIDA: The ocean.

TROILUS: With its cold waves rubbing against the shore, trying to include everything into itself, trying to make everything as black and cold as it is—and as beautiful.

CRESSIDA: The fires.

TROILUS: Which flicker and stop, then reappear again somewhere else at the edge of the distance. Always hungry too—eating everything they touch. Disappearing and reappearing again and again all through the night, all through our lives.

CRESSIDA: The moon.

TROILUS: The moon is death itself. The moon is where the ocean and the fires combine.

CRESSIDA: All of those for me.

TROILUS: All of them. I will give you everything in the world of darkness.

CRESSIDA: I think I see people walking around down there in the darkness.

TROILUS: Don't think about them. They are nothing—vague animal shapes that don't know how to die. Look out of the window again. There is only Cressida and Troilus and the ocean and the fire and the moon. (*CRESSIDA moves away from the window.*) What's the matter? I mean I hope you don't mind me talking this way.

CRESSIDA: It's just that it makes me feel afraid sometimes. Not of death —but because, well, because I can't feel the same way about you that you feel about me.

TROILUS: No two people ever do. I mean people love differently. I don't love you more than you love me. I love you differently. You don't measure love in bushels, you watch it in shapes. There's no question of more.

CRESSIDA: I can see you've thought a lot about this. It must have bothered you.

TROILUS: Is a lion more than an eagle?

CRESSIDA: Lions and eagles aren't lovers. I don't want to spoil things, Troilus, but sometimes I feel guilty that I can't love you enough. (*TROILUS starts to interrupt.*) Now don't start telling me about lions and eagles again. I've told you what I wanted to say. (*TROILUS has taken a rock and thrown it out of the window. CRESSIDA puts her arm around him.*) Yes, let's throw rocks.

(*They throw rocks out of the window in silence for a few moments.*)

TROILUS: Let's throw rocks at the moon. *(He throws a rock.)*

CRESSIDA: At my moon? *(She throws a rock.)*

TROILUS: Just look at your moon up there—how big and bare it is and fat enough to contain everything that has ever died.

CRESSIDA: And we're throwing rocks at it!

TROILUS: Call them honeycakes. Why we've discovered a whole new continent of the dead up there, a New Hades.

CRESSIDA: Where are the souls for it?

TROILUS *(throwing another rock)*: We'll find them. I'm loony Hades, lord of the moon dead, and you're my Persephone, my ravished bride.

CRESSIDA: Where was I kidnapped?

TROILUS: From the other side of the moon. We're the king and queen of the dead.

CRESSIDA: What will poor Hades do now we've taken over?

TROILUS: He can keep most of his dead. All that we'll ask for are those who have died in the moonlight. *(CRESSIDA has thrown several rocks at the moon again.)* Aim those honeycakes straight, Persephone!

CRESSIDA: If I'm to be Persephone, these had better be pomegranate seeds.

TROILUS: Isn't death wonderful!

(He takes her in his arms and they turn from the window kissing. The black figure, unobserved, kisses them both as the curtain falls.)

ACT III, Scene 1

> A few days later. CRESSIDA's apartment. Bedroom door is off at stage left. Front door at stage right. As curtain rises there is a heavy knocking at the front door and PANDARUS is calling "Troilus" from offstage. After a full minute the bedroom door opens and TROILUS comes out in a bathrobe, sleepy and puzzled, half-wondering whether he should open the door.

PANDARUS *(offstage)*: Troilus. It's me, Pandarus. *(TROILUS opens the door. PAN-DARUS enters, followed by AENEAS and PARIS.)* Troilus, you'd better sit down.

TROILUS *(sitting on the edge of a chair)*: What's the matter? Has father died?

PANDARUS: No. Look, they just told me. They kept this from you because there's nothing anyone can do about it. Cressida's been exchanged.

TROILUS *(looking involuntarily toward the bedroom)*: What?

PARIS: For Antenor. The Greeks offered the trade yesterday and father accepted it immediately. I couldn't stop him.

TROILUS: The old bastard. He probably cooked the whole thing up himself. Well, you can tell them she won't go.

AENEAS: I'm afraid she'll have to. Look, Troilus, none of us like this very much but there's nothing anyone can do about it. They'll be coming for her in a few minutes.

TROILUS: I'll be damned if they'll take her. Tell father to come and get her himself if he dares to. Tell him to bring a sword.

PARIS: Nobody's doing this out of spite, Troilus. Antenor's your brother too.

TROILUS: Tell me about it! You don't care how many brothers are killed for your woman.

PARIS *(gently)*: I knew you'd say that. Do you think I wanted to come here and tell you something like this? I did everything but fall down on my knees and plead with father.

AENEAS: There's just nothing that can be done.

TROILUS *(wildly angry, takes hold of AENEAS and tries to throw him out the door)*: Get out of here, you slimy hypocrite. Don't come back without a sword on.

(AENEAS does not resist but TROILUS is suddenly knocked down as if by an electric shock.)

PANDARUS *(runs over to TROILUS)*: Troilus! What did you do to him?

AENEAS: I'm afraid it's mother again. She must have thought I was being attacked. God, that means she's watching and enjoying this whole scene! *(TROILUS groggily starts to get up.)* Troilus, look, none of us wants this to happen. It's just one of those things.

PANDARUS: When Cressida sees Calchas she can convince him that she really wants to stay in Troy and get him to send her back and then we'll have both Antenor and Cressida. Isn't that right, Aeneas?

AENEAS: Maybe.

TROILUS (*starting toward the bedroom, the fight out of him*): Well, I guess I'd better tell Cressida.

PANDARUS (*embarrassed*): She knows.

TROILUS: She knows?

PARIS: We told her late yesterday afternoon. She didn't want to tell you and spoil your last evening together.

TROILUS: She knew.

PARIS: She felt as bad about it as you do, but she knew there just wasn't anything anyone could do about it. Don't worry, she'll be able to persuade Calchas to let her go back. He just doesn't understand.

(*The bedroom door opens and* CRESSIDA *comes out. She is fully dressed and has her make-up on.*)

CRESSIDA: You know now.

TROILUS: You knew.

CRESSIDA: I was afraid to tell you.

TROILUS (*formally*): Will you let me see her alone for a minute? (*PARIS, AENEAS, and* PANDARUS *all exit in silence.*) I always wondered how a person felt and what a person said at a time like this.

CRESSIDA: That's why I didn't tell you last night, Troilus.

TROILUS: One part of me wants to cry and one part of me wants to kill. Can't we do anything?

CRESSIDA: No.

TROILUS: Should I cry?

CRESSIDA: No.

TROILUS: My mind keeps swinging back and forth. Look, Cressida, you think that you can persuade your father to let you go back, don't you?

CRESSIDA: I don't know. I've told you how he is.

TROILUS: You can force him into it. Refuse to eat and all that. Make him cry.

CRESSIDA: Yes.

TROILUS: I'll write you letters every day. All you'll need is courage. I mean anyone can do anything if they have enough courage—everybody says that.

CRESSIDA: Yes.

TROILUS: You'll write me and tell me what's happening and I'll write and give you advice and courage.

CRESSIDA: Yes.

TROILUS: Everything I say sounds false and clumsy. I'm not even sure what I feel. Can't you cry?

CRESSIDA: I cried before I saw you last night.

TROILUS: You'll try to come back? I mean really—letting yourself believe that you can be strong enough to do it—all that?

CRESSIDA: Yes.

TROILUS: I'll help you. I'll write to you.

CRESSIDA (coming over and putting her arms around TROILUS): Oh, Troilus. (They kiss.) I'm not very good at making decisions. (They embrace for a moment. TROILUS breaks away.)

TROILUS (opening the door): All right. Come in and take her.

(AENEAS, PARIS, and PANDARUS enter followed by DIOMEDE.)

AENEAS (leading DIOMEDE over to CRESSIDA): Cressida, this is Diomede. He'll conduct you through our lines back to your father.

CRESSIDA (extending her hand): Hello.

DIOMEDE (smiling but slightly embarrassed): Hello.

AENEAS: I think you know Troilus.

TROILUS: We know each other.

DIOMEDE (to CRESSIDA): If you're ready, I think we'd better go.

CRESSIDA (going over to TROILUS and kissing him lightly): Goodbye, Troilus.

TROILUS (holding her head so he can see into her eyes): It won't be long. Just believe that. Goodbye. (Turns away so that he can't see CRESSIDA leave. All exit but TROILUS and PANDARUS.) Is she gone?

PANDARUS: These things happen.

TROILUS: Why? Why do they happen? Every time they happen they make love cheaper. Oh, I know, I shouldn't—. But even if she comes back tomorrow, I'll never feel safe again.

PANDARUS: You don't doubt her?

TROILUS: I don't doubt her, I doubt things that happen. This happened. Things like this are going to happen until the day both of us die.

PANDARUS: This can come out all right. All Cressida has to do . . .

TROILUS *(interrupting)*: That's not the point. Something else will happen as soon as this is fixed. Like mending a leaking boat. Oh, I know, it's amusing or touching or whatever you want—a callow youth discovering that things never work out. Old men know it and expect it, don't even talk about it. I know that.

PANDARUS: But . . .

TROILUS: Are we wrong? Are we wrong to be bitterly disappointed? You were young. Do you remember it? There's something inside you that tells you that there really is a land of heart's desire, that everything can come out in beauty. That there's a somewhere and a somehow that will repay all the disappointments and agonies of the present. And then the old men laugh when you find that you've had a liar planted in your heart, that there is no somewhere and somehow. Only the desire for them.

PANDARUS: I'm not laughing. I remember. But an old man has learned to compromise and look for partial solutions.

TROILUS: What are they? A man dies if he's given stone to eat when he's asked for bread, and the heart dies when it asks for beauty and is given —compromise.

PANDARUS: But the heart doesn't die. That's what old men can tell you. There's just enough bread mixed with the stone to keep the heart alive. That's why I've never been impressed by your talk about worshipping death. You're young and you're a war-child. The only death you've seen is death by violence. That's clean and only kills the heart —it doesn't starve it. It doesn't leave the heart locked alone in a prison cell, a cell that gets danker and slimier year by year, foul with its own excrement, stinking of unfulfilled desire.

TROILUS: Is that death too?

PANDARUS: It's the death most of us die. Your friend Hades didn't tell you about that kind of death.

TROILUS: Is it really so bad, Pandarus?

PANDARUS: No, not so bad. The human heart adjusts to anything. Year by year, the day you live merely seems less real, more like a dream —every new year less real than the years you remember. And the eyes begin to narrow in the darkness. You see less. If a man my age tried to live an hour with his eyes as open as yours are, he'd collapse like a man coming out into the open sun after years in the darkness.

TROILUS: Then this will go on for the rest of my life?

PANDARUS: It will. So you'd better learn to eat your mixture of stone and bread with the rest of the prisoners. *(Goes and gets glasses and a wine bottle.)* Have a drink and let's discuss our plans for getting back Cressida.

(Curtain.)

ACT III, Scene 2

> ZEUS *comes onto the stage dressed as before. He is carrying two large sacks.* THERSITES *is already on the stage curled up, asleep, with a wine bottle beside him.*

ZEUS *(to audience)*: I'll be with you in a minute. *(Walks over to* THERSITES *and shakes him.)* Wake up, Thersites.

THERSITES *(waking and looking at him)*: Get out of my dreams.

ZEUS: Don't be childish, Thersites. Anyone ought to be proud to have a god in his dreams. Come on, wake up, we're ready to talk to the audience. *(*THERSITES *gets up grumbling to himself and comes to the front of the stage with* ZEUS. ZEUS *faces the audience as if to make a formal speech.)* I think this is a good time to stop the action of this war for a while and comment on it. You're probably quite confused by what you've seen so far. It's this damned human time. Things go so fast for human beings that it's often hard to see what's happening if you let time go at their pace. It's already two weeks after the last scene ended. *(Turns to* THERSITES, *who scowls.)* This is Thersites. You've already met him. I've invited him to appear with me because he's such an amusing fellow and because no one would believe him if he told them about this and because Thersites used to be—No, I don't think I'll tell you what Thersites used to be.

THERSITES: I used to be what the rest of them are now. Don't pretend to be mysterious around me, you old fake.

ZEUS: Isn't he amusing? Well, I guess I'd better catch you up with the last two weeks of human time. I'll start with the touching love affair you've been watching. Troilus has been writing letters to Cressida every day and Cressida wrote him one last week in which she said that she was having a hard time persuading her father to let her go back and that she felt pretty discouraged. She was telling the truth too.

THERSITES: Telling what truth? She's been spending most of her time wiggling her ass at Diomede—and anyone else that would watch it.

ZEUS: But she hasn't slept with him yet. I think that's important. Anyway, to get to bigger things, the war has been relatively exciting. Ulysses decided a few days ago to execute his emergency plan—to let the Trojans through and let the Greeks be forced back to a new defensive line—this was supposed to frighten Agamemnon so much that he'd give back Breiseis to Achilles.

THERSITES: Defensive line my ass! Another few steps and the Greeks will be in the ocean.

ZEUS *(with dignity)*: I was about to tell them that. You see unfortunately Ulysses miscalculated and the Greeks weren't able to form that line and they've been driven back to a position around their ships. But, in the long run, it's worked out just as well. Achilles can't leave as long as the Greeks are in actual danger and he's wondering now if he shouldn't go back into the fighting for a while.

THERSITES: The stupid bastard doesn't even want to go home.

ZEUS: There may be something in that. Anyway, it's a kind of a half time in the action now and we have a chance to talk about motives without a lot of human beings fluttering around the stage and making us nervous. *(To THERSITES.)* Open the left-hand sack and bring out Achilles. We'll be impartial and do this in alphabetical order.

THERSITES *(goes to sack and after a moment's search brings out a doll almost a foot high which is the image of Achilles in face and costume. Handing it to ZEUS.)*: Here's your hero.

ZEUS: Not my hero exactly. Hasn't Achilles rather surprised you?

THERSITES: Human stupidity never surprises me.

ZEUS: I don't mean that. I mean how affected he was by Troilus's hints about the god of the dead. I had imagined that if any Greek understood Troilus it would be Diomede.

THERSITES: Maybe Achilles isn't so dumb. Maybe he guesses what you're cooking up.

ZEUS: I'm not cooking anything. I must admit though that I'm certainly glad that Calchas talked him out of that Hades nonsense. One Troilus is bad enough. *(Hands Achilles to THERSITES.)* Let's have Aeneas and Agamemnon next. There's not much to say about either of them.

THERSITES *(Gets dolls. Aeneas from right-hand bag, Agamemnon from left. Those from the Greek side, including Cressida, are always taken from the left-hand bag, the Trojans from the right. Brings them to ZEUS handing over Aeneas first.)*: You wouldn't think this one had a goddess for a mother.

ZEUS: He hasn't really had a chance so far. He hasn't had to make one decision yet. When he does then we'll see whether he has the blood of a goddess.

THERSITES *(handing over Agamemnon)*: And this one is just a wax-works dummy.

ZEUS: He still hasn't given back Breiseis. Not with his back to the wall. That takes a kind of courage.

THERSITES: A wax-works donkey then.

ZEUS: A leader of men. *(Puts the dolls on the ground next to Achilles.)* Cressida's next.

THERSITES *(gets Cressida)*: Here's Troilus's masturbation fantasy. Isn't she sweet?

ZEUS: She did seem to start out as an invention of Troilus, maybe even a fantasy. But she started to tell him something in the tower.

THERSITES: What could she tell him except that she's a whore and he's a double whore for inventing her. I suppose you want the next three now. *(Brings Hector, Menelaus, and Nestor out from the bags while ZEUS puts Cressida carefully down next to Achilles. THERSITES hands Hector to ZEUS.)* Here's another hero.

ZEUS: Well, I'll have to admit that he's been rather a bore and I can't conceive of his being anything but a bore. He'd work out better in one of Ulysses's poems.

THERSITES *(handing him Menelaus and Nestor)*: And these two.

ZEUS *(taking them and laying them down along with Hector)*: Well, you need people to fill out Councils. We've forgotten Calchas. What made me forget Calchas?

THERSITES: It was a good idea. *(Brings Calchas over.)* There he is, a metaphysical double-agent, the only man in the world with a square asshole.

ZEUS: We'll have to see. *(He playfully straightens Calchas's robes.)* He hasn't had a chance to make a choice yet.

THERSITES: Don't make me sick. Who did you ever give a chance to make a choice?

ZEUS: When people talk as much about conscience as Calchas does, I usually give them a chance to make a choice. By the way, we've forgotten Diomede too. Bring him over. *(ZEUS puts Calchas down away from both the Greek and Trojan dolls as THERSITES brings Diomede over and ZEUS stands waiting in silence as THERSITES hands Diomede over.)* Aren't you going to say something nasty about this one?

THERSITES: He knows what he is and he's not afraid to fight against the gods.

ZEUS: You admire that?

THERSITES: It's the least sickening thing a human being can do.

ZEUS *(dangling Diomede by one arm and looking at him)*: I wonder how Cressida will affect him. It would be ironic if *he* fell in love with her. A man who had the temerity to wound Aphrodite—.

THERSITES: She can't touch him. Aphrodite can't touch anyone who stands up and fights her. The people she picks on are the ones who talk against her, not the ones who fight against her.

ZEUS (*deliberately puts the Diomede doll in the Cressida doll's arms in a rather obscene position*): If—. Well, let's get on with this. Pandarus next.

THERSITES (*carrying Pandarus over*): You can do what you want with this one. He's the kind of man who listens at bedroom doorways.

ZEUS (*taking Pandarus*): I'm certainly angry with him at the moment. He told Troilus far too much. He'll spoil his own fun as well as mine if he isn't careful. (*Puts Pandarus down.*) Paris, Patroclus, and Priam now. God, there are a lot of P's in this war!

THERSITES (*brings all three over, straightens Paris's hair before handing him to* ZEUS): I rather like Paris. He at least knows that the war isn't about Helen.

ZEUS: He ought to. (*Points to Patroclus.*) That one knows it too.

THERSITES (*handing Patroclus over*): Oh, he thinks the war's a plot to keep him from sleeping with Achilles. He's single-minded, I'll give him that.

ZEUS (*putting Paris among the Trojan dolls and Patroclus next to Achilles*): I feel sorry for him. (*Taking Priam.*) Now Priam here . . .

THERSITES: Is the perfect person to be Troilus's father—incompetent, pigheaded, and hypocritical.

ZEUS: But he was a good king and a good father before the war started. It was the war that undid him. He's as much of a victim of it as any of his sons are. I don't know why I don't feel more sympathy for him.

THERSITES: Aren't you going to ask for Troilus now?

ZEUS: I suppose so. I wish I were sure how much he knows. (THERSITES *brings Troilus over to* ZEUS *who takes him in his hand and looks him over.*) Look at him. You wouldn't think I'd have trouble figuring him out, would you?

THERSITES: Love made him long-winded. That's why he puzzles you. I liked him better when he stammered.

ZEUS: Did love make him pretend to be Hades?

THERSITES: How do you know he was pretending?

ZEUS: He looks like he's listening. (*Hits the Troilus doll in the stomach brutally as it if were alive. Shakes it, then gives it to* THERSITES.) Oh, take him away. (THERSITES *puts Troilus down among the Trojans.*) Get Ulysses!

THERSITES *(bringing Ulysses):* Here's the last of them. An ex-poet. There's nothing worse than an ex-poet.

ZEUS: The thing that puzzles me about Ulysses is how he seems to love to play the fool. He doesn't let anybody take him seriously.

THERSITES: Troilus took him seriously.

ZEUS: Yes. I think Ulysses will never forgive Troilus for respecting him. *(Puts Ulysses down.)*

THERSITES: And for liking him.

ZEUS: It's a terrible thing to be liked by Troilus. *(Goes over and runs his feet over the empty sacks.)* Well, that's all of them. Any questions before we end this intermission?

THERSITES: Who was that figure in black that kept prancing around Troilus and Cressida in the tower?

ZEUS: What figure in black? I didn't see any figure in black. *(THERSITES walks away and lies down in the same place he was before.)* Come on, Thersites, help me put these things away.

THERSITES *(not moving):* Put them away for yourself. I'm going back into my own dreams.

(ZEUS is putting the dolls back in the sacks as the curtain falls.)

ACT III, Scene 3

> The evening of that day. HECTOR, TROILUS, and PANDARUS are standing in the darkness somewhere between the Trojan and Greek lines. TROILUS carries a torch.

HECTOR: I wish he'd come. I don't like this cloak and dagger stuff.

TROILUS: You didn't have to go with us.

HECTOR: I want to make it perfectly clear to Ulysses that this isn't an official Trojan action. We haven't any right to ask for Cressida's return and we aren't officially asking for it. This is merely an unofficial visit on your part to Calchas which Ulysses himself has arranged.

TROILUS: Don't rehearse your speech on me. I'm going to have to make a speech of my own soon. I wish he'd hurry. You don't think anything's gone wrong do you, Pandarus?

PANDARUS: He'll get you your interview.

TROILUS: You still don't want me to go, do you?

PANDARUS: I've told you what I think.

TROILUS: You think that I'll find out that Cressida doesn't want to come back.

PANDARUS: I didn't say that. I said that it's always a mistake to try to do something that someone else has to do.

TROILUS: Do you expect me to stay home and write letters? I know what I may find, Pandarus. I know.

PANDARUS: Things often work out better when you don't know. Do you hear somebody coming?

HECTOR: It's so damn dark you almost can hear anything. I heard a sound a minute ago that sounded like children crying. It's one of those nights when you're likely to hear anything.

TROILUS: I suppose it was the unburied dead calling out. It must have been a night like this when Orpheus was waiting to go down into Hades to get Eurydice, waiting for Hermes at the edge of a black cave with no moon in the sky behind him.

PANDARUS: Ulysses is a rather unpropitious Hermes.

HECTOR: And Orpheus didn't get Eurydice. I hope you aren't counting on this too hard, Troilus.

TROILUS: I'm not Orpheus. I'm Troilus. I don't have to sing for my supper.

PANDARUS: What are you going to say to Calchas?

TROILUS: I don't know. I don't think I'll have to decide. I mean the night is full of . . .

VOICE OFFSTAGE: Hey!

TROILUS: Here, Ulysses.

HECTOR: Let's hope it is Ulysses.

(ULYSSES *enters stage left carrying a torch.*)

ULYSSES (*calling*): Troilus! (*Sees them.*) Who are these people? (*Recognizes* HECTOR.) Hector? (*To* TROILUS.) They aren't coming with you?

HECTOR: No. I just came along to make sure you understood that this is in no sense an official Trojan mission.

ULYSSES: You don't have to worry. We understand. Who's this?

TROILUS: Pandarus. *(He waits for PANDARUS to say something but PANDARUS doesn't.)* He came along to say goodbye to me.

ULYSSES: You're not going that far. You two might as well wait here for him. This won't take long.

(TROILUS smiles nervously at HECTOR and then at PANDARUS. He gives the torch to PANDARUS and then he turns and follows ULYSSES.)

PANDARUS *(as TROILUS is about to leave the stage)*: Goodbye!

(Curtain.)

ACT III, Scene 4

> *A few minutes later. CALCHAS's tent, the front of which is the stage's fourth wall, is illuminated and CALCHAS is sitting there reading. It fills the middle of front stage. Above it on backstage is a platform with steps leading down to stage left. This cannot be seen in the darkness until ULYSSES enters on it carrying a torch. He swings the torch three times in the direction of stage left as if giving a signal. After this he turns.*

ULYSSES: This way, Troilus. *(TROILUS enters.)* We're almost there.

(There is a noise of running offstage and then CRESSIDA runs in closely followed by DIOMEDE. He catches her in the semi-darkness to the left of CALCHAS's tent. TROILUS, above them, sees this and starts to draw his sword.)

CRESSIDA *(quite happy about it)*: You caught me.

DIOMEDE: You didn't run very hard. I'll race you back now.

(TROILUS has looked at ULYSSES and then sheathed his sword.)

CRESSIDA: No, I'm out of breath. Let's rest here. *(She stretches out on the ground.)*

DIOMEDE: We're just outside your father's tent. He'll hear us.

CRESSIDA: He won't mind. *(DIOMEDE sits down and puts his arm around CRESSIDA. She whispers something in his ear.)*

TROILUS *(to ULYSSES)*: You knew I'd see this.

ULYSSES: You'd better be quiet. They'll hear you.

TROILUS: They won't hear me.

(DIOMEDE and CRESSIDA have been whispering during this.)

DIOMEDE *(aloud)*: You mean that fellow who pretends to be Hecate or something, the one you were with on the day I met you?

CRESSIDA *(softly)*: Yes. It's his ring. Take it. *(She takes it off.)*

DIOMEDE: It wouldn't fit me.

CRESSIDA: It fit him. He used to wear it on his little finger.

DIOMEDE: I don't like wearing somebody else's ring.

CRESSIDA: You ninny, take it! *(DIOMEDE embraces her instead.)*

TROILUS *(to ULYSSES)*: He doesn't want my ring.

ULYSSES: We'd better go now.

TROILUS: I'm going to watch this all the way.

(CRESSIDA in the course of the embrace has slipped the ring on DIOMEDES's finger. They break their clinch.)

CRESSIDA: You've got the ring now.

DIOMEDE: Have you got your breath back yet?

CRESSIDA *(breathing hard)*: Yes. Let's race back. *(He helps her up and they run off.)*

ULYSSES *(pulling at TROILUS's arm)*: Let's go. It's over.

TROILUS: It's not over. I've got to see Calchas.

ULYSSES: You want to see Calchas after that?

TROILUS: The evening isn't over. I still hear voices.

ULYSSES *(trying to block his way)*: Look, you're upset. I understand how you must feel but . . .

TROILUS (*grabbing his torch and pushing him out of the way*): Get out of my way—and I hope you dream of your woman tonight.

(*HE walks slowly across the ledge and down the stairs and then over to* CALCHAS's *tent.* CALCHAS *is still reading.* ULYSSES *exits.*)

TROILUS: Calchas!

CALCHAS (*surprised*): You're here?

TROILUS: I had an appointment.

CALCHAS: Yes, but—

TROILUS: You didn't expect me to keep it.

CALCHAS: No. You saw them, didn't you?

TROILUS: I saw them. I saw all you and Ulysses arranged for me to see. But what you don't understand is that I don't care what Cressida does with the Greeks . . .

CALCHAS: I don't think *you* understand.

TROILUS: Let me finish. What I want is my Trojan Cressida—I'd watch worse scenes than the one you staged for me to get *her* back. You thought you were being so clever arranging it so I'd see her being unfaithful. Unfaithful! Every single minute she's away from me she's unfaithful. Every second that we're not kissing each other, every instant that we're not laughing into each other's eyes she's unfaithful. Monstrously unfaithful. I don't care what she does outside of Troy, who she gives rings to or who she sleeps with. I want her back. I want my Trojan Cressida back.

CALCHAS: I was against this whole business.

TROILUS: I don't care who arranged for me to see them. It didn't work. Let her go back to Troy where I can love her.

CALCHAS: Would you like to know who arranged for you to see what you saw?

TROILUS: Ulysses, wasn't it? I trusted him. But I don't care.

CALCHAS: It was Cressida.

TROILUS: Cressida!

CALCHAS: She thought it would be easier for you if you hated her.

TROILUS: She wants me to hate her!

CALCHAS: Look, I didn't approve of her plan but you've got to understand what she was trying to do. She thought it would hurt you less this way than if she simply told you that she didn't want to come back. She wanted to kill your love.

TROILUS: Does she love Diomede that much?

CALCHAS: I don't think she loves Diomede. Certainly not as much as she says she used to love you. She just doesn't want to go back to being your Trojan Cressida. You never did understand her.

TROILUS: And she and Diomede played this scene for me.

CALCHAS: Diomede didn't know anything about it. She arranged for Ulysses to give a signal when you were coming and then did the rest by herself.

TROILUS: I went down into hell to rescue Eurydice and it turns out that Eurydice is the queen of hell.

CALCHAS: You'll forgive her in time.

TROILUS: Forgive her! You don't talk of forgiving Eurydice for dying.

CALCHAS: You take the old myths too literally, Troilus. The story of Orpheus and Eurydice is the story of the soul searching for divine wisdom, not the story of a young man who lost his girl-friend.

TROILUS: You have a chance to gloat over me now. It's good revenge for the past, isn't it?

CALCHAS: Maybe. I'm never certain of my own motives. But I'm still a priest of Apollo and, as a priest, I'm as ready to help you now as I was then.

TROILUS: To help me regain Eurydice? I don't think Apollo can shoot that far.

CALCHAS: To help you regain the true Eurydice, the thing my daughter was a copy of.

TROILUS: And Apollo owns the real Eurydice, the original Eurydice.

CALCHAS: He can help you find her inside yourself. He can help you find balance and pleasure.

TROILUS: Apollo, the god of balance, the juggler god. Come, brothers, let us worship the god of neither here nor there, the god who disappears before you touch him.

CALCHAS: You have locked your heart like a city.

TROILUS: Who taught me to lock my heart? Who built the walls around my city? You and the rest of your balance worshippers, your friends of Apollo. You gave me a war to play with when I was a child. You taught me how to build walls. Then you brought me Cressida and I moved the walls to make room for her—and so you took her away. Now my heart is empty and big like a deserted city and you tell me I've locked my gates. *(Pauses. Walks around the room.)* Cressida! Is she really lost?

CALCHAS: What you loved is never really lost.

TROILUS *(hesitates for a moment almost believing this, then)*: Orpheus goes down into hell to find Eurydice and finds a sermon. Shit on Apollo! I came here for Cressida, not for a plaster statue. *(He takes the statue of Apollo, which tonight is crowned with laurel, and throws it on the floor.)*

CALCHAS: It doesn't break.

TROILUS: Neither do I.

(He takes the torch and starts his long journey through the darkness as the curtain falls.)

ACT IV, Scene 1

> The next evening. The anteroom of a hospital tent behind the Greek lines. CRESSIDA and PATROCLUS are rolling bandages. A scream is heard from inside the hospital.

CRESSIDA: That must be the boy that was wounded through the stomach.

PATROCLUS: Or the one without legs. He may have discovered that he doesn't have legs anymore.

CRESSIDA: Do people get used to this?

PATROCLUS: Other people's pain? Yes. After a while you're angrier at the screamer than at the wound.

CRESSIDA: I never saw wounded men in Troy—not until they'd bandaged them up and given them wooden legs and stuff. They'd stopped screaming by then.

PATROCLUS: The Trojans must have a really professional hospital setup. I wish we did. We just use anybody for nurses that hasn't been fighting.

CRESSIDA: Achilles must hate doing this.

PATROCLUS: You stop hating it after a while. It's not really any more difficult than killing people. These people make more noise than the people you kill—but that's about all.

CRESSIDA: They look at you with the strangest eyes.

PATROCLUS: So do corpses. Do you remember the boy in the third bed on the left, the boy with the short-cut blond hair? The one with the long sword wound down his back?

CRESSIDA: Yes.

PATROCLUS: Ares, the Paphlagonian, his name is. That's a pretty funny name for a person dying in a hospital. Ares, the Paphlagonian, who was a beautiful boy of nineteen this afternoon and who will be an ageless corpse in anywhere between a day and a half an hour.

CRESSIDA: Did you know him?

PATROCLUS: No. The name just amused me. Ares, the Paphlagonian!

CRESSIDA: His god didn't seem to help him.

PATROCLUS: Ares? He's the least believable of all the gods. Imagine a god of war! War belongs to all the gods like a man's life does.

CRESSIDA: Or a man's death.

PATROCLUS: I don't know about that. Your friend Troi—. *(He stops in embarrassment.)*

CRESSIDA *(half amused)*: That's all right, Patroclus. I don't mind talking about him. I know that everybody knows what happened last night.

PATROCLUS: I was going to say that Troilus seems to think that death has a god of its own.

CRESSIDA *(ripping a bandage)*: I suppose you want to know why I did what I did to Troilus.

PATROCLUS: I didn't mean to bring up the subject. You don't have to talk about it. I can understand how you feel about Diomede.

CRESSIDA: Diomede was an excuse. I'm not in love with Diomede.

PATROCLUS: Well—.

CRESSIDA: I simply would rather be a Greek than a Trojan. That's all there is to it. But I couldn't tell Troilus that.

PATROCLUS: I don't think I understand what you mean.

CRESSIDA: Neither would Troilus. I simply would rather be a Greek than a Trojan. It hasn't anything to do with men or patriotism or anything else like that. It's more a matter of temperament.

PATROCLUS: And so you arranged the whole thing.

CRESSIDA: And so I arranged the whole thing. And do you know what Diomede and I did afterwards? We ran down to the water and sat there for an hour or so, watching the waves breaking in the darkness.

PATROCLUS: Achilles and I used to do that. Back in Greece that was. A long time ago. The water sounded different there.

CRESSIDA: I'd have thought that all oceans would sound the same — especially in the darkness.

PATROCLUS: Maybe they do. It was a long time ago. I remember once while we were lying there a big wave came and completely covered me without touching Achilles and Achilles jumped up, naked except for his sword, and ran into the dark ocean shouting curses at it. He thought Poseidon was trying to rape me. I'll never forget how the waves sounded that night and how black they were.

CRESSIDA: Troilus offered to give me the ocean once.

PATROCLUS: Did you accept it?

CRESSIDA: I forget. He offered me the moon and the campfires too. He doesn't know the ocean. He's not a Greek.

PATROCLUS: But the moon belongs to Troy.

CRESSIDA: Yes. He had a right to offer me that.

(ACHILLES *enters from hospital wearing a white nurse's coat which is covered with blood, as are his hands and face.*)

ACHILLES: They finally sent someone to relieve me.

PATROCLUS: You look like you've been bathing in blood.

ACHILLES: Dead men seem to have more blood than live men do. I've never looked this way after a battle.

(CRESSIDA pours some water in a basin.)

CRESSIDA: Here. You can use this to clean up.

ACHILLES *(sitting down)*: Not now. I'm too tired.

PATROCLUS: We were talking about watching the ocean at night.

ACHILLES: There's not much of an ocean here to watch. It doesn't go anywhere.

CRESSIDA: Is the Greek ocean so different?

ACHILLES: Different! Try watching the waves break on the edge of a Greek island some night. You'll see the difference.

CRESSIDA: What do they look like?

PATROCLUS: They look like someone who has been out on an impossibly long journey and has come home to die. They crash along the rocks like muscular old men.

CRESSIDA: The waves here die like butterflies.

ACHILLES: And at night, at Chios for example, you can stand on the rocks watching that black water and know that each dying wave connects with another wave and that with another all the way back beyond the Pillars of Hercules to where the ocean starts—and you wonder if there is any beginning.

PATROCLUS: Or any end to it.

ACHILLES: There's just the sound of the black water and the sudden whiteness of it as it hits the rocks. And we used to stand there alive on the little edge of it.

PATROCLUS: Achilles . . . *(at the same time)* CRESSIDA: Last night . . .

PATROCLUS: I'm sorry.

CRESSIDA: Last night when I watched the ocean I tried to think what it was. Diomede had his arm around me. I think he was asleep. The torch was burning, although it was low, and I could see the patterns the waves were making on the sand before they disappeared. I tried to think of it as Troilus would have, as another land of the dead out there beyond me, or, as you two did, as something black and limitless, or even as a woman—Diomede called it that before he went to sleep. But all I saw was an ocean with pieces breaking off from it in meaningless patterns, some coming close to our torch, some ending far away from it. Just a cold dark fact that no metaphor could make significant. It didn't even mean to be meaningless.

PATROCLUS: That must have been frightening to feel.

CRESSIDA: It was wonderful. I had nothing to do with the ocean and the ocean had nothing to do with me. There were no gods around to watch us.

PATROCLUS: Achilles and I will be leaving soon. Why don't you come along with us and see a real ocean?

ACHILLES: I'm afraid we won't be going.

PATROCLUS: What!

ACHILLES: Agamemnon has finally changed his mind. He's giving back Breiseis.

PATROCLUS: He couldn't.

ACHILLES: It was at the staff meeting today. He made a big speech about how each of us would have to make personal sacrifices to keep the Trojans from driving us into the sea. I yawned. Then he said, "To start with, I'm giving Breiseis back to Achilles." Everybody looked surprised and began to applaud.

PATROCLUS: With Ulysses leading the applause.

ACHILLES: It was his idea, of course. So I won't be going home.

CRESSIDA (after a silence): Who's Breiseis?

ACHILLES: That's what I almost asked Agamemnon. She was my excuse for not fighting. There's nothing I can do, Patroclus. Nothing.

PATROCLUS: You don't seem to care very much.

ACHILLES: What good would it do me to care? I'm a hero.

PATROCLUS: So it all begins again?

ACHILLES: It begins again.

PATROCLUS: What about me?

ACHILLES: You don't have to stay. You could go tomorrow and no one would blame you.

PATROCLUS: You could leave too. They wouldn't put up guards to stop you.

ACHILLES: A man can't violate his nature. I think I'm supposed to die here.

PATROCLUS: And I'm supposed to rot here waiting for you to leave.

ACHILLES: You don't have to stay.

PATROCLUS: I don't think I will. I'd like to see a city again. A real city. I'd like to see olive trees and wine shops and dogs in the street. I'd like to see ugly philosophers arguing with pretty boys in the square, and hear nightingales at night, and see a Greek ocean. I'm bored with blood and dirt and heroes.

ACHILLES: Then go! Then see them!

PATROCLUS: I don't know. Achilles, do you think there's any hope?

ACHILLES: Of what?

PATROCLUS: That the war will end. That either side will win.

ACHILLES: Frankly, no.

PATROCLUS: What makes me so unhappy is that you don't seem to care. Oh, I know, I know. Don't tell me again. You're a hero.

ACHILLES: I won't tell you again.

PATROCLUS: I'm going to take a walk. *(Almost runs out as he exits.)*

CRESSIDA *(after a long silence)*: He loves you very much, doesn't he?

ACHILLES: He did. I'm just a habit with him now.

CRESSIDA *(after another pause)*: Let me wash the blood off your face.

(She dips a rag in the basin and starts to wash ACHILLES's face. There is a scream from the hospital. He pulls her to him and they kiss. Curtain.)

ACT IV, Scene 2

> *An hour later. A dark part of the battlefield. PATROCLUS is stretched out on the ground facing the audience. He has been crying. TROILUS enters unobserved from the left in battle-gear. PATROCLUS is in casual clothes and has no sword.*

TROILUS: Patroclus!

PATROCLUS: Who's that? *(Raising up.)* Oh, it's you, Troilus. What on earth are you doing here?

TROILUS: I've come to kill you.

PATROCLUS (*annoyed*): Don't you Trojans get enough fighting in the day-time? Wait a few more hours and someone will fight you. (*TROILUS keeps advancing with drawn sword.*) Damn it, didn't you hear me? I'm not carrying a sword and I wouldn't feel like fighting even if I were.

TROILUS: I didn't say I wanted to fight you. I said that I was going to kill you.

PATROCLUS (*not taking this seriously*): Oh well, as long as there's no fighting involved. Sit down and tell me about it.

TROILUS (*sitting down*): I don't care much for fighting any more myself. I hid among the rocks up there all day today and watched the fighting. It looks pretty silly when you watch it.

PATROCLUS: You didn't go back to Troy last night after—. (*Pauses.*)

TROILUS: After seeing Cressida? No, I've been right here all the time.

PATROCLUS: I know how you feel, Troilus. Something like that happened once to me too. I was never able to forget it.

TROILUS: Cressida? I'm not thinking about her. That was all a trick.

PATROCLUS: You mean last night?

TROILUS: Oh, no. Last night was real. I mean my falling in love with her. Not a trick anyone *played* on me exactly, although I guess Aphrodite would take credit for it if you asked her—that is, if you're on speaking terms with her.

PATROCLUS: I'm not at the moment.

TROILUS: I never was. I hope you understand that I'm not going to kill you because of Cressida or anything like that. I mean it's not because you're a Greek or an enemy of Troy and so forth.

PATROCLUS (*still not taking him seriously*): You're the Lord of the Dead come to receive my soul.

TROILUS: I don't believe in him anymore.

PATROCLUS: Neither do I. I only believe in Ares, the Paphlagonian, and the sheer bitchyness of life.

TROILUS: Who?

PATROCLUS: Ares, the Paphlagonian. You don't know about him, but you know about the other.

TROILUS: That's why I'm going to end it.

PATROCLUS: No thanks. If I want to end my life, I'll do it for myself.

TROILUS: I don't mean just your life. I mean all of this. Everything. The war, the ocean, and the moon.

PATROCLUS: Do you think I'm responsible for the war, the ocean, and the moon? *(He has moved over next to* TROILUS *and puts his hand on his shoulder.)*

TROILUS: It isn't that at all. Killing you will be a trick—like what happened to me and Cressida. We humans get tricks played on us, but suppose we started playing tricks ourselves?

PATROCLUS *(moving still closer to* TROILUS*)*: And you want to kill me as a trick?

TROILUS: Yes, I want to kill you as a trick. I remember when I first killed something. It was an ant. I stepped on it and waited for something to happen.

PATROCLUS: And nothing happened.

TROILUS: No. Nothing happened when I killed an ant.

PATROCLUS: What will happen to me when you kill me?

TROILUS: I don't know. I don't think the gods know. I think that hell is just a place that things get lost in.

PATROCLUS *(still half-amorous)*: And you don't care?

TROILUS: Of course I don't care. If I cared, it wouldn't work.

PATROCLUS *(stands up, angry now)*: You war-people make me sick. Everybody says that war-people are practical. Practical! You're all a bunch of metaphysicians, crazier than the old men who lecture in the parks in Athens. Ulysses who wants a perfect war, Achilles who thinks that there's some ultimate reason he has to behave like a hero, and now you, who think you can solve all the problems men have struggled with through a hundred stupid centuries by a single act of violence. Don't you know anything about history? Don't you know there have been other Troiluses?

TROILUS: I hate history.

PATROCLUS: You mean the war that educated you hates history—the metaphysicians who taught you how to invent lies of your own, the fathers who enjoy teaching their sons how to kill them.

TROILUS: I know enough not to make that mistake. I'm killing you and not my father.

PATROCLUS: You're not killing anybody. You're going to do something sensible for a change. Look, Troilus, there are empty boats in the harbor. We could get onto one of them tonight and sail out of this whole damn war. *That* would be a trick on the gods. *That* would annoy them.

TROILUS: Where would we go?

PATROCLUS: Everywhere. I could show you the monuments men have built against the gods, towers centuries old that still raise a finger against death, huge statues, wild songs, all of them saying the same thing about life that you're trying to say.

TROILUS: I'm not trying to *say* anything.

PATROCLUS: We could travel through every land of the earth, sail on every ocean. India, Africa, even . . .

(TROILUS, *who has taken up his sword unnoticed by* PATROCLUS *or the audience, comes behind* PATROCLUS *and stabs him in the back with it.* PATROCLUS *dies looking surprised.*)

TROILUS (*looking around*): *Now* something ought to happen.

(*Curtain.*)

ACT IV, Scene 3

> The next day. The body of PATROCLUS has just been burned in a funeral pyre. A crowd of Greeks is gathered around the remains of the fire at the back of the stage and CALCHAS is standing on a raised platform about to pour wine on the ashes and make a funeral speech. ULYSSES, ACHILLES, and THERSITES are standing at the front of the stage completely separated from the crowd.

ULYSSES: I tell you he was murdered. You know he wasn't carrying a sword last night—and the wound was in his back.

ACHILLES (*hysterical*): What difference does it make? You tell me it was Troilus. All right, I'll kill Troilus, and Hector, and any other Trojan I can find to kill. Isn't that enough? Why do you want to keep telling me how he died? You've wanted me to kill Trojans and now I'm going to kill Trojans. Why aren't you satisfied?

ULYSSES: Because everybody is pretending it was a fair fight, that it wasn't murder. They're trying to fool us.

THERSITES: A poet never wants to let anyone else be a liar.

ULYSSES: Why are they lying, then? Just tell me why. You know there wasn't another sword.

ACHILLES: I suppose they're trying to protect his memory.

THERSITES: They don't care anything about his memory. They're trying to protect his world.

ULYSSES: His world? What on earth are you babbling about, Thersites? You're behaving as strangely as the rest of them.

ACHILLES: Thersites loved Patroclus too.

THERSITES: I liked him better than I liked any of the rest of you idiots. He was never fooled by the little-boy nonsense the rest of you go around playing at. He was only fooled by his genitals.

ACHILLES: I still can't believe that he's dead. Even with that pile of ashes out there.

ULYSSES: But why . . .

THERSITES: Shut up, poet. Calchas is about to make his speech.

(CALCHAS *on the platform takes a jar of wine and pours it on the still-smoldering ashes. Steam rises.*)

CALCHAS: May the gods rest the weary spirit of this warrior. May his spirit rest as these ashes rest now the fire is departed. As these ashes mingle with the clay of the earth and become a source of new life, so may his spirit mingle with the countless spirits of those that died before him. May it become a source of new life. May his name, which is now cast out upon history, so mingle with the names of other heroes. May it become a source of new life. May his memory remain in the memories of those who knew him as these ashes remain in the ground they were burned on. May it become a source of new life.

THERSITES: It looks like Patroclus is going to fertilize everything.

CALCHAS: The wine has now put out the last fire in his ashes. It is all over for Patroclus as a human. Even though most of us still really do not believe it, we shall never see him again. Never see him again. Never. Never—that is the hardest word for a human being to say. It is a word that the gods teach us. Never. Now there are only symbols left—the tired ashes representing his flesh, the fading steam representing his spirit, the dirty wine representing his blood.

ULYSSES (yelling): And who spilled that blood?

CALCHAS (ignoring the heckling): That is the flesh, spirit, and the blood. Symbols, mere symbols. But is that all of it? Not all of it. The elements that composed Patroclus have not died—they grow, they flower, all of them, separately and in different places. The flesh, which yesterday rode joyfully on his bones and made men look at him and his beauty, is already becoming seed in the warm earth, is already beginning to feed new beauty from its undiminished substance. The spirit, the spirit of a brave and beautiful boy, has already merged with the air, merged with the spirits of the dead, the beautiful spirits, the brave spirits—merged with them and in them, sometime, either in the future or in the past, to become a part of a new god—for gods, when they are created, are created only out of the spirits of the beautiful. And the blood—the blood is already beginning to flower into a legend, a riddle, a symbol of a new Patroclus who died in combat . . .

ULYSSES (yelling): Who was murdered at night.

CALCHAS: . . . at the hands of a mighty Trojan warrior . . .

ULYSSES (yelling): At the hands of a madman.

CALCHAS: . . . in defense of his comrades . . .

ULYSSES (yelling): Pointlessly.

CALCHAS (to ULYSSES): If you can't behave yourself, you'd better leave the funeral.

THERSITES (to ULYSSES): Keep it up. You're ripping the fabric.

CALCHAS: And so we, the living, whose flesh, spirit, and blood are still indivisibly chained together, say a last goodbye to this shining boy whose sources are now free. The fleshly Patroclus was slain gloriously . . .

ULYSSES (even louder): He was murdered like a sheep!

CALCHAS: Ulysses, calm yourself. What you are saying is nonsense and the gods do not allow nonsense.

ULYSSES: You're afraid Achilles will kill Troilus.

CALCHAS: I expect him to kill Troilus. I expect him to kill Troilus and Hector and a thousand other Trojans until the wrath of Achilles becomes so terrible that it will be remembered longer than this death. *(CALCHAS exits and crowd follows.)*

THERSITES: Calchas is a good tailor.

ULYSSES: Why are they all lying?

ACHILLES: I don't see why you care so much, Ulysses. Calchas is right. I'll be killing Troilus and Hector and anyone else I can find just as soon as I'm able to cry. That's what you always wanted, wasn't it?

ULYSSES: I want things to be real.

ACHILLES: Just as soon as I'm able to cry. *(Walks over toward the ashes.)*

THERSITES: Let's go. The poor booby will be crying in a minute.

(Curtain.)

ACT IV, Scene 4

> *A few hours later. An empty stretch of battlefield.* TROILUS, *very disheveled, is kneeling in the center of the stage praying.*

TROILUS: Zeus, father, god of all gods, lord of the living and the dead. *(Repeats this like one would repeat hail-Marys for a minute.* ACHILLES *comes in from stage right looking wild and carrying a bloody sword. He walks toward* TROILUS *who sees him but pays no attention—merely going on with his prayer.)*

ACHILLES *(walking with sword advanced)*: I've finally found you. *(TROILUS pays no attention.* ACHILLES *stands over him now.)* Troilus, I'm going to kill you.

TROILUS: Go away.

ACHILLES: I've killed five Trojans in the last hour and I'm going to kill more, but you're the one I really want to kill. *(TROILUS goes on praying, moving his lips silently.)* You killed Patroclus, didn't you?

TROILUS (*as if annoyed by the interruption*): Yes.

ACHILLES: You murdered him in cold blood. (*TROILUS is silent.*) Didn't you?

TROILUS (*annoyed as before*): Yes.

ACHILLES (*holding sword over him*): I'm going to cut your heart out.

TROILUS: Go away.

ACHILLES (*stands indecisively with sword*): Are you praying for forgiveness? (*TROILUS is silent.*) Are you?

TROILUS: I've done nothing that has to be forgiven. Don't bother me. Go away.

(*ACHILLES starts to wield the sword in earnest this time but suddenly changes his mind and plunges the sword into the ground and kneels down next to TROILUS.*)

ACHILLES: I'll pray with you.

TROILUS: Go away.

(*ACHILLES stays on his knees for almost a minute while TROILUS, ignoring him, moves his lips in prayer, then he hesitantly gets up and walks off the stage, looking back at TROILUS all the while.*)

TROILUS (*repeats the prayer formula out loud for a minute after ACHILLES's exit, then raises his head toward the sky*): Zeus, father, god of gods, lord of the living and the dead, let me see you in any of your disguises. I have torn away my own heart from my eyes so that I can see you. Take any shape. Become a cloud, a bird, or even death itself and I will see you. Become my eyes, my blood, or even my own heart that I have torn away and I will see you. I hold you in my hand. I love you. I love you. (*He waits in silence and then begins again.*) Zeus, father, god of gods, lord of the living and the dead, you are everything that I have loved and everything that I have hated. You are the body of Cressida and you are the hypocrisy of my father. You are the peace that I have never known and you are the war that has twisted my manhood. You are the beauty of desire and the anger of death. I love you. I love you. I love you. (*Waits again.*) Zeus, father, god of gods, lord of the living and the dead, I am going to wait here until I see you. Even if you appear as empty space, even if you appear as a lack, as a nothingness, I am going to wait here until I see you. I love you. I love you. I love you.

(As TROILUS is saying this, ZEUS comes in from stage left.)

ZEUS: I wish you could sing like Orpheus did. I'd have come sooner if you had.

TROILUS: I'm not asking for the same thing Orpheus asked for.

ZEUS *(wearily)*: What are you asking for?

TROILUS: To learn how to see you.

ZEUS: You're seeing me, aren't you?

TROILUS: I want to learn how to see you always, whatever I'm looking at.

ZEUS: Why do you want that?

TROILUS: Because you're Zeus and I love you.

ZEUS: I suppose you want to learn how to see me after death.

TROILUS: I'm not interested in death anymore. I suppose I used to love death because it resembled you.

ZEUS: You also loved Cressida.

TROILUS: I needed someone to help me find you. I don't need anyone now.

ZEUS: Well, if you love me instead of Cressida, the solution is pretty simple. I could use another boy on Olympus. *(He comes up and puts his arm around TROILUS.)* Ganymede's a blond and I like variety.

TROILUS: You don't fool me with your disguises. *(ZEUS takes his arm away.)*

ZEUS: Or I could make you into a chain of stars.

TROILUS: I want to learn how to see you always.

ZEUS: There's no trick to it, nothing to learn. You see me if I'm there, just like anything else. If I'm not there, you don't see me. Of course, I could make you think that you see me—.

TROILUS: I want to learn how to see you.

ZEUS: I'm sorry. It's impossible.

TROILUS: Impossible? I can't see you.

ZEUS: Not more than you have. Humans have to live like humans.

TROILUS: There'll be nothing more than this?

ZEUS: I'm sorry Troilus. *(Pause.)* I'll tell you what. I'll let you have one wish. Anything else you want. You can have Cressida back.

TROILUS: I don't want Cressida back.

ZEUS: I'll bring Patroclus back to life. You and he could go on that trip.

TROILUS: I don't want him back.

ZEUS: Well, what do you want? This is your last chance.

TROILUS: If all this has to go on—Let the war end.

ZEUS: The war end? You're wasting a wish. It will only go on for a couple of years anyway.

TROILUS: I know how long your years are.

ZEUS: What do you mean?

TROILUS: Your years have centuries in them.

ZEUS: So you know about that too.

TROILUS: Yes. I know about it. I'm asking for my wish now. Let the war end.

ZEUS *(rises and pinches* TROILUS's *ear)*: I'll think about it. I really will. *(He looks around toward where the Greek camp would be and then toward the Trojan camp, then pats* TROILUS *on the back.)* You're a nice boy. You're a nice bunch of boys.

*(*TROILUS *stares blindly at him as* ZEUS *leaves the stage. Curtain.)*

San Francisco, June 25, 1955

NOTES TO THE POEMS

Abbreviations

CP	Jack Spicer, *My Vocabulary Did This To Me: The Collected Poetry of Jack Spicer*, ed. Peter Gizzi and Kevin Killian (Middletown, CT: Wesleyan University Press, 2008).
H	Jack Spicer, *The House that Jack Built: The Collected Lectures of Jack Spicer*, ed. and afterword Peter Gizzi (Middletown, CT: Wesleyan University Press, 1998).
JSP 71/135	"Jack Spicer Papers," BANC MSS 71/135, Bancroft Library, University of California–Berkeley.
JSP 2004	"Jack Spicer Papers," BANC MSS 2004/209, Bancroft Library, University of California–Berkeley.
ONS	Jack Spicer, *One Night Stand & Other Poems*, ed. and Preface Donald Allen. (San Francisco: Grey Fox Press, 1980).
P	Lewis Ellingham and Kevin Killian, *Poet, Be Like God: Jack Spicer and the San Francisco Renaissance* (Hanover, NH: Wesleyan University Press / University Press of New England, 1998).
PJS	Daniel Katz, *The Poetry of Jack Spicer* (Edinburgh: Edinburgh University Press, 2013).

Notes for Collected Poems 1945–1946

University of California–San Diego Library Special Collections MSS 397 used as copytext. As a Christmas present in 1946, Spicer typed out and bound by hand a "Collected Poems" for his creative writing teacher Josephine Miles, which he gave her with the note "Dear Jo, You taught me how to look for poetry. Here is part of your return. Love, Jack." As the book's colophon archly notes, it was "designed and executed by hand" and "strictly limited to 1 copy." That copy is now held by the Mandeville Library at UC–San Diego. We publish the entirety of the contents in their original sequence here, the courier typeface a gesture to our desire to present the project as such, and not just the poems that comprise it. The *Collected Poems 1945–1946* might also be seen as a crucial transitional text: while the timespan this collection delimits corresponds to Spicer's residence at UC–Berkeley up to that point, having transferred from the University of Redlands in 1945, as of 1947 Robert Duncan would supersede all other friends, peers, and teachers in importance, and Spicer's work over the first few months of that year points more directly to his mature writing than most of the *Collected Poems*. Still, he did not leave this little book behind: quite a few of the poems found here remained important to Spicer, and were significantly revised and in some cases, published elsewhere. "The Bridge Game" and "The Inheritance: Palm Sunday" fall into this group, and, not appearing in *CP* (as two others of these poems do), are published here in their variant forms separately; their corresponding notes are keyed to those printings. In our republication here we have tried to remain true to the spirit of the unique one-off, hand-made object, and have restricted editorial corrections and interventions to a very few instances, which are discussed in the notes.

"Within the world of little shapes and sounds . . ." This poem was originally a sonnet, completed by the following sestet, which can be found cancelled in two surviving typescripts:

> Within no orbit can the mind escape
> No syllable is safe from prophecy
> No forest-branches and no mango-tree
> Will offer refuge to this maddened ape
> For it will overtake us as we flee
> And will embrace us in sublunar rape.

All surviving manuscripts record "dreams" of line 6 in the singular, respecting a full rhyme with line 7. Spicer may have mistyped here.

"Among the coffee cups and soup tureens walked beauty . . ." *ONS* follows typed MS from JSP 2004, which features very minor variants.

The Chess Game *ONS* adds a penultimate line consisting only of the word "Amen" followed by a period and enclosed within the preceding quotation marks. This is found in two JSP 2004 typescripts, but is cancelled in pencil in one of them. *ONS* and both typescripts render "four-dimensioned" in line 13 as "four-dimensional."

Berkeley Spring Typescript drafts in JSP 2004 show the poem exactly as here, except preceded by these three lines:

I wish my legs were wild with the odor of oranges.

I wish my lungs breathed like a sackfull of rain-clouds.

Spring has jumped me from behind.

Palm Sunday See notes to "The Inheritance: Palm Sunday," which is on page 36.

To the Semanticists *ONS* publishes this version.

Chinoiserie *ONS* publishes this version.

"I saw a thunder-blossomed tree . . ." Manuscript evidence in JSP 2004 suggests that the "too" in line 10 might be Spicer's misprint for "to," as found in a typescript variant identical in every other respect.

Berkeley Summer Spicer would have found Berkeley significantly cooler than the Los Angeles where he grew up, and September is routinely warmer than July or August.

Berkeley in a Time of Plague *CP* includes a revised version of this poem identical in its wording but with minor changes to punctuation.

A Girl's Song *CP* includes this version.

"A green wind rose in cones and shook our town . . ." Spicer wrote various "green wind" poems in high school; the rhetoric of the "bruising sweet" wind seen here will reappear a few years later in "Psychoanalysis: An Elegy" (*CP*, 31–33).

"The unrejected bronze lies slowly in my hall . . ." Spicer's original has "montheism" for "monotheism" in the poem's last line; I take this to be a typographical error rather than the sort of orthographical idiosyncrasy Spicer increasingly adopts as he matures.

A New Testament *ONS* publishes a manuscript version identical in wording to this, with slightly different punctuation and what appears to be a printer's error omitting final quotation marks. Spicer prized this poem, and listed it for inclusion in his "Selected Poems" project of 1958. There and in other MSS, variants include "spiritual" for "promise of" in line 14, and a line 8 reading "And though it hurts it fits you pretty well."

"The long wind drives the rain around me now . . ." Spicer closes the volume with what was probably his most ambitious poem to date, and one that points forward to both "An Arcadia for Dick Brown," which he would write over the first half of 1947, and the first three "Imaginary Elegies," which began to emerge shortly thereafter. The earliest drafts of this poem give it the title "A Long Poem for Gene Wahl," which becomes "An Elemental Poem for Gene Wahl" in a fair-copy typescript, identical to the version printed here except for very minor variants, mostly of punctuation. Did Spicer remove the title so as not to out or embarrass Wahl? Wahl was Spicer's close friend from the University of Redlands, who transferred with Spicer to UC–Berkeley in 1945. Famous for his good looks, Wahl was an early lover of Robin Blaser and in fact the person through whom Blaser and Spicer first met. See Miriam Nichols, *A Literary Biography of Robin Blaser: Mechanic of Splendor* (Palgrave, 2019), 35–36; and Robin Blaser, *The Astonishment Tapes*, edited by Miriam Nichols (University of Alabama Press, 2015), 53–55, for more on Gene Wahl. The epigraph is from *The Colossus of Maroussi*. For a sense of Spicer's thoughts about Miller around this time, see his review of *Remember to Remember* of 1947 (*H*, 227–28). *Board of Equalization*: the California state body tasked with tax administration.

Notes for Early Poems: Los Angeles, Berkeley, Minneapolis, San Francisco

"We bring these slender cylinders of song . . ." *ONS* used as copytext, with the replacement of "taken" in line seven with "take," as this seems an obvious error. In his notes to *ONS*, Donald Allen specifies that the manuscript to this poem was given to him by Spicer's mother, after Spicer's death. I have not been able to locate this MS, or any other. *Geneva*: Might Spicer here be thinking not of the city but rather the alcoholic beverage?

"There is an inner nervousness in virgins . . ." JSP 2004 typescript used as copytext. In *ONS* Donald Allen explains that this poem was reconstructed from memory by Ariel Parkinson; almost perfectly, as subsequently uncovered manuscripts confirm.

Hospital Scenes I, II JSP 2004 typescript used as copytext. Probably written in 1946, these poems are on Spicer's 1947 list of his favorite poems.

An Arcadia for Dick Brown JSP 2004 typescript used as copytext. Spicer wrote this poem for his friend, the conscientious objector Dick Brown, in the spring of 1947, concurrently with Robert Duncan's work on the same theme, "An Ode for Dick Brown: Upon the Termination of His Parole: March 17, 1947." A major project for the young poet, it is one of the earliest works Spicer retained for his "Selected Poems" selection of 1957–58. He also included it in an April 11, 1957 reading at San Francisco State University. But the poem evolved significantly over the decade. Originally destined for an unrealized poetry anthology to be edited by Kenneth Rexroth, the 1947 version was first published by ARK Press in 1974. The most important difference in the early version is an entirely different concluding stanza, which reads:

> I rise like moon when sun has fallen—glow
> With vestiges of light caught from below
> Upon the waxen mountains where I lost my faun.
> I am false dawn, the poet-moon,
> God's vampire, the all-reflecting one
> Who sucks the blood of beauty from the sun.

In addition to minor variants, the version published in *ONS* contains the final stanza that replaced the 1947 version above and which is also found in both the "Pook-Up" and the "Selected Poems" manuscripts. The latter has been chosen as copytext, though subject to minor corrections based on variances with the 1957 reading, the "Pook-Up," and other draft material. Aside from rewriting the last stanza, the most important revisions Spicer made were to line breaks.

Mr. J. Josephson, on a Friday Afternoon JSP 2004 typescript used as copytext in preference to *ONS*, where it is published with minor differences. Also proposed to Rexroth for his anthology.

Ars Poetica *ONS* used as copytext. In several drafts, including in the "Selected Poems" MS, this poem is untitled; in one variant it's called "A Criticism of Dylan Thomas' Poetry." Spicer included an untitled version in the sheaf of poems for Rexroth in 1947.

"Come watch the love balloon . . ." *ONS* used as copytext. This poem was also sent to Rexroth in 1947, and in ARK's publication they present the exact same poem twice, the first iteration labelled "I" and the second "II." I have not been able to find a MS that confirms this rendering.

The Bridge Game *ONS* used as copytext, except for minor divergences in JSP 2004 typescript from "Selected Poems" MS, where the latter is followed.

"Hereafter . . ." JSP 2004 typescript used as copytext. This poem figures on Spicer's 1947 list of his favorite work.

"There is a road somewhere . . ." JSP 2004 typescript used as copytext. This poem, from 1946–1947, is on Spicer's 1947 list of his best poems.

Riddle No. 1, Riddle No. 2 JSP 2004 typescript used as copytext. These two poems always appear together on all fair-copy typescripts, of which there are several. Probably written in 1947.

"The avenues of flame, paved with what fires . . ." JSP 2004 typescript used as copytext. Probably written in 1947 though possibly earlier, Spicer included this on his 1947 list of his best work.

Eucalyptus Leaves JSP pencil holograph used as copytext. Probably sent to Duncan in the same 1947 letter containing "A pulse," see below; contextual evidence suggests that the poem dates from around that time or earlier. Published in the journal *Acts* 6 in 1987 with minor variations.

"A pulse, a quiet lengthening of breath . . ." JSP 2004 typescript used as copytext. This poem was sent in a letter to Robert Duncan in 1947, though possibly written earlier, and was published along with "Eucalyptus Leaves" (see preceding note) in *Acts* 6, with slightly different punctuation based on Duncan's typescript.

A Poem for Nine Hours JSP 2004 pencil holograph used as copytext. Found in a notebook containing work from the *Collected Poems for Josephine Miles*, this poem possibly dates to 1946. The MS contains a teacher's marginal comments, presumably those of Miles herself: "All good—it's just that *bells* is so standard now for a climax."

The screamless voice . . ." JSP 2004 pencil holograph used as copytext; from same notebook as above.

The Inheritance: Palm Sunday *Occident* (Spring 1954) used as copytext. A favorite of Spicer's from among his earliest work, the poem was included in the "Selected Poems" project, and also printed in *ONS*.

A Heron for Mrs. Altrocchi *ONS* used as copytext. The "Selected Poems" MS omits stanza breaks and has "voyagings" in place of "voyaging" in line 7, creating a full rhyme. On a handwritten list of poems from the early 1950s, with brief comments on some, Spicer says of this piece: "Waiting at the pinball machine aching for a trick."

Re A Poem for Josephine Miles JSP 2004 pencil holograph used as copytext. Probably written in 1946–47. Though no colon follows the first word of the title, presumably "Re" should be read as a contraction of "regarding." If this is true, the poem can be read as a comment on Spicer's own "To Josephine Miles," which also uses cosmological vocabulary.

Breakfast / Realestate / Busfare JSP 2004 typescript used as copytext. These titles correspond to the first three poems of Robert Duncan's sequence "Domestic Scenes," written in 1947 and bearing a dedication to Spicer in early printings. This gesture was important to Spicer; he mentions it in a 1959 letter to Duncan, in which he also laments a late revision in view of Duncan's forthcoming *Selected Poems*: "Domestic Scenes made me cry. 'Friend' was originally 'Jack' which is much stronger. Why not cut the dedication and go back to that." (JSP 2004). He appears to be referring to the section "Matches" which begins "Friend, friend" (see Robert Duncan, *The Collected Early Poems and Plays*, ed. Peter Quartermain (University of California Press, 2012), 174.

Orgy, Porgy, Pumpernickle, and Pie JSP 2004 pencil holograph used as copytext. Spicer is responding here to Mildred Edie Brady's article "The New Cult of Sex and Anarchy," which appeared in *Harper's* magazine's April 1947 issue, and dealt with artistic and social circles in which Spicer travelled. The biographical sketch of Mrs. Brady is in fact not Spicer's invention, but lifted verbatim from *Harper's*.

Wham, Bam, . . . JSP 2004 pencil holograph used as copytext. Probably written in 1947.

"We who have wept at the shrine of the bloodless Apollo . . ." JSP 2004 pencil holograph used as copytext. Probably written in 1947. A pencil holograph variant loose-leaf appears on the same page as the copytext for "The sea is a mirror . . ."

And every boy and girl has a lover . . . JSP 2004 pencil holograph used as copytext. This poem and the next are found together in fair copies on the same sheet of paper, numbered i and ii. This might have been only the first page of a longer sequence. Probably written in 1947.

"Capone in the springtime has . . ." JSP 2004 pencil holograph used as copytext. See preceding note.

"If I could hear some whisperings . . ." JSP 2004 pencil holograph used as copytext. Probably written in 1947. Spicer returns to the theme around eight years later in "Babel 3" (*CP*, 63).

"If autumn was a time for love . . ." JSP 2004 pencil holograph used as copytext. Probably written in 1947.

"This angry maze of bone and blood . . ." JSP 2004 pencil holograph used as copytext. Probably from 1948, and possibly fragmentary.

A Night in Four Parts (first version) ONS used as copytext. This is the first version of the poem, which was published in *Berkeley Miscellany* 1 (1948); ONS reprints this, differing only in details of editorial style, while a heavily revised "second" version also appears in both *ONS* and *CP*. The "L. E." of the dedication is the Berkeley Renaissance poet Landis Everson; see *P* for more on Spicer's infatuation with him.

"The sea is a mirror . . ." JSP 2004 pencil holograph used as copytext. There is no clear contextual data for dating this poem, but in its rhetoric, imagery, and concerns, there is pronounced dialogue with both "A Portrait of the Artist as a Young Landscape" and "A Lecture in Practical Aesthetics." It was probably written, then, in 1948, during the period when Spicer was working through the concept of the "microcosm" by way of a long graduate school paper on Donne (see *PJS*, 22–27). The poem's first line echoes W. H. Auden's play "The Sea and the Mirror," first published in 1944.

Nunc, In Pulvere Dormio JSP 2004 heavily revised pencil holograph used as copytext; untitled by Spicer. Spicer might have found the Latin tag in John Skelton, who also uses it as a refrain in his poem on the death of King Edward IV, which is included in *The Mirror for Magistrates*. Skelton himself seems to be working from the Book of Job, 7:21: "ecce nunc in pulvere dormiam et si mane me quaesieris non subsistam" ("And why dost thou not pardon my transgression, and take away mine iniquity? For now I shall sleep in the dust; and thou shalt seek me in the morning, but I shall not be"). Drafts indicate that Spicer contemplated a section titled *The Soldier* but if he ever undertook to write it, no fragments have been found.

"The world I felt this winter every hour . . ." *ONS* used as copytext, with very minor changes to punctuation based on manuscript evidence from JSP 2004.

"Look / The king is on the stage . . ." JSP 2004 pencil holograph used as copytext. Contextual evidence suggests this poem was written in Berkeley in the 1940s.

"This is June . . ." JSP 2004 pencil holograph used as copytext for this poem, probably written in 1947 or 1948. It's worth noting that all of the place names mentioned in lines eight and nine also refer to cities in the American south.

"Flesh fails like words . . ." JSP 2004 pencil holograph used as copytext. Poem from same notebook as above, and probably written around the same time. In some ways a variant of "We find the body difficult to speak . . ." (*CP*, 22), which dates from the same period.

"It was so cold a night . . ." JSP 2004 pencil holograph used as copytext. Impossible to date with precision, the poem seems to be from the late 1940s. The idea of nonsense as magic would return in 1956 as a guiding theme of the Oliver Charming project, and appears in correspondence with Graham Mackintosh in 1955.

At a Party *ONS* used as copytext. In *ONS* Allen notes that he "retained" the second stanza of the poem, which Spicer "deleted in 1956" (xxxv), as can be seen in the holograph MS in JSP 2004 that Allen used as copytext, where lines are drawn through that stanza. Spicer's excision is reaffirmed in the MSS for the "Pook-Up" and the "Selected Poems" which both reproduce only the first stanza, but I follow Allen here, probably against Spicer's wishes, so as not to remove the second stanza from the record.

Remembering You, I Leave the Music of the Inner Room JSP 2004 pencil holograph used as copytext. Contextual evidence suggests that this poem was written in 1948. In its deployment of dashes, the phrase "door ajar," and its wider concerns, the poem seems to reflect an engagement with Dickinson.

"The forward wept . . ." JSP pencil holograph used as copytext. As above, the poem probably dates from around 1948. Spicer also writes about baseball and sometimes football, but this might well be the only reference to basketball in his work.

On Falling Into Your Eyes JSP 2004 pencil holograph used as copytext. Probably written in 1948 or 1949.

Lost Ulysses JSP 2004 typescript used as copytext. Written in 1948.

The old moon is still rolling . . ." JSP 2004 pencil holograph used as copytext. Probably written in 1948 or 1949.

You are made out of porcelain and black ink . . ." JSP 2004 pencil holograph used as copytext. From same notebook as previous poem. Spicer's spelling of "chizeled" has been retained.

Songs From An Enormous Birdcage . . ." JSP 2004 pencil holograph used as copytext. From same notebook as two preceding poems. "The Farm" is a common nickname of Stanford University.

To a Certain Painter *ONS* used as copytext. This poem was not included in either the "Selected Poems" project or the letter to Donald Allen of 1958 with Spicer's long-list of potential contributions to the *New American Poetry* anthology. Early drafts are found in the notebook mentioned in the immediately preceding notes.

"I wonder where Orpheus has been . . ." JSP 2004 pencil holograph used as copytext; from the same notebook as preceding poems.

"We were talking . . ." JSP 2004 pencil holograph used as copytext. Probably from the late 1940s. See "Whenever I love" (page 59) for a variation on this theme, and a poem that also reuses some of the material in this one.

"The laughing lady greets you . . ." JSP 2004 pencil holograph used as copytext. This poem, probably dating from the late 1940s, appears to be a revised extension of a draft fragment titled "The Fun House":

> He said, "Don't enter here." I saw the doll
> Laugh with her long doll's laugh. Her paper lips
> Part with a kind of joyous agony. Again, again.
> He said, "Don't enter here. The place is sad.
> The whistles and the creaking never stops
> The laughing lady laughs all night."

"We are too tired to live like lions . . ." JSP 2004 pencil holograph used as copytext. The phrase "we are too tired to live like lions" was important to Spicer during the late 1940s. In a prose text from the same period, in part about Spicer's break-up with Kate Mulholland, the narrator learns the day after a drunken night out that "I wrote WE ARE TOO TIRED TO LIVE LIKE LIONS on the wall of the lavatory of the First Last Chance" (JSP 2004). The phrase also appears in this short, perhaps fragmentary poem, which probably dates to 1947:

> We are too tired to live like lions.
> We are tired animals
> And beauty is just outside
> With the terrible eyes of a parrot,
> With terrible eyes.
> (JSP 2004 pencil holograph, Box 22, folder 6)

This poem in turn seems to have inspired a short fragment found scribbled on the opposite page of the fair copy of "Any fool can get into an ocean . . ." (*CP*, 23), in the later notebook from which the final copytext reproduced here is taken (Box 23, folder 11). Most intriguingly, this same notebook also has a page with the heading "Elegy IV," followed by the first line, "We are too tired to live like lions" and then a brief succession of false starts and fragments. The long untitled poem that follows in the notebook a few pages later and is included here can therefore almost be thought of as a ghost elegy—a rejected first meditation on Elegy IV of the "Imaginary Elegies," which wouldn't be completed for another five years. That Elegy returns at its close to the "amusement pier" and "giant funhouse" (*CP*, 49) evoked in so much more detail here. "We are too tired to live like lions," with its perhaps too obvious conflation of a pastiche of Pound's *Cantos* and Rimbaud's "The Drunken Boat," is clearly a crucial undertaking of this period, with ramifications for Spicer for years to come. Around forty years later in a poem for Duncan, Robin Blaser recalls what Spicer recounted in his story at the time: "Jack writing the Italian underground *we / are too tired to live like lions* on john walls and gay bars" (Robin Blaser, *The Holy Forest: Collected Poems of Robin Blaser*, ed. Miriam Nichols (University of California Press, 2006), 335; Blaser's spacing). Elsewhere, Blaser links the phrase to the Italian Resistance, claiming it was their response to Mussolini's insistence "we must live like lions," and confirms Spicer's love of it as well as his predilection for pinning things on bathroom walls (see Nichols, 201). In addition, in an interview with Kevin Killian, JoAnne Low, who knew Spicer in the 1950s, recounts the following: "You know, one time Jack told me that he believed that he inadvertently started the use of the term 'Beat.' That because of him the term 'Beat' was used. And he told me that he had written a line in the men's john at Vesuvio: 'We are too tired to fight like lions.' Maybe he was spinning a tale, but I sort of believed him. He was always convincing to me." See *Openings in the Veil: JoAnne Low and Kevin Killian in Conversation*, https://openspace.sfmoma.org/2018/12/openings-in-the-veil-joann-low-and-kevin-killian-in-conversation/.

Whenever I love . . ." JSP 2004 pencil holograph used as copytext. This poem follows the page of false starts under the heading "Elegy IV" mentioned above, and reprises the questions and some of the lines of "We were talking . . ."

"The New Aeneas . . ." JSP 2004 pencil holograph used as copytext. Probably from 1948; from same notebook as cited in preceding note. In a personal communication to this editor, Kevin Killian suggested that "Aeneas" might here function as a sly reference to Anaïs Nin.

"At the sound of Apollo . . ." JSP pencil holograph used as copytext. This poem is found in the same notebook as the one cited in the preceding notes.

"You thought . . ." JSP 2004 pencil holograph used as copytext. There is no contextual data that allows this poem to be dated, but late 1940s or early '50s seems reasonable.

Dardenella JSP 2004 used as copytext. *ONS* published a version broken into three quatrains, in which the first eight lines are identical to the version included here aside from minor points of punctuation, but the last four lines read as follows:

Such crazy songs. I wonder what he dreams
When kissing's over and he sleeps alone.
If something sings a lullaby for him
Out of the ancient tears when he was young.

There is a pencil holograph manuscript in Donald Allen's papers at the Bancroft Library that follows the *ONS* reading, except that the final stanza above is cancelled in Spicer's hand and replaced with the lines as presented in this volume. Aside from minor variants, that text, without stanza breaks, is chosen for both the "Pook-Up" of 1956 and the subsequent "Selected Poems" manuscript, which is used here as copytext; this is also the version Spicer read at San Francisco State University on April 11, 1957. The poem occupied Spicer from 1949 through 1960, where it appears with stanza breaks reintroduced and a new concluding quatrain as "Chapter 4: Rimbaud" in *A Fake Novel About the Life of Arthur Rimbaud* (*CP*, 288). Among other notable variants are versions that only contain the first eight lines, and one that largely follows the *ONS* reading, but uses the feminine pronoun throughout. "Dardanella" is a jazz standard dating to 1919, with markedly Orientalist lyrics presumably deriving from an implicit reference to the Dardanelles. In all of his drafts Spicer opts for the apparently erroneous spelling of "Dardenella."

A Translation of George's Translation of "Spleen" from "Les Fleurs du Mal" (Die Blumen Des Bösen) JSP 2004 ink holograph fair copy used as copytext. Probably written in the 1940s, this translation of a translation foreshadows the *After Lorca* project, in which an unending chain of translations of translations becomes the explicit model of poetic creation. And there is another mediation at work here: Stefan George had been the master of one of Spicer's own during the 1940s—Ernst Kantorowicz, who in his youth had been an ardent member of George's "Kreis."

When Your Body Brushed Against Me . . ." *ONS* used as copytext. Under the title "Butterflies" (which none of the extant MSS carry) this is included in the prospective table of contents for the "Selected Poems."

Coffee-Time JSP 2004 typescript used as copytext. The probably dates from the late 1940s.

Lives of the Philosophers: Diogenes *ONS* used as copytext. The poem, which Spicer retained for his "Selected Poems" project, can usefully be read as a companion piece to "Orpheus in Athens" in *CP* (39–40).

The Trojan Wars Renewed: A Capitulation, or The Dunkiad Robin Blaser's compilation *The Collected Books of Jack Spicer* (Black Sparrow Books, 1980) used as copytext, subject to minor correction based on the JSP 2004 typescript. This mock-epic poem, in some ways a summation of Spicer's experiments of living within academia as an institution, is of considerable biographical and historical importance. The main subject was the UC–Berkeley English Department's decision in 1948 to close the "Writers Conference"—a student-led group in which Spicer, Robert Duncan, and Robin Blaser were all prominent. While opinions differ as to the relative weighting of issues in play, there is general agreement that the plan to publish a short story with explicit depictions of gay sex was a main precipitating cause. The gay writers also felt that generalized homophobia was a major factor, as reflected in the worry of "Helen" (more or less Josephine Miles) that the participants were "too Greek." This conflict with Miles pitted Spicer against a teacher with whom he was close, as well as against his friend Tom Parkinson, qualified as such in the poem and spared opprobrium on that basis (the friendship with Parkinson remained intact). Among the antagonists, most prominent was Mark Schorer, who apparently personally insulted Spicer at a meeting and was met with treatment in kind from him and Duncan. While Ekbert Faas argues that the Homeric characters are largely composites and defeat attempts at one-to-one attribution, it's known that Leonard Wolf attempted to play the role of mediator. Likewise, the description of Achilles as the "oldest Sophomore" encourages an identification with Duncan, then around thirty, as does the reference to "last year's masque"—a form Duncan was experimenting with at this time. While the final stanza could be read as implying that Ajax is Spicer himself, Robin Blaser identifies Schorer as the "Safeway bard," Miles as Helen, Tom Parkinson as Hector, and Leonard Wolf as Agamemnon (see *Astonishments*, 213). As a record of Spicer's feelings about UC–Berkeley, especially interesting is the original version of the penultimate stanza in the typescript Blaser used as copytext, cancelled and replaced in Spicer's hand with the final rendering. The earlier draft of this stanza read:

> The battle waxed and waned and leaped like fire.
> Then from a fabulous and distant land
> Called Santa Barbara, ultimatums dire
> Descended on the Greek and Trojan band.
> These princes asked for oaths from all on hand

They were not Amazon nor did conspire
With Amazons. We'd better stop the brawl
Trojan or Greek, this oath will get us all.

It's fascinating that Spicer ultimately chose *not* to close the poem on the note of a new unity established in face of the graver threat of the anti-communist loyalty oath, the measure that ultimately drove him from Berkeley in 1950. The original version's implicit opposition of the censorship of the Writers Conference to that imposed by the loyalty oath was abandoned, perhaps suggesting that Spicer came to see these two initiatives rather as of a piece. For more on the Writers Conference affair, see *P*, 24–25, and Faas, 274–78. In a letter to Robert Duncan written when Spicer was in Minnesota (probably dating to 1950), Spicer includes the new stanza, writing, "I looked over the Trojan War Satire the other day preparatory to sending it to Landis. I like it better now and can see its connection with the rest of my (and your) mythology. Its magic is awfully thinly spread but it's there. I wrote a new next to last stanza where I had had that unsatisfactory one about the oath" (Poetry Collection, University of Buffalo Libraries). The new penultimate stanza, with a reference to Shakespeare's *Troilus*, heralds Spicer's subsequent interest in that tale. *Epigraph*: See "Sometimes our feelings are so mild / they are like a day when rocks / seem mere extensions of the sea" from Duncan's "Heavenly City, Earthly City" (*Collected Early Poems*, 92). *Gayley*: Charles Mills Gayley, legendary former Chair of the UC–Berkeley English Department, who died in 1932. *Applejack*: distilled spirit derived from apples or cider.

The Panther - After Rilke Published in *ONS* as "The Panther." JSP 2004 preferred as copytext to *ONS*, which prints a version Spicer later revised in pencil holograph; these revisions were retained in the typed fair copy in the "Selected Poems" manuscript, which is used here.

All Hallows Eve JSP 2004 used as copytext. The copytext used in *ONS* consists of a typed MS in four stanzas, with significant pencil holograph revisions in Spicer's hand. These revisions are incorporated in two identical fair copies, one typed and one a pencil holograph, which remove the stanza breaks and carry additional small changes.

Midnight at Bareass Beach *ONS* used as copytext. An early draft of this poem titled "At Night at Bareass Beach" was far more explicit regarding nudity than the ultimate version, closing with these lines:

Stiff with a cold hard cock a boy
Runs through the water and I hear the sound
Of running back and forth across the beach
And I want to meet him on the edge

Turning the draft upside down reveals an additional stanza, of which the intended placement in the poem cannot be determined:

You whom I love and talk to in this room
As yet unknown however take my hand
Black with the washings of eternity
And we will lead each other to the sea

JSP 2004 and the Jack Spicer Papers, 1938–1973, in the Stuart A. Rose Manuscript, Archives, and Rare Book Library at Emory University contain several versions of a very stable text with almost no variants, save one that recurs in several places, including in papers from Allen's *ONS* collection: "His flesh" in place of "My flesh" in the poem's ultimate line. Allen chose the reading found in both the "Pook Up" and "Selected Poems" MSS, and I follow him here, while it seems possible that Spicer himself oscillated throughout.

"The audience was sad to see . . ." JSP 2004 pencil holograph used as copytext. The poem was probably written in 1952.

Christmas Eve: 1952 *ONS* used as copytext.

A Prayer for Pvt. Graham Mackintosh on Halloween *ONS* used as copytext. Graham Mackintosh was one of Spicer's students at the California School of Fine Arts in San Francisco in 1953, and he quickly became a close friend and love interest. In the autumn of 1954, Mackintosh, in military service, was stationed at Ford Ord, California, and at that point Spicer began a long and important correspondence with him, which was taken up and reworked a year later in Boston in the "Oliver Charming" project (see *PJS*, 84–85). This poem marks Halloween, 1954.

Epiloque in Another Language JSP 71/135 typescript used as copytext. Published as "Epilogue in Another Language" in *ONS*, that title does not agree with the typed MS used as copytext. Given the distance between /g/ and /q/ on the keyboard it's reasonable to assume this misspelling was intentional; moreover, not only does it conform to the distorted English throughout (foreign accents exist which would transform the velar stop as above), but additionally this shifts the phantom etymology in the direction of the Latin "loqui" from the Greek "logos." This is the sort of joke that Spicer, a trained linguist, unquestionably enjoyed. The *ONS* version appears to suffer from some mis-transcriptions, for example, "I" for "Is" in the penultimate line; a reading that occurs in neither extant MS, and which is not particularly legible within the poem's structure.

"These woods, so fit for emperors . . ." *ONS* used as copytext. No extant manuscript of this poem has been found; Allen's suggestion that it dates from 1955 seems plausible.

"As if a Chinese vase were filled with blood . . ." JSP 2004 pencil holograph used as copytext. From a notebook which contains drafts of the play *Troilus*, dating the poem to the first half of 1955.

IMAGINARY ELEGIES I–IV (**early version**) Transcription in Kevin Killian, "Under the Influence: Jack Spicer, Robin Blaser, and the Revision of 'Imaginary Elegies,' 1957," *Exact Change Yearbook*, no. 1 (1995) 133–40, used as copytext, subject to minor correction. When published in Donald Allen's *New American Poetry* anthology, "Imaginary Elegies I–IV" were listed with a composition date of 1950–1955, and indeed, Elegy IV harps on the five years separating it from the previous three. That said, the "Elegies" as published by Allen in both his anthology and *ONS*, and which also appear in Blaser's *Collected Books* and *CP*, did not arrive at their final version until summer or fall 1957, as Killian details in "Under the Influence." Moreover, their origins extend before the start date of 1950 too: a notebook in the Simon Fraser University archives contains a full holograph ink MS of the final versions of the four elegies, bearing the dateline "1947-1957." As late as April 1957, Spicer was publicly reading significantly different versions of the first four Elegies than those that were to appear subsequently, as can be heard on a recording from April 11, 1957, which is the basis of the early versions published here: https://diva.sfsu.edu/collections/poetrycenter/bundles/191198.

Notes for Manhattan and Boston: 1955–1956

Manhattan *ONS* used as copytext. The poem was sent on a postcard to Allen Joyce from New York on August 7, 1955, and was published untitled in *Sulfur* 10 (1982), 141. JSP 2004 contains a very similar notebook variant bearing the title "Hisperica Famina."

"White as southern blindness . . ." JSP 2004 pencil holograph used as copytext. From a notebook Spicer kept in Manhattan during the summer of 1955.

On August 28 of that year, fourteen-year-old Emmett Till was murdered in Mississippi by two brothers who would be acquitted by an all-white male jury the following month. There was national news coverage of the story, which remained vivid when the Montgomery bus boycott began in December. Could this inform the blindness Spicer evokes here?

"When the moon comes out . . ." JSP 2004 pencil holograph used as copytext. One page after "White as southern blindness . . ." in the Manhattan notebook.

Central Park West *ONS* used as copytext. Spicer included this poem in the "Selected Poems" MS.

"And no one is around to see my tears . . ." *ONS* used as copytext. This excision from or instigating fragment of "Central Park West" was sent in a letter to Allen Joyce in the summer of 1955, and was published in *Sulfur* 10, 140.

"Easy on squeezing . . ." JSP 2004 pencil holograph used as copytext. This quatrain features in lieu of a return address on a postcard Spicer sent from Boston to Don Allen in New York in September, 1956. "J. Spicer fecit" possibly alludes to Ezra Pound's Canto XLV.

"Orpheus was a poet . . ." JSP 2004 pencil holograph used as copytext. This prose piece from the "Oliver Charming" notebooks seems a rejected fragment from that project. See *CP*, 86–88, for Orpheus's appearance in the final version.

Hell JSP 2004 pencil holograph used as copytext, untitled by Spicer. From the same "Oliver Charming" notebook as the related piece, "Imagine Lucifer" (*CP*, 61–62). "Able" is Spicer's spelling.

The Waves JSP 2004 pencil holograph used as copytext. Several drafts of this poem are found in the "Oliver Charming" notebooks. At one point Spicer projected it as the first of a series to be titled "Four Sea Pieces." The others — "The Red Sea," "Song for Hart Crane," and "The Pacific" — have not been found. Or was Spicer planning to slot in here sections from "A Portrait of the Artist as a Young Landscape," which he had written much earlier, and which bear the titles "The Indian Ocean: Rimbaud," "The Atlantic Ocean: Hart Crane," and "The Pacific Ocean"?

"If I had invented homosexuality . . ." JSP 2004 pencil holograph used as copytext.

Translator JSP 2004 pencil holograph used as copytext. Probably a note towards a longer text, this short aphorism was written just when Spicer was beginning what would become *After Lorca*, in which translation is one of the major themes.

Goodnight. I want to kill myself . . ." JSP 2004 pencil holograph, found in the "Oliver Charming" notebooks, used as copytext. Barton Barber and Donald Bliss were both acquaintances of Spicer from Berkeley. He wrote this poem while living in an apartment in a building adjoining that of Carolyn and Joe Dunn, the latter the addressee of one of his most notable poems of the Boston sojourn: "Five Words for Joe Dunn on His Twenty-Second Birthday" (*CP*, 58–59). It is perhaps this younger couple who are imagined in the "next room" and with regard to whom Spicer imagined himself thrust into the role of "Big Uncle." A recording of Kevin Killian reading the poem was released in on the compact disc *Harry's House*, vol. 1 (Fast Speaking Music, 2012).

Notes for San Francisco and Berkeley: 1956–1965

For Kids JSP 71/135 typescript used as copytext. This manuscript is untitled, but *P* details that the poem also circulated under the title "For Kids"—using John Wieners's nickname for Joanne Kyger—and could be considered in the context of the dedicated poems of *Admonitions* (see *P*, 122–23). This would date the poem to late 1957 or early 1958.

Sonnet Exercise JSP 2004 pencil holograph used as copytext. This poem was sent in a letter to Robin Blaser, probably in November or December 1956. Spicer explains there that the poem arose from the exercise of taking the rhyme words from one of Shakespeare's sonnets and writing a new poem around them: "This was my result and I like it mainly because the imagery was irresponsible" (JSP 2004). The source poem is Sonnet 76, beginning "Why is my verse so barren of new pride?" and Spicer seems to have cheated: the rhyme-word in line three is "aside," and in line five "same." That said, were he looking at a facsimile of the 1609 Quarto and only scanning the rhyme-words outside of context, he could easily have misconstrued the printer's "s" for a modern "f" in line five.

Buster Keaton's Shadow JSP 2004 pencil holograph used as copytext. A companion to the two other "Buster Keaton" plays eventually retained for *After Lorca*.

"The boy . . ." JSP 2004 pencil holograph used as copytext. For more on John

Ryan, a love interest of Spicer, see *P*, especially pp. 56–62. Manuscript evidence indicates the slash in the last line is a textual element and not an editorial indication.

"They are going on a journey . . ." JSP 2004 pencil holograph used as copytext. This is an early variant of "Radar," the final poem in *After Lorca*.

"Hmm. Tahiti . . ." JSP 2004 pencil holograph used as copytext.

"I feel a black incubus crawling . . ." JSP 2004 pencil holograph used as copytext.

"It was like making love to my shadow . . ." JSP 2004 pencil holograph used as copytext.

Romance Sonámbulo JSP pencil holograph used as copytext. Untitled in Spicer's notebook, this poem is in fact a largely faithful translation of about the first half of Federico García Lorca's "Romance Sonámbulo," which Spicer would have found in the New Directions edition of Lorca's *Selected Poems*, edited by his close friend and future editor Donald Allen, wherein it is translated by Stephen Spender and J. L. Gili. There's no evidence as to why Spicer left this piece unfinished, but it's worth noting that he breaks off just where the mode shifts from lyric to narrative.

A Poem Against Dada & The White Rabbit JSP 2004 pencil holograph used as copytext. Spicer wrote poems for "Dada Day" at The Place—a favorite North Beach hangout—in 1955 and 1958 (see *CP*, 46 and 180), and it's very possible that this piece was a 1957 iteration in the series. Spicer's friends Joe Dunn and Graham Mackintosh were both involved with White Rabbit Press, which published *After Lorca*, and both figure frequently in Spicer's poetry, often as objects of unrequited love. "Ken" is Ken Austin, a Fairfax High School friend of Spicer's who died young of rheumatic fever, and Lee Hough was a star basketball player at Hollywood High School, whom Spicer later befriended at University of Redlands. (Thanks to Kevin Killian for this information).

THE CLOCK JUNGLE JSP 2004 pencil holograph draft used as manuscript. This poem exists only as a very rough draft in one of the *After Lorca* notebooks, which places it in 1957. The manuscript contains many corrections and even more variants, which Spicer apparently never ultimately accepted or rejected. Given the poem's interest I have decided to publish it, but the text cannot be considered altogether stable.

"Ridiculous is a word . . ." JSP 2004 pencil holograph used as copytext. This poem and the following represent an interregnum between *After Lorca* and the series of poems that will evolve into *Admonitions*. As a completed typescript of the latter was finished by December 1957, it seems reasonable to date this notebook—and therefore, the beginning of the detective novel—to autumn 1957.

"Hunters in the great Southwest . . ." JSP 2004 pencil holograph used as copytext.

For Bob JSP 2004 pencil holograph used as copytext. The "Bob" in question is the Beat poet Bob Kaufman, who lived in San Francisco around that time (1957–58). This rejected "admonition" needs to be read in the context of the intense and public sexual infatuation that Spicer's then boyfriend Russell Fitzgerald had attached to Kaufman; a fixation that ultimately proved fatal to his relationship with Spicer. Although verbal assault and obscene and occasionally derogatory language are formal characteristics of *Admonitions*, Kaufman himself used the word "negro" very frequently in his own work, at this period and subsequently. Beyond this, while Spicer's white-splaining here, if campy, is still highly offensive, the poem also engages with Kaufman quite seriously in several important ways. For example, the strange locution, "I / Told your voice," could refer to the fact that Kaufman disseminated his poems almost exclusively by reciting them aloud—many if not most of his poems that we have come from tape recordings, or transcriptions made by others—in a form of "unpublishing" that might be seen to mirror Spicer's own. Even more important is the poem's one clear demonstration of sympathy, the line, "It is terrible to be anything people wanted you to be." For this begs to be heard as a response to Kaufman's Whitmanesque catalog poem, "I, Too, Know What I Am Not," a twenty-two-line poem in which every line begins with the words, "No, I am not . . ." and which mostly devotes itself to denying racist and stereotyped figures of black identity. For more on Spicer, Fitzgerald, and Kaufman, see *P*, 118–39. Sadly, the biography's account confirms that Spicer's jealous rage did on occasion take racist forms in relation to Kaufman. Still, this probably rightly rejected "Admonition" does not reduce itself to that.

For Tom JSP 2004 pencil holograph used as copytext. Another rejected "Admonition."

For Jerry JSP pencil holograph used as copytext. An entirely different "For Jerry" appears as the penultimate poem of *Admonitions* (*CP*, 167–68).

"An island is a herd of reindeer . . ." JSP 2004 pencil holograph used as copytext.

"And he said there are trails . . ." JSP 2004 pencil holograph used as copytext. Against expectations, there is no possessive apostrophe in "hearts" in line 8, whereas the clearly written one in "it's" in line 10 turns what feels like a possessive into a contraction. As Spicer rarely makes punctuation errors of this kind, I have retained these oddities.

"Dear Russ" JSP 2004 pencil holograph used as copytext. This letter to Russell Fitzgerald, in a similar style to the *Admonitions* letters to Joe Dunn and Robin Blaser, is found in the same notebook that contains the first of the *Book of Music Poems*, itself immediately following the notebook with the last-retained pieces for *Admonitions*.

Vistas: On Visiting Spinoza's Grave JSP 2004 pencil holograph used as copytext. The painting reproduced in the postcard would seem to be Goya's "The Third of May, 1808." Goya also rendered a version of "Cupid and Psyche," which is discussed in detail in Robert Duncan's "A Poem Beginning with a Line by Pindar," written at about the same time as this piece. "Sea surge" alludes to Pound's Canto II: "And poor old Homer blind, blind, as a bat, / Ear, ear for the sea-surge, murmur of old men's voices."

Lamp JSP 2004 typescript used as copytext. Retained by Spicer for the "Selected Poems" project, this poem was originally written as a contribution to Eugene de Thassy's semi-fictional autobiographical memoir *Twelve Dead Geese*, which Spicer edited and helped to write in 1955–56.

Carmen JSP 2004 typescript used as copytext. Drafts confirm Spicer's decision to write "someoneelse's" as one word. Grouped like "Opera" with *A Book of Music* poems, this one seems to echo the songs of the "Thames daughters" in *The Waste Land*.

Opera JSP 2004 typescript used as copytext. The only known manuscript is from the "Selected Poems" project, where the poem is grouped among others from *A Book of Music*, and where I shall leave it though it's not certain to have originated in the same notebook as the others here.

Mazurka for the Girls Who Brought Me Tranquilizers JSP 2004 typescript used as copytext. Draft found in the same notebook as "Carmen," and placed with *A Book of Music* poems, as above, in "Selected Poems" table of contents.

The Birds JSP 2004 typescript used as copytext. Another provisional *A Book of Music Poem*, apparently written shortly after the preceding.

Song For A Raincoat JSP 2004 typescript used as copytext. A holograph draft is found in the same notebook as "The Birds." This figures as another apparent *Book of Music* outtake in the "Selected Poems" project.

Birthday Pool JSP 2004 typescript used as copytext. Retained for the "Selected

Poems" project, the title might refer to schemes where co-workers "pool" money, creating a fund from which each will receive a present on their birthday.

Poet JSP 2004 typescript used as copytext. This is the poem Spicer chose to close his "Selected Poems" manuscript. A pencil holograph version titled "Portrait" contains this variant in place of lines 8–9:

> Droid constructed of all our poems.
>
> Petrouchka
>
> Wearing a beaver shirt

"Three little waves . . ." JSP 2004 pencil holograph used as copytext.

Hotel JSP 2004 pencil holograph used as copytext.

"No daring shadows . . ." JSP 2004 pencil holograph used as copytext.

The Pipe of Peace JSP 2004 pencil holograph used as copytext. In the same notebooks where the detective novel peters out, *Billy the Kid* tentatively takes shape. This poem is from the last of the "Tower of Babel" notebooks, which also contains three other poems that were retained for *Billy the Kid*.

"Billy came into the bar . . ." JSP 2004 composite pencil and green ink holograph used as copytext. From a notebook containing finished versions or advanced drafts of over half of the *Billy the Kid* poems, this one begins on a single page in green ink, and then proceeds to offer three alternative endings on separate pages, two in ink and one in pencil. The pencil version has been retained, as most complete. The friends Spicer refers to here are George Stanley, Russell Fitzgerald, and Dora and Harold Dull.

"This poem has to do . . ." JSP 2004 pencil holograph used as copytext. This is a variant of the tenth poem in "Fifteen False Propositions Against God" of 1958 (*CP*, 199), referring as does the other to William Carlos Williams's "The Last Words of My English Grandmother." In addition to its intrinsic interest, it's included here on the principle that seriality also implies a reticence to banish the ghosts of final versions.

Notes for Hokkus *and* Poems from J

Sometime in 1959 Spicer began experimenting with the name "Hokku" as a way of thinking about his short poems and how to bundle them together into larger structures. There's a notebook from this period with a poem ("Bitterness / Bitter-ness") titled "Hokku" on its first page. Following this, interspersed with other material, are ten other short pieces. While these were untitled in the notebook, some were later published under the title "Hokkus" in Spicer's own mimeographed magazine, *J*. A second notebook bears the title "10 Hokkus for Dorrie" on its first page and contains sixteen poems in sequence followed by a concluding excerpt from Sigmund Freud's *A General Introduction to Psychoanalysis*, much as *Lament for the Makers* ends with a citation from a biography of D. H. Lawrence. It is tempting to see "Dorrie" as a serial poem, except apparently Spicer didn't: as early as the first issue of *J* in the fall of 1959, Spicer was pilfering some of the most recent poems from "Dorrie" as well as earlier ones from the "Hokku" notebook, and recombining them together in ways that respected the sequencing of neither notebook (this *a posteriori* refashioning is different from the situation of Spicer's penultimate book *Language*, in which the poems appeared pretty much as they were being written in the journal *Open Space*, and were collected into a "book" after, in a version that followed the original sequencing). Moreover, there is yet another potential grouping for these works: poems from both notebooks, either in pencil manuscript, in *J*, or both, occasionally bore the pseudonym of "Mary Murphy" (a Hollywood leading lady of the 1950s, who notably played opposite Marlon Brando in *The Wild One*), implying still another relational device that cuts across the two notebooks. The decision here has been to privilege the versions in *J*—which Spicer edited, after all —using these as preferred copytext (checked against holograph manuscripts for minor errors) for all poems published therein, and to group the "Mary Murphy" poems together. The remaining poems from the two notebooks are given in the order found in the notebooks, with one fascinating exception. The fourteenth poem of "Dorrie" has long been known to Spicer readers, but in another book: it is a pencil holograph fair copy of "This ocean, humiliating in its disguises" —the first poem of Spicer's penultimate book *Language*, normally thought to have been written in 1964. There is every reason to believe that this iconic poem, which features neither in *Open Space* nor in the ink holograph manuscript of *Language* held by Simon Fraser University, was in fact written over four years earlier. This is all the more plausible as the "hokkus," especially in the "Dorrie" notebook, frequently make use of the morphological splitting of words that was to figure so prominently in *Language*.

Hokkus *J* 1 used as copytext. The three-level indentation of the poems here follows the page layout of the six poems in *J*, where they took up an entire page.

ONS also follows *J*, but mistakenly prints the title in the singular. *"Past / Re-membering"*: *J* doesn't split the final word "seed" over two lines, but the holograph manuscript clearly does, and is preferred in this instance. *"Sure / Eurydice is dead"*: holograph manuscript clearly indicates the extra spacing between "hell" and "or," which *J* does not reproduce.

"In- / Visible zombies" *J* 2 used as copytext, where this poem is attributed to "Mary Murphy"; a pencil holograph fair copy is found in the "Hokku" notebook.

"The skull is not the bones." *J* 3 used as copytext, where the poem is attributed to "Mary Murphy"; pencil holograph draft is found in the "Hokku" notebook.

"Lack of oxygen puzzles the air." *J* 5 used as copytext. Both there and in pencil holograph draft in "10 Hokkus for Dorrie," the poem is attributed to "Mary Murphy."

"Down to new beaches . . . JSP 2004 pencil holograph from "Hokku notebook" used as copytext. Published in *J* 2 and *ONS* with minor variants.

"The slobby sea . . ." *J* 3 used as copytext; also published in *ONS*.

Last Hokku *J* 3 used as copytext; also published in *ONS*.

Jacob *J* 4 used as copytext; also published in *ONS*.

"Mar - tar - dumbs - ville . . ." JSP 2004 pencil holograph used as copytext. First poem of "Ten Hokkus for Dorrie" notebook.

"At the back of the age . . ." JSP 2004 pencil holograph used as copytext. Second poem of "Ten Hokkus for Dorrie" notebook.

"I make difficulties . . ." JSP 2004 pencil holograph used as copytext. Third poem of "Ten Hokkus for Dorrie" notebook.

"A hokku is something . . ." JSP 2004 pencil holograph used as copytext. Fourth poem of "Ten Hokkus for Dorrie" notebook.

"No one can rescue anyone from hell . . ." JSP 2004 pencil holograph used as copytext. Fifth poem of "Ten Hokkus for Dorrie" notebook.

"In the smallest corner of words . . ." JSP 2004 pencil holograph used as copytext. Sixth poem of "Ten Hokkus for Dorrie" notebook.

"What I miss . . ." JSP 2004 pencil holograph used as copytext. Ninth poem of "Ten Hokkus for Dorrie" notebook.

"Get away zombie . . ." JSP 2004 pencil holograph used as copytext. Tenth poem of "Ten Hokkus for Dorrie" notebook.

"Saying love . . ." JSP 2004 pencil holograph used as copytext. Twelfth poem of "Ten Hokkus for Dorrie" notebook.

"Extend it in words . . ." JSP 2004 pencil holograph used as copytext. Thirteenth poem of "Ten Hokkus for Dorrie" notebook.

"Hell, / If you have a horror . . ." JSP 2004 pencil holograph used as copytext; from the "Hokku notebook."

"No real resting place . . ." JSP 2004 pencil holograph used as copytext; from the "Hokku notebook."

"You have to make moral decisions . . ." JSP 2004 pencil holograph used as copytext; from the "Hokku notebook."

"A million carpenters work on this single deal . . ." JSP 2004 pencil holograph used as copytext; from the "Hokku notebook."

"It is as if / Love had wings . . ." JSP 2004 pencil holograph used as copytext; from the "Hokku notebook."

Hokku ("Not / Even / Hatred remains . . .") JSP 2004 typescript used as copytext.

"It is impossible to stop . . ." JSP 2004 pencil holograph used as copytext. From the "Homage to Creeley" notebooks and drafts.

Blood and Sand JSP 2004 pencil holograph used as copytext. From the "Homage to Creeley" notebooks and drafts.

AN EXERCISE Boundary 2 (1977) used as copytext, subject to minor revision based on archival sources. Robin Blaser and John Granger edited this poem, which they provisionally dated to 1959, though more recently uncovered contextual evidence indicates a far more probable date of 1961. Working from loose-leaf sheets, the editors remark that the order of poems is given "as found." Since then, an earlier draft in a bound spiral notebook has been discovered, and this manuscript slightly differs in sequencing. However, since Spicer also added two new poems and made other (mostly minor) revisions, I have let the *Boundary 2* sequencing stand. *Epigraph*: while this passage is not a direct quote, in *Of Modern Painting* John Ruskin argues that innocent animals tend to be brightly colored and dangerous ones dull and dusky. *"Death to the murderers of Jacques Molay"*: a reference to section 7 of W. B. Yeats's "Meditations in Time of Civil War"; Jacques de Molay, the last Grand Master of the Knights Templar, was burned alive on March 18, 1314. *"Ebbe Borregaard"*: bearded poet and member of Spicer's circle. *"Translation"*: in Spicer's first draft, this poem was titled "Magic." *"Always in October"*: this is a revised version of "All Hallows Eve," probably written around ten years earlier. Blaser assumed that Spicer was working from memory here. *"Congratulations,*

George Stanley . . .": This piece appears to be a title without a poem, rather than the more familiar phenomenon of poems without titles. *"George Stanley"*: a poet and member of Spicer's circle; see *P* for details of his relationship to Spicer. *"Beatitude"*: a well-known Beat journal, edited by C. V. J. Anderson. *"On Listening To A Game . . ."*: Blaser and Granger point out that the Angels and Giants were in different leagues, and would not have been able to play against each other except in the World Series. While Spicer's enjoyment of listening to baseball games on the radio is legendary, Maurice Cigar does not appear to be a real person. *"Shit-eaters"*: in a move recalling "Congratulations . . ." above, Spicer here puts the "body" of the poem above its title, as the use of capitalization indicates.

"Do what thou wilt . . .": a reference to Alaister Crowley's notion of Thelema, which stipulates "Do what thou wilt shall be the whole of the law."

FOR MAJOR GENERAL ABNER DOUBLEDAY INVENTOR OF BASEBALL AND FIRST AMERICAN PRESIDENT OF THE THEOSOPHICAL SOCIETY JSP 2004 pencil holograph used as copytext; contextual data suggests 1961 as year of composition. Though Doubleday's status as the inventor of baseball is no longer widely credited, Spicer follows the conventional wisdom of his day. Doubleday was certainly President of the American branch of the Theosophical Society. Did Spicer know that he also once held a patent for the San Francisco cable car system that is still operational? The title joins baseball to a consideration of the supernatural, which Spicer continues in *The Book of Magazine Verse* (see Gizzi, "Afterword" in *H*, for more on this). And just as Spicer's Vancouver Lectures pointedly remind us that theosophist W. B. Yeats's spiritualist automatic-writing sessions kicked off in San Bernadino, California, Doubleday is another figure for Spicer who links the most radically "modern" elements of the United States to the sort of mythopoetical structures from which the new world could seem to be *a priori* excluded. *"Quondam et Futurus"*: anticipates *The Holy Grail*, which Spicer would write in 1962. *"Mary Murphy's Chowder"*: Around this time Spicer occasionally used the pseudonym "Mary Murphy" for his own writings, as published in *J*. *"Krazy Kat"*: American comic-strip character running from 1913–1944. *"Concerning the Future of American Poetry II"*: See *AN EXERCISE* for "Concerning the Future of American Poetry." *"Hypocrite lecture"*: either Spicer has mistaken "lecture" ("reading" or "text") for Baudelaire's *"lecteur"* ("reader") in the opening poem of *The Flowers of Evil*, or he is making a joke.

"Daily waste washed by the tides . . ." JSP 2004 pencil holograph used as copytext; probably written in 1961.

Shark Island JSP 2004 pencil holograph used as copytext; probably written in 1961.

Stinson JSP 2004 pencil holograph used as copytext. The title refers to Stinson Beach, California, just north of San Francisco, where Robert Duncan and Jess Collins lived intermittently for several years in the 1950s and '60s, with Spicer an occasional visitor. Probably written in 1961.

For B. W. I, II, III JSP 2004 pencil holograph used as copytext for the three poems in this series.

"It's dark all night . . ." JSP 2004 pencil holograph used as copytext. From the "Red Wheelbarrow" notebook.

"Love has five muscles . . ." JSP 2004 pencil holograph used as copytext. This lyric is also from the "Red Wheelbarrow" notebook; eight of the nine lyrics there have the word "Love" in their title.

Thank you all for your fine funeral . . ." JSP 2004 pencil holograph used as copytext. From the "Red Wheelbarrow" notebook.

"Jesus came to me in a dream . . ." JSP 2004 pencil holograph used as copytext. Probably from late 1950s or very early '60s. Spicer might be conflating two different men named William Law. The first was an Anglican priest and author of *The Absolute Unlawfulness of the Stage Entertainment*, who, in fealty to the House of Stuart, refused to swear allegiance to the House of Hanover after the Glorious Revolution, and has thus been considered a "non-juror." He lost his position at Emmanuel College, Cambridge, over this stand, and perhaps reminded Spicer of himself, another "non-juror" in the context of the University of California's anti-Communist Loyalty Oath, which he refused to sign in 1950. The other William Law was an early follower of Joseph Smith but later broke with the Mormon Church and founded the dissident "True Church of Jesus Christ of Latter Day Saints." This Law objected particularly to Smith's practice of polygamy.

"Orpheus / Purposes . . ." JSP 2004 pencil holograph used as copytext. Probably from 1961–62.

Against Corso JSP 2004 pencil holograph used as copytext. From same notebook as previous poem. The title refers to Beat poet Gregory Corso, while the quotation (unverified) from Trotsky would be in the context of early Soviet debates on military doctrine, in the course of which Trotsky argued that there was not a specifically "proletarian" or "Marxist" science of war; www.marxists.org/archive/cliff/works/1990/trotsky2/09-debate.html#n9/. "If the salt has lost its savour" is from Matthew, 5:13. The line "The enemy is in your own country" will return in "The Book of Merlin" in *The Holy Grail* (*CP*, 348). In his "Poetry and Politics" lecture, Spicer attributes the phrase to Rosa Luxemburg, and Peter Gizzi's accompanying note points to her mobilization of that idea in her essay "Either/Or" (*H*, 169, n2), but the phrase is more usually associated with her fellow Spartacist martyr, Karl Liebknecht.

SPIDER MUSIC JSP 2004 pencil holograph used as copytext. This serial poem from 1962 consists of torn-out notebook pages, and therefore the sequencing is uncertain. The first poem, "Spider Music," also exists under the title "Spider Song" in two different typescripts, with very minor variants. "Spider Song" was submitted to and rejected by the local magazine *M*, edited by members of Spicer's coterie, primarily Stan Persky. See *P*, 203–205, for Spicer's angry response, which noted that Persky was Jewish. The last lines of "Nikko San" might have him in mind. *"Laredo"*: Spicer refers here to the Western-themed folk song, "The Streets of Laredo." His collapsing here of folk material and song with Greek myth is typical of his practice.

For Harris, For Harris II JSP 2004 pencil holograph used as copytext. The Harris in question is Harris Schiff, who entered Spicer's San Francisco orbit in 1963, when these poems were almost certainly written. For more on Schiff, see *P*.

Ch'ang Ch'eng JSP 2004 pencil holograph used as copytext. The manuscript attributes this work to Mao, and in his Berkeley Lecture of July 1965, Spicer refers to Mao as a "damn good poet" (*H*, 153), however this text isn't a rendering of any of Mao's poems. Rather, it's a mash-up of phrases from two different sources: "A Single Spark Can Start a Prairie Fire" (www.marxists .org/reference/archive/mao/selected-works/volume-1/mswv1_6.htm) and the code of conduct for Red Army soldiers (see Rebecca Karl, *Mao Zedong and China in the Contemporary World: A Concise History* [Duke University Press, 2010], 39). The title is a transliteration of the Chinese term for the Great Wall.

"Be brave to things . . ." *ONS* used as copytext except for minor points of punctuation, in which cases the version in *Open Space* 2, where the poem was first published (late winter or early spring 1964), is preferred. The poem was submitted to that magazine's Valentine poem contest and won, apparently as the only submission. An editor's note explains "in lieu of other entries, M. Spicer to be winner by default."

"With fifteen cents . . ." JSP 2004 photocopy of a pencil holograph notebook page. Robin Blaser used this as epigraph for his path-breaking essay on Spicer, "The Practice of Outside," first published in 1975. There, he dates the piece to late 1964.

A NEW POEM (**texts and fragments**) Spicer's apparently unfinished serial poem of 1958, *A New Poem*, while containing examples of Spicer at the top of his form, also presents insuperable editorial problems. The bulk of the work was written in late summer or autumn 1958 in a notebook in which the poems are interspersed with some of the later pieces from *Fifteen False Propositions Against God*; drafts of letters to Russell Fitzgerald, whose rupture with Spicer informs the entire notebook; and the poem "For Steve Jonas Who is in Jail for Defrauding a Book Club" (*CP*, 192), as well as other material that does not unequivocally belong to the "New Poem" project. Indeed, it's entirely conceivable that while he was writing these poems Spicer wasn't sure which belonged in *Fifteen False Propositions* and which didn't; *A New Poem* might have evolved out of leftovers from *False Propositions*—out of works that Spicer came to realize belonged not in that book, but rather themselves constituted *a new poem*. At some point, at any rate, a typed fair copy was produced, bearing a title page reading *A New Poem* and seventeen lyrics, each on its own page. The problem is that the manuscript as found was clearly out of sequence, and establishing reliable sequencing has proved impossible. One cannot simply follow the notebook sequencing, because five of the poems in the typed manuscript are without any extant draft. Moreover, of the twelve poems for which holograph drafts exist, three are found on loose-leaf, ripped-out notebook pages which had been placed inside the notebook covers, making their sequencing with regard to the others unknowable. That one of them bears the title "A New Poem" ("The rope. A beginning") and is the only poem of the sequence that has a title at all, indicates that it should probably be placed first, but this still leaves the placement of the other two loose-leaf poems up for grabs. If this weren't enough, eight of the seventeen typed poems bear hand-written numbers in their top-right corners, but unfortunately, there are two each of numbers one, two, and four, and one three and one five. No clear principles of sequencing emerge from the content of the numbered texts. Was Spicer thinking of two sequencings of separate sections? Are the numbers even his? Which "one" goes with which "two"?— etc. But it's worth noting that the poem that bore the title "A New Poem" in holograph is one of the two "number ones." While it's reasonable to wonder if the duplicate numbering might mean texts from an entirely different project got mixed up with the *New Poem* manuscript, *both* the poems numbered as "one" contain the phrase "a new poem." Even more, there's also one holograph poem from the notebook that clearly speaks to the other "New Poem" lyrics, but does not appear in the typescript. The problem, then, is that short of the miraculous appearance of another manuscript in a more reliable state, any publication of the poem is inevitably an editorial fabrication, based on no solid principles or evidence. On the other hand, too much of this material is too good to leave out. I've chosen to simply include all of the work from the typescript, and one holograph poem from the notebook that the typed manuscript does not reproduce. After starting with the one poem that does seem clearly marked as inaugural, the sequencing given here is loosely informed by that found in the notebook and that indicated on the typescript, bearing in mind that those two are of course themselves impossible to collate without some contradiction.

"Heurtibise": the emissary between the underworld and the world of the living in Jean Cocteau's movie *Orphée*, a major and recurring influence on Spicer, especially in *The Heads of the Town up to the Aether*. I have retained Spicer's spelling here. *"Lament of the makiris"*: Scottish poet William Dunbar's famous elegy, "Lament for the Makaris"; it contains the Latin refrain "Timor mortis conturbat me," or "The fear of death terrifies me." In 1961, Spicer published a book titled "Lament for the Makers" with White Rabbit Press (*CP*, 317–22). *"Tom Parkinson"*: Spicer's friend and UC–Berkeley English professor; also a noted Yeats specialist. *"Sunya"*: a Sanskrit word meaning "zero," "nothing," "empty," or "void." Etymologically related to the important Buddhist term *sunyata*. *"The Gentleman wants to know . . ."*: parentheses left open in copytext.

BIBLIOGRAPHY

Blaser, Robin. *The Astonishment Tapes: Talks on Poetry and Autobiography with Robin Blaser and Friends*. Edited by Miriam Nichols. Tuscaloosa: University of Alabama Press, 2015.

———. *The Fire: Collected Essays of Robin Blaser*. Edited by Miriam Nichols. Berkeley: University of California Press, 2006.

Brazil, David, and Kevin Killian, eds. *The Kenning Anthology of Poets Theater, 1945–1985*. Chicago: Kenning Editions, 2010.

Damon, Maria. *The Dark End of the Street: Margins in American Vanguard Poetry*. Minneapolis: University of Minnesota Press, 1993.

Davidson, Michael. *Guys Like Us: Citing Masculinity in Cold War Poetics*. Chicago: University of Chicago Press, 2004.

———. *The San Francisco Renaissance: Poetics and Community at Mid-Century*. Cambridge: Cambridge University Press, 1991.

Dickinson, Emily. *The Poems of Emily Dickinson*. Edited by R. W. Franklin. Cambridge: Harvard University Press, 1998.

———. *Selected Letters*. Edited by Thomas H. Johnson. Cambridge: Harvard University Press, 1986.

Ellingham, Lewis, and Kevin Killian. *Poet, Be Like God: Jack Spicer and the San Francisco Renaissance*. Middletown, CT: Wesleyan University Press, 1998.

Faas, Ekbert. *Young Robert Duncan: Portrait of the Poet as Homosexual in Society*. Santa Barbara: Black Sparrow Press, 1983.

Jarnot, Lisa. *Robert Duncan: The Ambassador from Venus*. Berkeley: University of California Press, 2012.

Katz, Daniel. *The Poetry of Jack Spicer*. Edinburgh: Edinburgh University Press, 2013.

Nichols, Miriam. *A Literary Biography of Robin Blaser: Mechanic of Splendor*. London: Palgrave Macmillan, 2019.

Smith, Simon. "General Purpose Love Poem," in *Some Municipal Love Poems*. Colchester, UK: Muscaliet Press, 2018.

Spicer, Jack. *The Collected Books of Jack Spicer*. Edited and with a commentary by Robin Blaser. Santa Barbara: Black Sparrow Books, 1980.

———. *The House that Jack Built: The Collected Lectures of Jack Spicer*. Edited and with a afterword by Peter Gizzi. Middletown, CT: Wesleyan University Press, 1998.

———. "Letters to Allen Joyce." *Sulfur* 10 (1982): 140–53.

———. "Letters to Graham Mackintosh." *Caterpillar* 12 (1970): 83–114.

———. *My Vocabulary Did This To Me: The Collected Poetry of Jack Spicer*. Edited and by Peter Gizzi and Kevin Killian. Middletown, CT: Wesleyan University Press, 2008.

———. *One Night Stand & Other Poems*. Edited and with a preface by Donald Allen. San Francisco: Grey Fox Press, 1980.

———. "Selected Letters from the Spicer/Duncan Correspondence." *Acts* 6 (1987): 13–30.

INDEX OF TITLES FOR POEMS

INDEX OF FIRST LINES FOR POEMS

ABOUT THE AUTHOR AND THE EDITOR

Jack Spicer (1925–1965) was an American poet often identified, along with his friends Robert Duncan and Robin Blaser, with the San Francisco Renaissance. Proudly queer at a time of legal and social oppression, Spicer was also charming, truculent, inspiring, and enraging to those in his artistic and social circles. During his short but prolific life, he published numerous books with small presses, including *After Lorca* (1957), *Billy the Kid* (1958), and *The Holy Grail* (1965). In 2008, Wesleyan University Press published *My Vocabulary Did This to Me: The Collected Poetry of Jack Spicer*, which won the 2009 American Book Award for poetry.

Daniel Katz is professor of English and Comparative Literary Studies at the University of Warwick in Coventry, England. He has been an executive board member of the Samuel Beckett Society, and co-director of Warwick's Centre for Research in Philosophy, Literature, and the Arts. He is the founding editor of the Bloomsbury Studies in Critical Poetics book series and author of *The Poetry of Jack Spicer* (Edinburgh University Press, 2013) as well as many other contributions in the fields of modern literature and poetry and poetics.